KU-575-445

TWO WEEKS IN NOVEMBER

The astonishing untold story
of the operation that toppled Mugabe

CHESHIRE LIBRARIES	
A 81878791 X	
Askews & Holts	09-Apr-2019
968.91	£16.99

Author's Note

This book is a work of narrative non-fiction. It's a true story based on actual events gleaned from hundreds of interviews and conversations as well as research and personal experience of the period in question. The protagonists in the story are real, although I've changed some names to protect identities. There are instances where I've compressed conversations and relationships that took place over a longer period of time, and where I've described scenes and written dialogue I was obviously not present for. I've done this in the interest of story and narrative, using my best understanding of the characters, locations and historical period involved. It goes without saying that any errors are mine and mine alone.

———————————————

Published in 2019 by
Short Books, Unit 316, ScreenWorks, 22 Highbury Grove,
London, N5 2ER

10 9 8 7 6 5 4 3 2 1

Copyright © Douglas Rogers 2019

Douglas Rogers has asserted his right under the Copyright, Designs and Patents Act 1988 to be identified as the author of this work. All rights reserved. No part of this publication may be reproduced, stored in a retrieval system or transmitted in any form, or by any means (electronic, mechanical, or otherwise) without the prior written permission of both the copyright owners and the publisher.

A CIP catalogue record for this book
is available from the British Library.

ISBN: 978-1-78072-368-6

Cover design by Two Associates
Printed at CPI Group (UK) Ltd, Croydon, CR0 4YY

Not for sale in South Africa or Canada

For Grace, a different one, without whom none
of this would have been possible

CHARACTERS

Robert Gabriel Mugabe – President (1980–2017) and leader of ZANU-PF; aka Bob, the Old Man

Grace Mugabe – First Lady and leader of Generation 40 (G40) faction within ZANU-PF; aka the First Shopper, Gucci Grace, Lady Gaga

Emmerson Dambudzo Mnangagwa – Vice-President, former Security, Defence and Justice Minister and leader of the Lacoste faction within ZANU-PF; aka ED, the Crocodile

Emmerson Mnangagwa Junior – son of ED; aka Junior

Ambassador Christopher Mutsvangwa – chairman of Zimbabwe National Liberation War Veterans Association and former Chinese Ambassador; aka Chris

General Constantino Chiwenga – Commander of the Defence Forces

Jonathan Moyo – former Information Minister and senior G40 faction member; aka the Professor, Jonso

Saviour Kasukuwere – ZANU-PF Political Commissar and former Indigenisation Minister; aka Tyson

George Charamba – President's Spokesman

Senator Monica Mutsvangwa – wife of Christopher

Kudzai Chipanga – ZANU-PF Youth League leader

Augustine Chihuri – Police Commissioner

Auxillia Mnangagwa – wife of ED

Northgate Declaration team:

Tom Ellis – businessman and political fixer

Agent Kasper – CIO operative

Agent Magic – CIO operative

Agent Horse – Military Intelligence operative

Gabriel Shumba – human rights lawyer, ZEF Chairman; aka Gabe

ABBREVIATIONS

ANC – African National Congress

AU – African Union

CIO – Central Intelligence Organisation

EU – European Union

G40 – Generation 40

GNU – Government of National Unity

MDC – Movement for Democratic Change

MI – Military Intelligence

PSU – Police Support Unit, aka Black Boots, paramilitary wing of police

SADC – Southern African Development Community

ZANU-PF – Zimbabwe African National Union, Patriotic Front

ZBC – Zimbabwe Broadcasting Corporation

ZDF – Zimbabwe Defence Forces

ZEF – Zimbabwe Exiles Forum

ZNLWVA – Zimbabwe National Liberation War Veterans Association

"Don't pursue big plans in November, my child; the ancestral spirits are restless, still deliberating which prayers to answer."

Words on the portentous month of November in Shona culture, as told to a Zimbabwean boy by his father.

Introduction

Every day for 37 years since Zimbabwe's independence in 1980, there has been a police roadblock at the foot of Christmas Pass, the precipitous mountain traverse that connects the Mutare River valley, where I was born and raised, with the city of Mutare on the Mozambique border. I've approached that roadblock a thousand times over the years, always with the same dread of the coming shakedown: the demand to see ID, passport, driver's licence; to pay a fine for some minor offence.

On the night of Thursday, November 16th 2017 there was still a roadblock at the pass, but it was now manned not by police but soldiers of the Zimbabwe National Army.

In Harare the generals were denying it, but a military coup was underway, and in this corner of the country the police, long loyal to President Robert Mugabe and his wife Grace, had turned tail and fled.

I pulled up and waited anxiously as a flak-jacketed soldier approached, wielding his AK47 like a club.

He leaned in the open window.

"Got any bombs?" he asked.

Then he grinned, burst out laughing, offered me a fist bump and waved me on.

The soldier's surprising wit was the first sign of a thaw in the air: after 37 years of rule by one man, Mugabe – at 93, the world's oldest leader – a changing of the guard was at hand.

I was in the country of my birth by chance.

I'd flown in from my home in Virginia, outside Washington DC, two weeks earlier to briefly visit my parents before picking up a vehicle and driving into Mozambique with three friends. The vehicle was a vintage white 1971 Mercedes Benz 280 SE – of the kind popular with African dictators in that faded decade – and my plan was to write a book about the trip. It would be the story of four middle-aged men in mid life crisis, in search of adventure and lost youth: The Hangover set in Latin Africa, if you will.

We were three days into the journey, closing in on a far northern Mozambican port, when we learned that back in Zimbabwe the country's Vice-President, Emmerson D Mnangagwa, the man next in line to the presidency, had been summarily fired by his one-time friend and mentor, Mugabe. Mugabe was clearly paving the way for his glamorous and controversial wife, Grace, 41 years his junior, to take power.

A day later we learned that Mnangagwa, also known as ED or "The Crocodile", had fled the country in fear for his life, and had almost been captured in a gunfight at the exact same Mutare–Mozambique border post through which we'd crossed days earlier. We wondered if he might turn up at our guesthouse.

Instead, a day later he turned up in South Africa, from where he released a statement saying that he would be back in Zimbabwe "in a few weeks" to remove Mugabe, free the country and take power.

That seemed optimistic, if not delusional, but we toasted

it from a cantina on Ilha de Mozambique.

The truth is, I wasn't much bothered either way. I had long since grown exhausted with Zimbabwe. I've written about the country for 15 years, and the cycle of hope followed by despair (and usually violence) has worn me – and everyone else – down. Mugabe was going nowhere and his wife would succeed him.

That view started to change slightly on the evening of Monday, November 13th, when we learned, via a sudden barrage of WhatsApp and Facebook messages, that the head of the military, General Chiwenga, an ally of The Crocodile, had given a blistering press conference in Harare at which he berated Mugabe, and warned him that the army would intervene to stop his wife and her cohorts from seizing power.

I'm a travel writer, not a conflict reporter, but I also know a story when I see one. The Zimbabwean military is a dark and brutal force, not given to idle threats, and if Chiwenga was threatening military action, he meant it.

"Shit is going to kick off back home," I told my friends. "We should be there for it."

After all, how better to complete a book about four guys in search of an adventure than by getting caught in an actual coup or revolution, in their own country, as it went down?

The four of us were in nervous agreement and we raced back to Zimbabwe.

It took us three days, but we entered the country on the night of Thursday, November 16th, and it was a few miles from my parents' home near Christmas Pass that I had that interaction with the soldier.

On the morning of Saturday 18th my three friends and I raced west for the capital Harare to attend a march that had been hastily arranged to persuade Mugabe to step down. Suffice to say, the march was one of the most extraordinary events in Zimbabwean history: organised in 36 hours, it went off like clockwork, with the kind of precision and unity unknown to Zimbabwe. There must have been a million people on the streets that day, watched over with professionalism by the much-feared armed forces – not a shot was fired, not a stone thrown in anger.

Three days later Robert Mugabe did indeed resign and the country broke into raucous celebration.

Back home in the US, I wrote a magazine piece about the events – "Coup Fever" it was titled – for which one of my travelling companions, Michael Bowles, a photographer, took the images. I then contacted my publishers and pitched them a book about four middle-aged men who set off on a road trip in search of adventure and who discover it when they get caught up in a real-life revolution back in their home country. I had already written the first half of it; all I needed was to tack on the story of the coup.

I would try to speak to The Crocodile and find out how he escaped the country; I would speak to the military and ask them how they planned and carried out the entire operation; and I would try to find out how that march was so well organised.

My publishers liked the idea and in March 2018, I was back in Zimbabwe asking questions.

Which was when the problems started.

For men who had carried out what appeared to be "the perfect coup", the Zimbabwe military didn't want to speak about it. The Navy Seals revealed all about Zero Dark 30; Mossad still boasts about the raid on Entebbe, but the Zimbabwe military were saying nothing about what they had dubbed Operation Restore Legacy.

I asked multiple contacts to put me in touch with any senior commander, even off the record, but I met a brick wall. I did speak to the President's son – I was the first journalist he spoke to about his dramatic escape with his father – but when I asked him about the military he said he doubted they would talk.

Even Zimbabwean journalists with close ties to the armed forces got nowhere.

It was then that my story took a strange turn.

I had called a businessman friend in my parents' home town, Mutare, a very connected man, to ask if he knew any officers who would speak.

"No," he told me. "But I do know someone who has a story to tell."

"What story?"

"I'll text you his number," he replied.

I got the text. It was a South African cell phone number and it came with a single name, "Tom".

"Has he got a last name?" I asked.

There was no response.

The following night, at a dimly lit veranda table in the courtyard of the Bronte Hotel, in the Avenues area of Harare, I met with another contact. He was a black Zimbabwean opposition party activist who had spent the past 13 years in exile in South Africa, and had only returned to Zimbabwe following Mugabe's removal.

The man spoke in a whisper. He was still wary of the secret police. He told me he had no military connections and he doubted anyone in the military would speak about the coup, but there was someone he knew who had a story to tell.

"Who?" I asked.

He gave me a number and a surname – Ellis.

"What's his first name?"

"Just call him," the man said quietly, and then he changed the subject.

The number was for a South African cell.

I frantically searched my phone for the number that my businessman friend had given me the day before.

My heart was now pounding: they were the same numbers! Who was this Tom Ellis?

I called the following day.

He was in Johannesburg and had been expecting my call. He was clearly a white man, and had a Zimbabwean accent and an easy-going manner. He said he had liked my book, *The Last Resort*, a dark comedy about my parents' struggle to hold onto their home and backpacker lodge in eastern Zimbabwe during the violent land invasions.

"Listen, mate, you want another book to write?"

"Ya, sure."

"Well, let me tell you the story of the coup. I'll tell you from my side – what we did."

"What do you mean 'we'?"

"Do you want to hear it or not?"

And so it began.

The story Tom Ellis told me on that call was so outrageous and unbelievable that at first I thought he was bullshitting. It was a tale of spies, assassins, double agents, secret meetings, seedy Johannesburg bars, Harare restaurants, parking lot pacts – and one-time enemies coming together to work for a common goal.

It was hard to keep up. But, after further WhatsApp calls and multiple meetings with Ellis in Johannesburg and Harare, I started to understand.

And then, when he introduced me to members of "The Team", things got really wild.

By this point I had called my publishers and asked if we could table the comic travel memoir for a later date. I said I had stumbled on another story that was more incredible and pressing.

They kindly agreed, and I'm eternally grateful to them for giving me the freedom to do it.

There are other books on the coup in Zimbabwe and hundreds of magazine and newspaper articles. The story that follows is different: it's a human story about brave, driven, flawed individuals caught up in a life-or-death struggle for the future of the country they love.

It's time to pull back the curtain on one of the most surreal and dramatic events in modern African history, the consequences of which are still reverberating.

Let's go.

Douglas Rogers,
Waterford, Virginia
February 2019

PROLOGUE:

TERMINATED

The Vice-President received his letter of termination early afternoon, Monday, November 6th.

He knew, even before reading it, what it would say.

In some ways it was the most predictable thing that had gone down these past few months. November had landed hot and heavy on Harare's high plateau – not the cobalt skies and dry heat that usually precede the summer rains. But still, the humidity of the weather was nothing compared to the sultriness of the politics.

The factional war that had been simmering within the ruling ZANU-PF party for more than a year had now exploded very publicly, and the weekend rallies had been brutal. Robert Mugabe's wife Grace – Vice-President Mnangagwa's rival to assume the presidency – was taking no prisoners.

"We must deal with this snake," she had railed at a packed religious gathering in Harare's Rufaro Stadium 24 hours earlier. "The snake must have its head crushed!"

Dressed in the serene white of the apostolic sect whose congregants packed the stands, she declared her husband to be a messenger of God, which meant death to Mnangagwa for daring to succeed him: "If you fight those who are anointed by God, you are as good as dead. You will never rise again. You will be walking but you will be a grave, you will be breathing but you will be dead."

The gloves had come off the day before that, at a Presidential Youth Interface Rally in Zimbabwe's second city, Bulawayo – the ninth of ten planned youth rallies that had taken place in the provinces through the winter. At rally after rally the First Lady, 51, long-limbed as an antelope, glamorous in designer glasses and chic beret, had prowled the stages, mic in hand, verbally assaulting her elder rival as he sat numb and emotionless just yards away from her. He was a "usurper", she said, a "traitor"; he was plotting a military coup against her husband. At the Bulawayo rally, however, something snapped. No sooner had she uttered the words – "Mnangagwa is the cause of factionalism" than elements in the crowd, supporters of the VP bussed in for the purpose, started booing her. It was unheard of.

Grace hit back: "Let me tell you this, bring soldiers with guns to shoot me – I don't care!"

Then, incredulous, Mugabe himself, a frail 93 now, stumbled to the microphone and waved a bony finger in the air. "We are denigrated and insulted in the name of Mnangagwa?" he said with disgust. "Did I make a mistake appointing him as my deputy? Because if I did I will drop him as early as tomorrow. I will remove him!"

And through it all, just as he had at the previous rallies, Mnangagwa, 75, a veteran of the country's liberation war from white rule, for 54 years a friend and comrade of the President, the second-most powerful man in the country, who, over the years, had run the state's most powerful ministries –

Security, Defence and Justice – sat implacably on stage, staring at distant clouds, as if in a trance, as humiliation heaped upon humiliation.

Some saw his stony silence during those months as strength: "He's not known as The Crocodile for nothing," they said. "He is waiting." But most recognised it for what it was: weakness in the face of the new reality. Mnangagwa – henceforth referred to as "ED" – was losing the succession battle to Grace and her henchmen in G40.

❖ ❖ ❖

For 37 years, since independence from British rule, the story of Zimbabwe had been dominated by one man: Robert Gabriel Mugabe, the liberator turned tyrant who won a war for freedom, but then led his country into a ditch. By November 2017, however, the only story in Zimbabwe was of palace intrigue: the game of thrones within the ruling party to succeed the nonagenarian President. Mugabe had never anointed a successor – having rivals fight each other had kept the scale balanced in his favour – but time was running out. He was no spring chicken (he fell asleep in meetings, slurred lines in his speeches), and the party's congress, at which a new VP, and thus a certain successor, would be chosen, was to take place in early December. National elections loomed in 2018.

If you wanted the throne, it was time to make your move.

Two factions vied for power, both with names that sounded like a reality TV show. The First Lady's group was known as Generation 40 – G40 – a reference to the youthful demographics of the country: G40 were the young ones, the under 40s, unencumbered by history. The term was coined by Grace's

Svengali, a tall, slim, University of Southern California-educated professor and master tactician named Jonathan Moyo. A former Information Minister and a brilliant media manipulator, Moyo had fallen out with the Mugabes frequently, yet somehow always found his way back into their good books. Grace also had a charismatic Young Turk named Saviour 'Tyson' Kasukuwere in her corner, a former state security agent turned politician with a trombone voice, a pugnacious style and a devoted youth following.

They had the ruling party's Women's League and the Youth League on their side too, and whatever they lacked in experience, they made up for in energy, commitment and a fanatical devotion to the President.

ED's faction, on the other hand, was known as Lacoste, after the French fashion brand with the crocodile logo – a reference to his nickname. Lacoste represented the old guard, the establishment. The base of ED's support were the war veterans who had liberated the country from white rule, and who, for so long, had been the enforcers of Mugabe's power. But the war had ended 37 years previously, the country's youth had no memory of it and the veterans were dying off. True, he was also said to have the support of the military – he had served as Defence Minister, and was close friends with the Commander of the Defence Forces, General Constantino Chiwenga – but when had the military ever gone against Mugabe, at least publicly? It was unheard of. Even the name Lacoste seemed retro and dated, unlike the crisp, clean Twitter-friendly G40.

And so it was that on the first weekend of November, the two factions made their move. One side heckled and booed; the other threatened violent death in the name of God. It was no contest. On Monday, November 6th the President made his choice: he unceremoniously fired ED and sided with his wife.

❖ ❖ ❖

The VP read the termination letter and walked across to the window. He gazed out over the tiled rooftops towards the horizon. The sky was overcast and broiling, as it had been for weeks.

Then he sat down to write a letter of his own.

Some speculated later that it was a gambit – that if Mugabe's feared secret police were about to come and arrest him or try to assassinate him, the letter, tender and respectful as it was, could not help but move the President to call off his dogs. In it, he thanked and honoured his friend and teacher Robert Mugabe. He traced their first meeting back to 1963, the start of the liberation struggle against white rule that they had fought together. They were, quite literally, the last of the 60s generation to have taken up arms:

I have regarded you as my mentor and father figure and have been loyal to you, the Party and the revolution... I... wish to express my gratitude for the role you played in saving my life in 1965 when I was facing the death penalty, which was consequently commuted to ten years. . . I also remember with pride your guidance during the armed struggle in Mozambique, when you nurtured and inculcated in me the lasting values of the sanctity of human life and a profound sense of natural justice.

But he ended the letter on a maudlin note, as if he knew what was coming:

However, today, my enemies have prevailed. I could have recently lost my life through poisoning, but survived through God's grace... I shall forever remain loyal and committed to you, my party and the revolution, although I am aware of uncanny attempts by unscrupulous elements to assassinate me.

Then he packed his US$8,000 Louis Vuitton Président briefcase – he'd only come to his office to get documents – and made his way to his car. When he got home to Helensvale, in the affluent northern suburbs, half an hour later, he noticed the security had been removed from the front gate. Inside, his wife Auxillia was waiting for him. The two chefs provided by the state had been removed too. The tail riders on his motorcade peeled off.

And so it was. For 37 years you're part of the system; and then you're left high and dry.

He was entering the unknown.

❖ ❖ ❖

At 4pm that afternoon, the Information Minister, in a slow, stilted delivery, relayed the news to the nation via the national broadcaster, the ZBC. "In accordance with the Constitution of Zimbabwe... His Excellency has exercised his powers to relieve Honourable Vice-President ED Mnangagwa of his position as Vice-President with immediate effect."

Zimbabweans are a literate people, with a dark humour, and, as he wound his announcement up, the Information Minister could not resist a final alliterative flourish: "The Vice-President has consistently and persistently exhibited traits of disloyalty, disrespect, deceitfulness and unreliability."

No one any longer watched the national broadcaster, a ruling party mouthpiece, especially not at 4pm on a Monday, but within minutes footage of the statement was zinging around Facebook, Twitter and WhatsApp, the encrypted messaging service used by most Zimbabweans, to avoid detection by the secret police.

The country was entering the unknown too.

❖ ❖ ❖

Two miles away, at Freshly Ground coffee shop in Sam Levy's Village, an upscale shopping precinct in Borrowdale suburb, Emmerson Mnangagwa Jr, the now ex-VP's eldest son from his marriage to his second wife Auxillia (ED is said to have fathered 18 children), was uneasy. He was with his friend Karan "KC" Shetty, an Indian national with whom he ran an investment company, Connecor Global Advisory Group, on the second floor of a handsome colonial building on Josiah Chinamano, downtown in the Avenues. The two friends hadn't done much work that morning; instead they'd sat in the office fielding calls from friends and relatives commiserating over the weekend rallies and asking whether rumours of ED's firing were true.

Needing a break, they drove to Borrowdale for a coffee. It was then that they saw the VP's motorcade heading for home down Borrowdale Road, earlier than usual. It looked forlorn. Soon after that, Junior got a call. The voice was calm, but urgent: "Listen carefully. A unit is going to come for him at home this evening and take him away. There is a cell waiting for him at Rhodesville Police Station. They are going to poison him and hang him. It will look like a suicide. He must leave. Don't let him sleep there tonight."

The line went dead before he could respond.

Junior, 34, stocky and broad-shouldered like a rugby prop forward, has a deep voice, broad smile and easy-going manner. Unlike most children of the political elite, he had attended a government school, Prince Edward, in the centre of Harare, and although he was a member of the ZANU-PF Youth League and well known in political circles (he'd gone to every one of the brutal interface rallies with his father over the winter) he was an everyman: likeable, laid-back, married with two young kids.

You don't grow up in the second-most powerful political family in Zimbabwe without connections, though, and he knew the security agent wasn't kidding. Heart pounding, panic rising, he phoned his younger brothers, Sean, a military officer, and Collins, a mining engineer – pint-sized identical twins with a penchant for fashionable, tight-fit designer suits – and they all agreed to go straight over to their parents' house in Helensvale.

They had to persuade their father that he was going to be murdered if he didn't run.

❖ ❖ ❖

It was one of the more surreal aspects of Harare's affluent northern suburbs in November 2017 that the two rival factions – Lacoste-leaning military generals, G40 bigwigs and their wives – lived side by side there in extravagant high-walled mansions; they dined in the same restaurants, and said hello to each other on the school run. Perhaps this was inevitable given the way the ruling party's allegiances had waxed and waned like the moon during its 37 years in power.

Put pins in a map of Harare where the ruling elite live and

you'll see that they cluster around a handful of north-eastern suburbs, about ten miles from downtown with names such as Greystone Park, Glen Lorne, Helensvale, Hogarty Hill and Borrowdale Brooke. The area is still generically referred to as Borrowdale, after the 55,000-acre estate established here in the 1890s by Henry Borrow, a friend of the great British Empire builder Cecil John Rhodes, from whom Rhodesia got its name.

In the 1950s Borrow's estate was subdivided into farms and 10-acre plots that were soon snapped up by the colonial horsey set. They built stables, jumping arenas and a horse racing track – Borrowdale. After independence in 1980 the area became a haven for Harare's affluent white urban gentry, a sort of Hampshire on the savannah. The boutique silversmith Patrick Mavros, jeweller to British Royals, lives here. Olive groves, golf courses and elite private schools sprang up, and by the late 90s the black nouveau-riches had started moving in. Who could blame them? It was idyllic: savannah grasslands and acacia-covered hills that afforded sweeping views from your veranda at sunset.

Among the political elite, the President and First Lady arrived first, establishing the Blue Roof, a sprawling 44-acre estate on Borrowdale Brook Road in Helensvale in 2003. Built in faux Imperial Chinese style for an estimated US$23 million, it had two lakes, a garden pagoda, a pine forest, a herd of antelope and a 25-room mansion with an interlocking dougong-style roof of dazzling, midnight-blue tiles imported from Shanghai. It was there, behind high mile-long walls protected by state-of-the-art radar and armed Presidential Guard soldiers, that Mugabe and Grace spent their time, eschewing State House, the President's official residence closer to town.

Being in the 'burbs also gave Grace easier access to the orphanage, fruit farm and dairy she ran in Mazowe to the north, on land seized from a white farmer.

Borrowdale Brook Road is not to be confused with Borrowdale Brooke, the most exclusive gated residential community in the country, which is literally across the road from the Blue Roof. Comprising some 500 homes on 620 acres of landscaped grounds, a lake at its centre, "the Brooke", as it's known, has a private golf course designed by Zimbabwe's champion golfer Nick Price, who lived there for a while before leaving the country in disgust after President Mugabe and ZANU-PF's war veterans sanctioned the invasion of mostly-white-owned commercial farms in 2000.

The biggest mansion in the Brooke, overlooking the entire community from a high rocky promontory, is the private residence of General Constantino Chiwenga, head of the country's armed forces. Of a contemporary design with an angular façade that juts out like a cruise ship (locals dubbed it the Titanic), it bears the giant initials C & M on its walls, M being for Marry, his second wife, a model and Miss Zimbabwe beauty pageant patron. The initials used to read C & J, but after an acrimonious divorce in 2009, "J", Jocelyn – who famously said during the farm invasions that she had "not tasted white blood in years", relocated to a home on a lower level. By all accounts she now has friendly relationships with her white neighbours in the Brooke, many of whom are dispossessed white farmers.

Such is the moving feast of Zimbabwean politics.

Back in November 2017, ED and Auxillia Mnangagwa lived two miles south of the Brooke, in Helensvale, in a comparatively low-key home on a dip in El Shaddai Road, concealed from view from passing traffic by a thicket of palms and banana groves at its front gate. With a modern, open-plan design – three adjoining seating areas under high angled ceilings – it suggested a rare modesty, if only for being hidden.

A neighbouring mansion on a steep hillside had no such qualms: the modern, cream-coloured, triple-storey palace of Saviour Kasukuwere, the ZANU-PF Political Commissar. Along with Grace and Jonathan Moyo, Saviour was the power and face of G40 and his house matched his garrulous personality. With its Gatsby-like gables and reinforced walls and floor-to-ceiling bulletproof windows it looked like something out of Malibu. Ironically, as things were later to turn out, it was designed by the same architect as Chiwenga's home in the Brooke, for Chiwenga had been a mentor and father figure to Saviour. Indeed, ED had been too. Saviour was a daring young intelligence agent in the late 80s and 90s during and after the period that ED, as Minister of State Security, oversaw the Central Intelligence Organisation (CIO), the country's secret police. Saviour gained renown for a hair-raising 1991 operation when, aged 21, he helicoptered into the remote mountain hideaway of Mozambique's RENAMO resistance rebels disguised as a journalist, locating the camp's coordinates. ED used to walk to Saviour's house for tea; Saviour would visit Chiwenga at the Titanic to watch Wimbledon tennis and Premiership soccer games. Chiwenga bought Saviour his wedding band as a token of their friendship; Saviour did the same for the General. Now they were at war.

With other G40 kingpins – Jonathan Moyo (Greystone Park) and Finance Minister Ignatius Chombo (Mount Pleasant) – living nearby, Borrowdale boasted the richest real estate in the country. In the days to come it would also become the stage set for the most dramatic and closely watched political and military operation in modern African history.

◈ ◈ ◈

Junior and KC pulled up at El Shaddai Road at 4pm, noted the absence of security on the gates, and raced inside. They thought they were too late. Instead, Junior found his parents chatting away on the sofas in the furthest living room. Junior was astonished at how calm his father was, and shocked that he still believed Mugabe – "Robert" as he called him – would not let any harm come to him. "I thought he was crazy," Junior said later, although he never dared say that directly to his father.

If Robert Mugabe was bookish, wiry and erudite, ED was his physical and verbal opposite: burly and broad-shouldered, he had the lumbering gait of a buffalo, and an inscrutable, taciturn manner. One of his daughters told a friend that their father had a strange form of discipline for them when they were kids: if they had done something wrong he would call them into his office, listen quietly as they explained what they had done, then dismiss them, telling them he was going to consider a suitable punishment. The punishment was to leave them in a state of anxiety for days wondering what the punishment might be. He was good at the waiting game.

Outside, the driveway was filling up; Sean and Collins arrived, as did lawyers, advisors, relatives and security personnel. According to Collins, Auxillia had spent the morning trying to contact Grace Mugabe to ask if there was anything she could do to mend things. They'd been friends once; they'd attended Grace's lavish wedding to the President and were near neighbours. Grace never answered.

Now the three sons set out to convince their father that

the threat to his life was real and he needed to leave. There had, after all, been a string run of attacks on him dating back more than a year: break-ins at his offices; a car crash that wasn't investigated; and, the big one, the poisoning…

It had happened three months earlier, Saturday, August 12th, at a rally in Gwanda, Matabeleland, in the far south of the country. ED had flown to the rally from Harare in a military helicopter, with two fellow cabinet ministers, one a medical doctor. They were served fruit and sandwiches on the chopper, in separate marked boxes. Later, at the rally, lunch was served under a tent – chicken, samosas and ice cream. The President was there, served by his own private chef, as in Nero's court. It spoke of the paranoia of the time. Forty minutes later ED got stomach cramps and sweats and began projectile vomiting. Someone diagnosed food poisoning and suggested he go to the local hospital. ED refused. He wanted to go to his personal doctor in Gweru, north of Bulawayo. It wasn't paranoia: he'd received warnings from his own allies in intelligence that there were plans to poison him. Now, in his delirious state, he was convinced that they'd done it.

It was Chiwenga who stepped in to save him. He had ED flown by military helicopter to Gweru, where "shivering and experiencing memory lapses", he was sedated by his doctor to ease pressure on his organs. Chiwenga then flew him to Manyame military base in Harare, and from there an emergency medivac charter flight was arranged to Johannesburg. ED would spend a week at the Donald Gordon Medical Centre where his system was washed out and the poison detected – an arsenic-related hard-metal toxin.

Now, three months later, there were still traces of it in his blood, and he claimed he knew who did it.

It was only at around 5.30pm, when ED himself got a warning call – the same message Junior had received – that he finally agreed to leave. "It was the first time my father ever listened to us," said Junior. But, before doing so he wrote another letter. The family waited anxiously in the living room or made emergency calls in the driveway as the patriarch retired to his study. He emerged almost an hour later with a letter and his Louis Vuitton briefcase. He gave the letter to his lawyer with express instructions: "Release it when you get news I am safely out the country."

❖ ❖ ❖

The problem was, they didn't know where to escape to, or how to get there. They had no plan.

KC Shetty had been dispatched to ask the Indian Ambassador if ED might get asylum in his embassy. Junior had called the CEO of a local chrome company owned by a South African friend and business associate of ED, the billionaire tycoon Zunaid Moti, to request emergency use of his private jet parked at Robert Mugabe International. But the CEO told Junior the plane wasn't working, and besides, Moti Group didn't want to "get entangled" in Zimbabwean politics. "We are just here for business."

"We were abandoned by everyone," said Junior.

If the Helensvale house wasn't already being watched it soon would be, so they decided to relocate to a nearby property to work out what to do: a half-completed house Collins was building on Crowhill Road, Hogarty Hill, just past The Brooke.

At 6.30pm, with the sun dipping over the hills, two vehicles made their way past the palms and banana trees at the gate, turned left and left again, keeping an eye out for tailing cars. There were seven in the party: ED; his three sons; their cousin Tarirai (Tarry); a baby-faced giant of a man named Richard Mavhoro who worked for a private security company ED often used; and a business and political consultant to Junior, Dr Jenfan Muswere. They were soon joined by Hosea Manzunzu, a friend of ED's from the guerilla war, and his driver Wise Jasi. Manzunzu limped from an old war wound and was known as Limping Jack.

For the next four hours the group hunkered down in Collins's roofless house, using cell phones and car headlamps for light. It smelled of wet cement. Mosquitoes buzzed around their heads and when a gust of wind rippled through the trees they all jumped. By now they had heard from friends at Robert Mugabe International Airport that it was teeming with police and security agents. And they got word that the family farm, outside Harare, was also being watched. The net was closing in.

Junior came up with one last gambit. He made a WhatsApp call to a friend, Ameerh Naran, a young Indian-Zimbabwean entrepreneur who owns Vimana Private Jets, a London-based company that arranges private jet charters for the world's elite – anything from 787 Dreamliners to Gulfstreams. Kanye West and the Kardashians are among his clients. If anyone could get them out, he could. Naran, 31, who is also a racing-car driver and has the licence to import Good Vibrations sex toys into Zimbabwe, just happened to be in Harare at the time, and was dining with a friend, Aron Vico, at Chang Thai, a popular restaurant on Churchill Road in leafy Gunhill suburb.

Naran told Junior he would make some calls and see what he could do.

He phoned Junior back 15 minutes later. Charles Prince, a private airport west of the city, was teeming with CIO officers so that would not work, but they could try a medical air evacuation; that was how ED had got to the South African hospital after the poisoning three months earlier. The problem was the medivac company needed a doctor's note to confirm the passenger was ill, and the passenger would have to get picked up by an ambulance with a nurse on board who could confirm the diagnosis. Jesus, thought Junior. How to pull all this off? It was late on a Monday night in a city with dysfunctional communications and crumbling infrastructure and assassins were after them.

Furthermore, when Junior relayed the news of the medivac plan to his father, he wasn't happy.

"But I'm not ill," ED told him.

"You have to pretend! You've not recovered from the poisoning and you collapsed!"

"How do I do that?"

"Just pretend!"

By now Junior was cursing his father for not having made his own escape plan.

After frantic cell phone calls the group located a military doctor at the Ministry of Defence who agreed to write a note. The former VP was suffering from heart-related stress brought on by his firing, it would read. The doctor sent a driver to deliver the letter to Naran at the restaurant, who was to forward it to the airport to get clearance for the medivac.

If Junior needed confirmation that all their phones were bugged, they soon got it. The Chang Thai restaurant has a large solid metal gate that opens up onto the wide expanse of Churchill Road. Naran got a call from the driver carrying the doctor's letter to meet him outside the gate. He duly stepped out, and seconds later a Toyota Prado with Ministry of Defence plates pulled up across the road. Its window was rolled down and the driver held out the doctor's letter. Naran was crossing the street to take it when suddenly two unmarked white vehicles pulled up behind the Prado in a cloud of dust, two men in each. He knew they were CIO, secret police.

"You're being followed!" Naran shouted.

The driver didn't hang around. He threw the letter at Naran – who caught it – and sped off. Naran ran back into the restaurant, knowing the police had likely ID'd him and would follow him in. Frantic, he asked the restaurant owners to close the automatic metal gate, while his dinner companion, Aron, collected his vehicle. Five minutes later, the gates reopened and sure enough, four CIO officers hovered outside. They had no interest in the white Jewish guy driving out, but if they'd searched his boot they would have found Ameerh Naran, racing-car driver, sex-toy importer and friend of the Kardashians, hiding in it with the doctor's note. Naran was at that point cursing his decision to make a quick visit to his family in Zimbabwe; he could have been in Monaco or Miami or Aspen with his fancy friends.

Incredibly, the medivac ploy almost worked.

A medical plane at Robert Mugabe International was fuelled and cleared, and an ambulance with a nurse on board was dispatched to Hogarty Hill. But whether out of gut feeling or over-caution, ED nixed the plan. He thought that the ambulance might be stopped, so he wasn't getting in it.

They put their heads together again and came up with a plan of last resort: since the action was all focused on the airports south and west of Harare, why not head east? Mutare,

Zimbabwe's fourth city, on the Mozambique border, is over 200 miles away. They could drive there and cross the border when it opened at dawn. Oddly enough, Limping Jack and Wise Jasi had been at that very border that afternoon: they were planning a business trip to Mozambique when ED had called them back to Harare to assist.

Meanwhile, as the failed medivac was being arranged, Jenfan Muswere had driven back to the Helensvale house three times to get food, clothes and documents. "I drove the back way, down Borrowdale Brook Road, past the Blue Roof to avoid suspicion." Presidential Guard soldiers stood sentry at its ornate gates. Behind its high walls, the President and First Lady were enjoying a peaceful night.

At around 11pm the nine-strong party made their way out of Collins's property in a three-car convoy, lights on dim. They needed to avoid intelligence agents, but also the police. The Police Commissioner was an ally of Grace and G40, and his men were all over the country's roads and highways at the time, stopping and harassing motorists for any minor offence.

They had a problem straight-away. Two of the vehicles needed fuel. It was late on a Monday and their options were limited, though there was a 24-hour ZUVA station on Enterprise Road near Harare Drive, the road they would need to take out of town. They headed there.

They hadn't got far when they hit more serious trouble.

A speeding vehicle, lights on full glare, as if to blind them, appeared out of nowhere and tried to overtake the back car – a C-class Merc – carrying Sean, Collins and Junior. A common method of political assassination in Zimbabwe is vehicular: mysterious car accidents have wiped out many a political opponent. ED would have known this, as would his sons. ED had run the Security Ministry that oversaw the CIO when the method was perfected; only a month earlier, ED had been the victim of a suspicious car accident himself.

The boys panicked.

Was this a CIO hit team? Did they know ED was in the front car of the convoy? Sean acted fast. As the tail car tried to pass, he blocked it, then pushed it off the road. The two vehicles came to a halt in the roadside dust. Sean and his brothers leapt out and rushed the driver before he could react. One of them dragged him out; the other leaned in, removed the keys and threw them into the bush. It was over in seconds. Then they leapt back in their car and sped on, catching up with the front two cars that had slowed ahead.

Minutes later, adrenaline pumping, they reached the ZUVA station and began filling the vehicles.

It was then that Junior suddenly began to have doubts. The driver had smelled of alcohol… There was loud music blaring in his car… He was alone… What CIO agent operates alone? It dawned on him: the man was likely an innocent drunk driver, emboldened by alcohol, just speeding home. "I felt bad," Junior recalled later. "I still wonder what the guy told his wife when he eventually made it home."

This was no time for doubt, though.

And so it was that in the early hours of November 7th, 2017, three vehicles, tanks full of gas, made for the outskirts of the capital then headed east.

Chapter 1

ELLIS: THE WHO THE HELL IS HE MAN

On a bright afternoon in the spring of 2015, driving past the mall near his suburban Johannesburg home, Tom Ellis spotted his assassins. He didn't know they were his assassins – they hadn't introduced themselves to him yet – but for the past 20 minutes, since he'd left his meeting at a Sandton hotel, a white Toyota Legend, two black men inside, had been on his tail, and Ellis knew they were bad news.

A good-looking man of 55 – slim, tall with a healthy mop of salt-and-pepper hair and hazel eyes that glistened like a leopard's – Ellis had faced his share of danger. He had smuggled an activist in the boot of a car across the Zimbabwe–Botswana border, been arrested during a violent election season in Zimbabwe; met with fugitive exiles from the Mugabe regime in the sketchier parts of Johannesburg. But this was different. This was blocks from his Randburg home, where his wife Clare and four kids would be waiting for him to get back. Clare had been followed recently – a black Merc with tinted windows had tailed her to the school gate on the kids' run – and the couple were wary. Ellis had a good idea who the men were. He knew the game. He'd expected as much, ever since he and his friends had taken a new direction. When you set out to remove a dictator – when you reach out to those close to the dictator – the dictator is eventually going to find out about it.

Approaching a set of lights at Northgate, Ellis made his move. He slowed his vehicle on green, watched the car behind him get close, then simply stopped and waited for red. The Toyota bakkie, unable to keep its distance, was forced to pull up behind him. Ellis exited his car and walked towards his tail.

He could see the men were dressed casually in polo shirts. The passenger was in his late 30s: a slight, bony, clean-shaven man with thick wire-rimmed glasses and hollowed-out eyes; the driver was a bit older, in his early 40s, and thick-set, with the harder features – a scar on his left cheek, a missing front tooth – of someone who'd known a rough life. Ellis reckoned he might be handy with a knife or a gun.

He walked to the driver's side.

"Guys," he said, leaning in as the driver rolled down the window. "I know you're following me. Let's go get a drink."

The driver, irritated and aggressive, scowled at him; his passenger stared straight ahead, pretending he wasn't there. "*Shamwaris*," said Ellis, mangling a plural out of the Shona word for "friend", "I know you're following me. You've been on me since the hotel. So, let's talk. I know a place."

The men in the car looked awkwardly at each other for a while, then shrugged and nodded. They could use a beer. Ellis smiled and sauntered back to his car. The two vehicles pulled away as the light turned green.

Ellis liked to work in bars. A builder by trade, he ran a small home maintenance company but, much to his wife's alarm, he'd largely abandoned that over the years to focus on his "thing". His thing – his love, his passion, his all-consuming obsession – was the politics and business of Zimbabwe, the country of his birth, a country he'd left in 1980 as a 15-year-old kid and not lived in since. He wasn't built for desk work, though, and the Sundowner bar in Randburg had become an informal office for him over the years. It was a run down, working man's joint with rugby on the TVs and the permanent smell of cigarette smoke and spilled beer. The Rundowner, he and his mates called it. They didn't stand on ceremony. He'd held countless meetings here: with potential investors, opposition activists, human rights lawyers and displaced white farmers. He had planned visits to the International Criminal Court at The Hague, even brainstormed a visit to the Obama White House to press the case for human rights in Zimbabwe.

The vehicles parked and Ellis, wearing slim-fit jeans, short-sleeved checked cotton shirt and the trademark Veldskoens common to white Zimbabweans of his generation, led the way, the two men following awkwardly behind. Ellis clocked their well-worn trainers: footwear to move fast in. Ellis hugged Heidi, the owner, a bob-haired blonde, chose a table at the back by the pool tables, and ordered his usual drink, a cold Hansa. The two men ordered Castle.

They introduced each other. As Ellis had guessed, they were Zimbabwean. The driver, Kasper, the senior of the two, said he was a plumber. The passenger, Magic, said he was an accountant. Ellis knew they were more than that and these weren't their real names. South Africa is a hot bed of Zimbabwean spies – freelance and full-time agents for Mugabe's expansive CIO, keeping an eye on the three-million-strong diaspora – but he didn't push it. Besides, he was enjoying their company. They talked about work, family and home; how the country they loved was tearing itself apart.

The two men were both supporting relatives back in Zimbabwe with remittances; Kasper had six children and a wife to feed in Harare. It was hard. He wished he was around for his young boy like his dad had been for him. He said his father had been a policeman in Harare. Ellis flinched a little. His father had been a policeman too, in a different era, when Zimbabwe had a different name, but he kept quiet about that.

It was during the third round of drinks, his guests switching to Johnny Walker, that Ellis asked the question again.

"So guys, why were you following me?"

They looked embarrassed but denied it.

"We are not, we are just driving to the shops," muttered Kasper, who did most of the talking.

Ellis smiled and gave them his pitch.

"Just so you know. I'm not political. I don't care what political party you are. All I want is good governance in Zimbabwe. Your families are hungry; you have to live here to feed your children back there. That's stupid. People don't even like us Zimbabweans in South Africa. Me, my sister lost her farm in Bindura in 2005. She's now in Zambia. My family is broke. My wife is angry at me. I'm spending all our money on this game. The question is – how do we get a fair system in Zimbabwe? How do we get a fair election, one where the people's choice wins and the military accept the results?"

They nodded their heads in agreement. It was the odd thing about Zimbabweans. Everyone, whatever their race or their politics, knew there was a problem – the disease had been diagnosed – but they all claimed someone else was to blame and that their man was the one to fix it.

By 6pm Ellis was getting text messages from his wife, asking where he was. He wanted to keep talking but he had to go. He was about to ask for their contact details when Kasper requested his and said he'd like to see him again. And so they ended up communicating on WhatsApp, the encrypted messaging platform.

❖ ❖ ❖

They met the following month, the month after that, and again a few months later, at the same table on different days. Mostly it was just Kasper. Magic had apparently landed an accountancy job at the South African Rugby Union in Newlands, Cape Town, and only occasionally came up to Joburg.

Ellis's wife Clare recorded the dates of some of the meetings in her diary. A tall attractive blonde from a farming family in Zimbabwe, she had first met Ellis when he was 15. He had visited her grandfather's farm with his best friend. She married the friend. They split up and she and Ellis got together.

It was the late 1990s. Ellis wanted to move back to Zimbabwe to be with her – he hadn't lived in Zimbabwe for 18 years now and was desperate to go back. But politics interfered: after years of one-party rule, Zimbabwe, once the model post-colonial African nation, was in economic turmoil and a popular opposition party, the Movement for Democratic Change (MDC), led by Morgan Tsvangirai, had risen to challenge Mugabe.

Rebuked at a referendum in 2000 – when he shockingly lost a vote to change the constitution, his first defeat in any national poll – Mugabe set out to crush the MDC. He used veterans of the liberation war and a violent youth militia called Green Bombers to invade mostly white-owned commercial farms. Agriculture, the backbone of the country, collapsed, the West imposed sanctions and the economy went into freefall. Between 2000 and 2010 some four million Zimbabweans fled the country, Clare among them. Instead of Ellis joining her in Zimbabwe, she joined him in the Joburg suburbs, and here they were many years and four children later. Although, in truth, Ellis wasn't here at all; mentally he was *there*, obsessed with the politics of a country he hadn't lived in since he was 15 years old.

Clare knew it was his mission.

"I could ask him to choose – me or Zimbabwe," she once said, "but I know what he would say, so I don't ask." And she had to admit; he was bloody good at it. He had a gift. There was no official role with any political party and few people knew his face or his name; he worked behind the scenes, connecting people. They came to him for advice, contacts, funding, legal aid, strategies, and he hooked them up.

A white Zimbabwean farmer named Pete Drummond (who appeared in travel writer Paul Theroux's African masterpiece *Dark Star Safari*) once received help from Ellis. It came out of the blue, without fanfare but it saved Drummond at a desperate time in his life. Drummond called Ellis "The Who the Hell Is He Man". He was an African Pimpernel. Good things happened if you knew Tom Ellis. People trusted him. It was partly the leopard eyes. Those eyes looked straight at you when you spoke so you knew he was listening, that he cared. But it was also the voice. White Zimbabwean men of Ellis's generation can be loud and aggressive, especially when they drink, but Ellis spoke softly, and the more he drank the quieter he got, so it was as if he was confiding in you. You ended up liking him and wanting him to like you.

It was on the seventh or eighth meeting, nudging into 2016, that it happened.

Ellis met Kasper on a weekday afternoon at the same window table in the back room at the Sundowner, a view of Johannesburg's skyline before them. Pool balls cracked; afternoon drinkers watched English soccer on TV, sitting on pine benches Ellis had recently installed for the owner. Ellis was starting to grow tired of Kasper. He gave nothing away and Ellis had started to doubt his instincts: maybe he and Magic weren't CIO spies; maybe they really were who they said they were – just a plumber and an accountant, part of the vast rootless diaspora.

But mostly he was annoyed because he was paying for all the food and beer and whiskey for them and he couldn't afford it. There was a time, in the early days of the game, when donor money had poured in. Mugabe was on the ropes and there was a belief that he could be toppled. They almost succeeded, too. In 2008 the MDC actually won the elections. Except the result was the same. The ruling party massaged the tallies, forced a rerun and then – there's no other word for it – the military went to war on its own citizenry, bludgeoning them into submission to keep Mugabe in power.

By the time the 2013 election rolled around there wasn't much money left. And when the MDC lost that too (they claimed it was rigged), the bottom fell out. Donors were exhausted and funds dried up. The energy that once defined the opposition dissipated; MDC leaders fell out with each other and formed splinter groups. A Zimbabwean writer living in the US, Dominic Mhiripiri, wrote an essay "A Breakup letter to Zimbabwe; I really just don't care anymore", that perfectly summed up the mood.

Ellis and his colleagues grew tired too.

Not of the goal – a new government for Zimbabwe – but of the method. What they were doing clearly wasn't working. What was the point of winning elections and never winning power?

And so, in 2015, they tried a new direction. They approached their once sworn enemies, those within ZANU-PF, the ruling party, who might be tired of Mugabe too, to see if they could work together.

Mugabe was getting old and the ruling party was riven with faction fighting, a vicious internal war to succeed him. Ellis chuckled. He thought his side had problems? What about theirs? Jesus, it was like Game of Thrones up there. In 2014 the party had got rid of the last Vice-President – and Mugabe's likely successor – Joice Mujuru. Mujuru was a female veteran of the liberation war against white rule who claimed to have shot down a Rhodesian helicopter in battle. She had been married to General Solomon Mujuru, the revered commander of the guerilla army that brought Mugabe to power. But in 2011 he'd died in a mysterious house fire on his farm. That had left his wife exposed. In 2014 a vicious character assassination campaign began against her. She was accused of treason, of plotting against Mugabe, of being a secessionist. The incredible thing was that the campaign was led by another woman, a 49-year-old political novice: the President's wife, Grace Mugabe. Up until 2014 Grace had been best known for her profligate shopping sprees and rapacious accumulation of money, mansions and farms. She was known as Gucci Grace, the First Shopper. But Grace was fast coming into her own and, in the space of a few months, with her advisors whispering in her ear, she had destroyed the female VP, her husband's former friend and ally.

Ellis and his colleagues had actually met with Joice Mujuru in Johannesburg in 2015, after her fall, to consider working with her, but what was the point? She had no power; Grace had seen to that.

So, who to work with? Obviously not Grace and G40. As Ellis well knew, Mugabe's wife meant more Mugabe – even worse!

That left the other group, Lacoste, led by the veteran politician and current VP, Emmerson Mnangagwa – the Crocodile – and, incredibly, there were openings. In late 2015 Ellis had met with an emissary of ED's in King Pie, a pastry shop in Northgate shopping centre, and over cokes and steak pie sounded him out. According to him, if ED came to power he would hold free elections and open the country to business. "Open for business" – Ellis liked that; it sounded just like the opposition MDC party's platform. Meanwhile, the war veterans – once one of the main pillars of Mugabe's power – appeared to be on the outs with Mugabe too, because they were loyal to the Crocodile and didn't fancy being ruled by the President's vulgar wife. Beyond her lack of sophistication, she hadn't taken part in the country's liberation war, which meant to them that she lacked the credentials to rule. And so Ellis and his allies approached the war veterans. What surprised him was how the more they inquired, the closer to the top they got. Which was why, he suspected, Kasper and Magic were on his tail: Mugabe's secret police knew who he had been meeting with…

❖ ❖ ❖

Then, out of the blue that weekday afternoon, in the back

room of the Sundowner, Kasper told him. He had strong Shona-accented English that was tough to make out. He wasn't educated like his friend Magic, but what he lacked in eloquence he made up for with a blunt, plain-speaking manner that Ellis found honest and refreshing. It was obvious to him that Kasper had power.

He told Ellis he was from Central Intelligence in Zimbabwe and he had a job to do.

"What job?" said Ellis softly.

"I was sent to kill you," said Kasper.

Ellis felt a rush of blood; Jesus – he was very much in the game.

"How would you do it?" he said, his voice a near whisper now.

"At the ATM by the Total station near here. You would be drawing money. It would be a robbery."

Ellis nodded, sipped his beer, never taking his leopard eyes off Kasper's.

"So why haven't you done it?" he asked.

Kasper looked straight at him, his eyes bloodshot.

"Do you know what they call me, Tom? *Wairasa*. I am unpredictable to everyone, even the bosses. Left signal, I turn right. Come on, we can't kill people like cockroaches lest we be haunted by their dead spirits. Sometimes my team is on a mission to kill someone; I say – this mission is not working. We stop. My hands are clean, Tom, my hands are clean."

The way he spoke, Ellis found himself believing him.

He had never met a man more persuasive.

A weight was lifted that afternoon; it was as if a married couple had made a breakthrough in therapy. Ellis still didn't trust him – he was a killer and a spy after all, and spying was a con game – but they spoke more freely now: about the politics of ZANU-PF, about the two factions, who was winning the game, and who was more likely to change things. Kasper was an ED guy – Lacoste. He didn't like the President's wife, how she insulted people, and he didn't like what she and the President were saying about the war veterans. Kasper's uncle was a war veteran; he had grown up on stories of the liberation war heroes.

They finished talking after another hour and this time Ellis was okay picking up the tab.

Then, as they walked back to their vehicles, Kasper turned to Ellis in the darkness of the parking lot and said something that took his breath away.

"You should know," he said. "There is someone on your team. He is not with you. He is with us."

Ellis felt winded. That there might be a spy in his camp didn't shock him that much. He met with dozens of activists in the MDC and the diaspora all the time. He couldn't keep track of all of them, or plan for it.

What shocked him was that Kasper was *telling him.*

"Who is it?" he asked.

Kasper grinned.

"*Shamwari,*" he said. "Wait, relax yourself. I will show you. Then, we can discuss."

And so it began.

Ellis had a name for Kasper from then on. When he recalled how they first met, how they got to know each other, how they started working together, how their team of two became four, then four became six, then six became a "Dirty Dozen" then, by the time the deal went down, those glorious two weeks in November, when a network of 50 men and women, sworn enemies turned brothers, rivals turned comrades, working out of hotels and bars and boardrooms and parking lots for a common goal – the removal of a dictator – Ellis chuckled to himself. He called Kasper "my assassin".

Chapter 2

KASPER: THE ASSASSIN

Agent Kasper parked his white Toyota Legend on Kotze Street, Hillbrow, and sat in it for a while checking his phones. He had seven of them and needed to answer dozens of text and WhatsApp messages – some from HQ in Harare, others from the embassy in Pretoria; still more from family, friends, contacts and other agents at what he called "The Institute".

He replied quickly, keeping one eye on the street. Then he messaged friends and sources he hadn't heard from that day, usually with just a simple "Hi" or "*Shamwari*" on WhatsApp. He'd followed this routine so long now it was second nature. He liked routine. His father, a policeman, had taught him that routine gave you discipline and discipline gave you a work ethic and a work ethic meant you would go far in life.

He watched the busy street. Pimps and drug dealers loitered in doorways; cop cars cruised by.

Kasper had certainly come far but he wasn't sure it was much of a life.

His full name was Charles Wezhira and he was a 16-year veteran of Zimbabwe's CIO. He was born in 1971 and grew up with his mother in a village in rural Mutoko, northeastern Zimbabwe. Home was a thatched mud hut. He spent his childhood herding cattle. In his early teens he moved to live with his father in the capital. Dad's place was a one-bedroom shack in the sprawling high-density suburb of Mufakose, west of the city. His father worked at Morris Depot Police Station in town and would wake at 5am to get to work. Kasper got in the habit of waking up with him, and every morning before school would go to the Area J gym down the road to pump weights. Four nights a week he took karate lessons at the local community centre. He made black belt and won city-wide tournaments. It was all because of routine.

❖ ❖ ❖

At around 6pm he saw the man he was looking for – an elderly black gentleman in a suit – enter a tavern across the road, and he stepped out of the car and followed him.

Hillbrow is a frenetic high-rise neighbourhood on the edge of inner-city Johannesburg. One of the most densely populated square miles in the world, its residential skyscrapers are decked like dominos along a narrow ridge. Its most prominent landmark, the cylindrical Ponte Tower Apartments, the third-tallest building in Africa, towers over the cityscape, a blinking electric advertisement on its top floors flashing like a warning sign for all the city to see.

Up until the early 1980s Hillbrow was a miniature Manhattan, a cosmopolitan borough of Italian sidewalk cafés, Jewish delis and late night-bars. In recent decades it has become first-stop for millions of African migrants fleeing war and poverty in their homelands to the north for the promise of riches in the City of Gold. They arrive in Joburg with nothing and lodge ten to a room in those cheap high-rises. Crime, drugs and prostitution are rife. The dominant migrant group in Hillbrow is Zimbabwean, and since spying on Zimbabweans was what Agent Kasper did, he spent a lot of time there.

He entered the tavern and found a stool at the bar two seats away from the man in the suit.

It was quiet and dimly lit. A few single men sat at corner tables with prostitutes. There were two TVs on; one showing English soccer, the other ETV News. The men watched the game while the girls whispered in their ears and sipped vodka from straws. Kasper ordered a Castle, said "hi" to the man he had followed in, and made small talk with him in Shona. Presently, another man joined the suit, and the two spoke more quietly. Kasper listened intently to what they were saying but it wasn't of much interest.

A prostitute came over and introduced herself to Kasper. He had seen her around the clubs and bars before.

He asked her where she was from.

"DRC," she said.

Kasper knew the Congo. He'd spent time there, in 1998–2000. He didn't want to be reminded of it and he wasn't in the mood for small talk. He was working.

"Fuck off," he told the woman, and she cursed him and slunk away.

The TV news turned to Zimbabwe – something about a riot in Harare; liberation war veterans had been tear-gassed by police – and the two men next to Kasper stopped talking for a while and watched. Back home the purges against the war veterans, the ZANU-PF old guard, were continuing. Kasper ordered another beer, slugged it, then got up to leave. As he did so he bumped into the man he had followed, dropping his phone. The man kindly picked it up and handed it back. Kasper thanked him. Outside he put the phone in a zip-lock bag. He had the man's fingerprints now. They could soon be on a file in Harare.

❖ ❖ ❖

Hillbrow was heating up. Police sirens blared, city lights made the night sky glow. He heard a distant gunshot. He did the rounds in the busier clubs and hotel bars – the Summit, the Diplomat. By 10pm he had made his way to the Hillbrow Inn on Van der Merwe Street. He was a regular there. It was a seedy 18-storey high-rise with a thumping bar and strip club on the ground floor. On the upper floors were the rooms where the women would take the men. "Eighteen floors of whores", people called it. Most of the working girls were Zimbabwean. He drank another Castle and watched women in their underwear gyrate on a stage. Some were as young as his daughters back in Harare. It depressed him.

How had it come to this?

Up until 1995, the 15th year of Robert Mugabe's rule, Zimbabwe had been the envy of Africa. It had the most educated and literate population on the continent, a sophisticated healthcare system, thriving tourism, and rich and fertile farmland that fed the region. Kasper was a proud and loyal patriot then. He graduated from high school in 1989 with four O-Levels, worked as a plumber, then as a welder for Budget Steel, making trailers. He was good with his hands. In 1994 he followed his father into the Zimbabwe Republic Police. He loved the crisp brown uniform. When he visited his mother in Mutoko he would wear it and he could see how proud she and the other villagers were of him.

Tough, fearless, confident, a karate black belt, he was soon recruited to the much-feared Police Support Unit (PSU), the Black Boots, a paramilitary wing of the force. It was with the PSU that he was sent to the Congo in 1998. The government told them they were going on a mission to support the Congolese government. In reality it was a bloodbath, Africa's first "world war": the armies of 16 African nations split into two sides, fighting over minerals buried deep in the central African soil. Zimbabweans seemed to do most of the fighting – against Rwandans. In one battle, 500 Zimbabweans dug deep in trenches on a ranch north of Lubumbashi and were shot at and shelled for days by Rwandan soldiers from a trench 80 yards away. It was like that Great War Kasper had read about. They ran out of water at one point and had to drink their own urine. Only the helicopter gunships saved them.

To Kasper, the Congo fiasco was the beginning of the decline in Zimbabwe. The liberation war veterans, who had won the country's independence from white rule in 1980, had already seen the political elite living the high life, and demanded their share. In 1997 Mugabe agreed to pay them cash handouts, and to do so he started printing money. That set off hyperinflation. Zimbabweans soon needed a brick of dollars to buy a beer; later they would need a wheel barrow. Mugabe went to war in the Congo to generate income, but that just turned out to be another way for the elite to get rich. In 2002 a UN Security Council investigation into illegal exploitation of natural resources during the Congo war found that Mugabe, Defence Minister Sydney Sekeramayi, along with ED Mnangagwa as "key strategist", had been engaged in a complex network of companies exploiting minerals and land in the Congo in partnership with Zimbabwe's top military brass, including General Chiwenga and Air Marshall Perence Shiri. The political and military elite cashed in, but back home the cost of the war – US$27 million a month – crippled the economy and made people very angry. The MDC, a popular opposition group sprung up as a result. Now Mugabe needed spies to infiltrate and take down the opposition. And so it was that in 2000 Kasper was recruited to the CIO – the Institute, as he called it – and that had been his life ever since: "Spying, spying, spying."

The CIO, already ubiquitous (it was set up by Rhodesian police in 1963 and had links to Britain's MI6), became a hydra-headed monster after 2000. It had nine branches, covering everything from counter-intelligence and military intelligence to a foreign bureau. Each branch had its own director, who reported straight to the President, bypassing the main director, as well as the Security and Defence ministries.

It was the beginning of what the Zimbabwean academic Ibbo Mandaza called the Securocrat State: "the primacy of 'national security' over political and economic reform," with Mugabe, the Big Man, as its all-powerful head. By the mid-2000s it was said that one in five Zimbabweans was a spy of some sort: your waiter, taxi driver, gardener, kids' primary school teacher – even the homeless man on the street – all could be informing on you. And since all intelligence was routed to Mugabe, he knew everything about everyone. It gave him enormous power, and kept his internal rivals – and the opposition – off balance.

Kasper's handler and mentor at the Institute was a veteran agent named Willard Badza who had trained in Russia, China and North Korea. Badza assigned Kasper to infiltrate the MDC. It was easy. Kasper joined the Mufakose branch of the party, demonstrated his police and paramilitary bona fides, and, before long, he was a body guard, working security for the opposition leadership, including Morgan Tsvangirai himself. The MDC was riddled with Mugabe's spies: it was how ZANU-PF always stayed steps ahead of them.

Kasper was a natural. Spying is a confidence game and he had confidence in droves – the confidence of a rural kid who'd grown up rough, without privilege. He was physical, with a meaty face and hands like shovels. He also spoke fast and looked you in the eye, and that intimidated people. Even his wife never knew what he did. "I can see beyond," he would say. "My words, which come from my heart, are too straight. I can persuade you of anything. Already I can see your weaknesses. If you like women, or money or beer or if you are a coward, then bang," – he would punch his fist into his palm – "you are mine."

He said it helped that he wasn't overly educated. Education took away your instincts. "When you are educated, you delay, it takes you in a wrong direction. My education is already here," he would say and point to his head. "It comes not from books."

He reeled off success after success working undercover, but after a few years in the game he grew stressed and despondent. He was the one taking all the risks, "making the big moves" while his boss, Badza, was taking all the credit. "He could see I could make things happen, but he steal my ideas and get glory for himself." He noticed his boss driving better cars, living in bigger houses. Kasper, married now, already with four kids, was renting a two-bedroom shack in Mufakose where the children slept in a single pull-out. There was only space for a small fridge; they filled the sink with ice at night to keep the meat and milk cold and used a broken washing machine as a pantry. They had an old TV with shitty reception. By 2004 he couldn't even afford school fees. "Sometimes, when I see how little my son has, I drop some tears," he would say. At that point he tried leaving. He planned to join the exodus of Zimbabweans to London – Harare North. Three million Zimbabweans had fled the country by then, many to the UK. "But my passport was a fail," he said forlornly. "I was made to remain."

And so he stayed, "Spying, spying, spying."

He almost got caught once. At Harvest House, MDC headquarters in 2005, a group of party youths turned on him, accusing him of being a sell-out. They started punching him, knocked him to the ground then picked him up to carry him off. Then, a miracle: the dictaphone he kept in his sock to record meetings fell out. They never noticed. The security bosses called off the youths and told them Kasper was trustworthy. Even Tsvangirai, their leader, trusted him.

He claimed to have saved Tsvangirai's life once. In 2006 Tsvangirai was detained and severely beaten at Borrowdale Police Station in Harare. Kasper learned that his colleagues at the Institute planned to release him and then finish the job. Kasper kept Tsvangirai inside the police station until the media learned where he was and reported it. "If I let him go before then, he was dead."

He came to like and respect Tsvangirai, but still he spied on him. That was Zimbabwe: the line between friend and enemy had blurred.

It was in 2007 that the Institute transferred Kasper to Johannesburg. The MDC was growing in strength. It had money and a vast support network in the diaspora. His job now was to spy on the diaspora working with, and funding, the MDC. Over the years he had built a team of loyal foot soldiers who revered him. One was a guy with thick glasses codenamed Magic – from the Shona *Magirobho,* meaning "big globes", in reference to his large glasses. Magic. Agent Magic was smart, with a university degree, a certified accountant. Kasper had plans for him.

And it was while working in Johannesburg over the years that he came to find out about a white man named Tom Ellis. It seemed to him that Ellis was some kind of lynchpin. He knew everyone and yet no one seemed to know anything about him. So he spied on Ellis, started a file on him and sent reports to Harare. Then word came down that he should eliminate this Ellis. Kasper ignored the order.

"You call me *wairasa*, right?" he said to his team. "And I will tell you right here: *mava kuirasa* – you are going off course. What do we get from killing this man? We can use him."

He drank beer and smiled as he thought of Ellis.

He had plans for Ellis too.

❖ ❖ ❖

Kasper snapped out of his reverie at the bar.

One of his phones was buzzing.

He saw he had a dozen WhatsApp messages and missed calls from another CIO agent, DeeZee.

Comrade, whr u?

Cmde, whereabouts?

Coms... location?

DeeZee was always pestering him. Kasper didn't reply. He didn't want to see DeeZee. He didn't trust him. He had the feeling DeeZee was following him, checking up on him and his moves, and he didn't like that. He liked being his own man, independent, running his own operations. And he had never seen anyone so devoted to Mugabe and G40 as Dee-Zee. DeeZee had told him once that his uncle was a brigadier general, a senior military officer loyal to Mugabe, tipped to become commander of the defence forces when Grace and G40 came to power. It was why DeeZee was such a big supporter of G40.

Then Kasper felt a tap on his shoulder.

He knew who it was before he turned around.

DeeZee was standing there with his slab of a face, scarred hands, bloodshot eyes.

"I've been messaging, why you don't reply?"

Kasper shrugged.

"So, it's on," said DeeZee. "I have a meeting. The Ambassador is coming to town."

Kasper nodded but said nothing.

"This time he is finished – *handei tione!*" said DeeZee, laughing.

"I am sure," said Kasper with a shrug.

"Come, let's go drink in Yeoville," said DeeZee.

Kasper said he might see him there later; he still had work to do.

Then he went back to his beer.

He sat there alone, watching the naked girls dance for the men. He thought of his wife back home, his six children – four daughters, two sons – and the choices he had made in his life.

On the one hand, coming to Johannesburg had been a good move. It gave him freedom. He had set up front companies – a plumbing business; a solar power company. They were covers for his intelligence work but they also earned him a little cash, which came in handy because, by 2016, he and his team were often not even paid. He knew of staff at the embassy in Pretoria who never got paid.

Johannesburg gave him opportunities but it was also a cruel place.

He thought of what Ellis had said: "South Africans don't even like us Zimbabweans."

It was true. Once, on a plumbing job in Benoni, he had seen a white man assault a black Zimbabwean in the street. He could have intervened, could have killed the man with his bare hands, but it would have blown his cover. Black South Africans were even worse. He had seen them chase Zimbabweans with clubs and machetes during waves of anti-immigrant attacks. They said Zimbabweans came down here and took all their jobs. Which was also true. Zimbabweans with three A-levels and university degrees were all over South Africa, working as waiters, taxi drivers and petrol pump attendants.

Kasper shook his head and guzzled the last of his beer.

So many wasted lives.

Then he pulled out a phone and sent a message to a white man he was getting to know.

He liked this white man. The white man was brave and he had some good moves.

Shamwari, u at Sundowner? Let us talk – he wrote.

And he waited for a reply.

Chapter 3

CHRIS: THE AMBASSADOR

Christopher Mutsvangwa was furious. What did these G40 neophytes know of history and war? What did they know of the ruling party bloodline – and who should lead? They hadn't even fought in the war! They'd been mere children then – or they had fled like cowards and knaves! Yet now they threw insults and threats around at men like himself and ED and other veterans – those who had made *sacrifices*.

It was mid-2016, the winter of Mutsvangwa's discontent, and he was making the rounds in Harare, telling anyone who would listen that the country had been hijacked by the President's mad wife and her "consortium of hoodlums". For all his passion, though – and even his close friends called him a loudmouth and a loose cannon – deep down he must have known: his side, the ED faction – Lacoste, the media had taken to calling them – was losing the succession battle to G40. They just kept coming at you, these young ones. They had the ZANU-PF Youth League and Women's League on their side and, in elevating Grace, they had found their Kryptonite, immunising themselves from attack. After all, to attack the First Lady was to attack the man she shared a bed with – President Mugabe – and that was treason.

A broad-shouldered middleweight with a perfectly round shaved head and a penchant for sharp suits and colourful silk ties, Mutsvangwa, 61, knew all about history and war. Hell, he wasn't shy; if you were to ask him, he'd say he understood a lot more than that. His resumé was that of the ultimate ZANU-PF insider; he was a blue blood, a Brahmin. He had run the Zimbabwe Broadcasting Corporation (ZBC) from 1991–94, the party's single most powerful propaganda tool; he had chaired the country's Mineral Marketing Corporation from 2010–13, overseeing sales of diamonds, platinum and other minerals worth billions; he was a liberation war veteran – indeed had abandoned a law degree scholarship at the University of Rhodesia in 1975 to join the struggle – which was why he was now Chairman of the Zimbabwe National Liberation War Veterans Association (ZNLWVA). He was also, at least up until three months before, a cabinet minister in charge of War Veterans Affairs with a seat on the politburo.

None of which is to say he *wasn't* a loose cannon.

But there were two strings to Mutsvangwa's bow that made him more than a loud mouth caricature. For all his volatility, he was a diplomat, and a brilliant one at that. In 1984, when newly independent Zimbabwe was the darling of the Western world, he was posted to Brussels to oversee relations with the EU. This was followed by a spell at the UN in New York, and several Africa postings.

Then, in 2002, when Zimbabwe became the pariah of the West in the wake of the violent farm invasions, Mugabe entrusted him with the big one: Ambassador to China. He would guide Zimbabwe's new "Look East" policy when they turned to Beijing to bail them out of the economic morass.

Mutsvangwa moved his family to China for four years. He picked up some Mandarin and his younger children spoke it fluently. Yet, throughout this time, when most of the ZANU-PF hierarchy wore their crude anti-white, anti-Western ideology on their sleeve, he kept his door open.

Leon Hartwell, a senior policy officer at the Netherlands embassy in Harare from 2012–13, recalls a visit by the Dutch Director for Africa, just before the elections of 2013. The Dutch are large trading partners with Zimbabwe and big hitters at the EU; cash-strapped Zimbabwe could have benefited from good relations with them. Meetings were arranged and confirmed with politicians across the political spectrum. The timing was bad because of the elections; most of the MDC officials not only failed to turn up, they never even called in their apologies. Some ZANU-PF officials also missed meetings, but at least they called to cancel. Mutsvangwa, on the other hand, phoned personally with his apologies and asked to reschedule. When told the Director was flying out that evening, he said he would drive to the airport to meet with him.

"He was different," said Hartwell. "He had a tactical mind and a vision for the future. He can appear a bit abrasive on camera but he's a damn good diplomat and unlike a lot of ZANU-PF apparatchiks he had spent enough time abroad to know most of Zimbabwe's problems were self-inflicted."

The other string in Mutsvangwa's bow was his wife, Monica. She was a fellow war veteran, a sitting senator, and an ex-cabinet minister. Monica was 15 years old when she joined the guerilla war in 1976, crossing into Mozambique from eastern Zimbabwe with four girlfriends. Three months later she was at the Nyadzonia training camp on the Pungwe River in Mozambique when it came under a surprise dawn attack by the elite Rhodesian special forces unit, the Selous Scouts. Over 1,000 guerillas were killed that day, the biggest single-day loss of life in the entire war. "We were not trained," recalled Monica. "We ran using our hands to block bullets. I saw something I never thought possible – people running without heads... By the grace of God I escaped." Such an experience could break a human being, especially one so young, but she stuck with it. She met Chris Mutsvangwa at another training camp where he was a political commissar. In 1978 they were both posted to Maputo. He worked for Radio Zimbabwe, broadcasting nationalist propaganda into Rhodesia; she became private secretary to the Special Assistant to the President of ZANU. The President of ZANU was Mugabe; the Special Assistant was ED Mnangagwa. They had been Mugabe people first, ED people second ever since, but now they were losing faith in Mugabe.

It may be rare for a marriage forged in war to survive so long, but here they were, almost 40 years on, still in the thick of it. Monica softened Chris's abrasiveness. A European ambassador to Zimbabwe in 2016 got to know the Mutsvangwas and respected them. "They are the power couple of Harare," she said.

Well, not *the* power couple.

There was another couple in Harare in the winter of 2016, with a lot more power: President Mugabe and the First Lady, Grace...

The barbs and insults against the war vets had been started in 2015 by the First Lady, and she'd kept the abuse coming. She accused them of trying to replace her husband with ED; she said the war vets were arrogant and entitled: after all, no one forced them to go to war. Her jaunty sidekick, Saviour Kasukuwere, now the ZANU-PF Political Commissar, once alluded to them as drunks and lunatics.

On February 18th 2016, Mutsvangwa organised a war veterans' march in Harare to protest against the insults. Denied a venue at ZANU-PF headquarters, they gathered on a nearby parade ground. And it was there that the unthinkable happened: police ran at them with batons and fired tear gas and water cannons. The war vets fled, humiliated. The country was stunned. To Mutsvangwa it was the ultimate insult. He had lived and studied in America – Boston and New York – and found it as shocking as if state troopers had begun assaulting Vietnam veterans during a Memorial Day parade. He lashed out, accusing Saviour of "disrespecting the institution of marriage" – insinuating that he and Grace were having an affair.

By now President Mugabe had had enough. To him, the war vets were annoying and ungrateful. He kept giving them things and they repaid him with insults.

He had a point. Mugabe *did* keep giving them things. Those enormous cash payouts in 1997 that forced him to print more money, setting off inflation. Those farms taken during the land invasions, which ruined the country's agriculture.

And they kept demanding more.

Now it was time to cut ties. Besides, Mugabe saw the future was not with the veterans; they were dwindling in number and the memory of the war was fading. The future was with the country's youth – the under 40s – and his wife and Professor Moyo and Saviour Kasukuwere had had the vision to see that. Even the authoritarians had to play the political game, and if ZANU-PF wanted to stay relevant, it needed to appeal to young people, the majority of voters.

And so Mugabe cut Mutsvangwa loose. On March 4th, 2016 he expelled him from the politburo, along with a dozen other ED allies, and the following day he fired him as cabinet minister. Monica Mutsvangwa was expelled too, and dismissed from the Women's League, which Grace now ran.

Mutsvangwa swaggered out of the politburo meeting, all bravado. "I neither care for that politburo post, nor indeed for the ministerial appointments," he said, adding that he had asked to be fired. "War veterans chairmanship, yes – politburo and cabinet appointments, I don't care."

He had already spoken of his disappointment in the President, a man he had once revered, days earlier after a private meeting. "The man I had trusted and served for 40 years was no longer there. I came out unsure of whether I could hang onto his word. I left with a distinct feeling of mistrust."

If it wasn't a complete severing of ties between the war veterans and Mugabe, it came close.

But instead of going quietly, like so many before him, Mutsvangwa now embarked on a quixotic one-man campaign against the President and his wife. He held meetings with senior military officers in their barracks, warning them that cabinet and politburo meetings under Mugabe were a disaster, that his economic policy was leading the country off a cliff. He told how Grace, as the Women's League Secretary, had sauntered into politburo meetings and sat right next to her husband at the head of the table from where she lectured her seniors, many of whom were war veterans. "A mad woman latched onto the tenuous blessings of a marriage certificate!" he ranted, the words seemingly sent to his mouth from his brain via a thesaurus.

The military officers listened – horrified and amused. The

life and times of Grace Mugabe had become a long-running soap and it was impossible to look away. Grace had been a typist in the President's secretarial pool at State House when Mugabe first noticed her in 1988. He was then still married to Sally, his first wife, but Sally was terminally ill, and the President and the typist, 41 years his junior, began an affair. Grace was married too, to an air force pilot. They were soon divorced. Grace bore Mugabe two children out of wedlock and a third after their wedding in 1996, but no one ever considered her a political player. She would become known for her orphanage, that fruit farm and dairy in Mazowe, and lavish shopping sprees in Hong Kong, Singapore, Malaysia, Dubai and Paris. She had a penchant for Gucci, hence Gucci Grace. There were constant rumours of extramarital affairs, and at least one of the purported partners wound up dead in a car crash. Then, in early 2014, she registered for a philosophy PhD at the University of Zimbabwe. What was that about? She was 49 years old and had failed her O-levels. Little did the country know that this was the start of her political career. Lo and behold, she graduated in three months – credentialled with a doctorate that would take the finest minds in the country years to attain. Sure, her dissertation was not filed, and it was noted the President had just reappointed the Vice-Chancellor for an unprecedented third term, but who were Zimbabweans to quibble?

Besides, she was now Dr "Amai" (Mother) Grace Mugabe – and insisted on being called that. Mutsvangwa said he refused to.

Indeed, he told the soldiers he had seen the writing on the wall years earlier, when he was still in Beijing. In the mid-2000s the President and First Lady made an official visit to

China and Mutsvangwa, as ambassador, had overseen the visit. He said he had watched appalled as Mugabe kowtowed to his bossy and domineering younger wife much of the time – behaviour unbecoming of a leader and a war veteran. Yes, he had had his doubts for a while now…

Most of all he spoke to the media. Not merely to rant, but because he understood the importance of having a public presence. He would attend the opening of an envelope if there was a journalist with a camera present. Friends implored Monica to tell him to wind his neck in or it was going to be chopped. It was one thing to get fired, they said, but to keep attacking Mugabe and his wife – that was a death wish. When Mugabe accused his war veterans group of being "dissidents" – equating them with the Ndebele rebels whom he had crushed in the early 1980s – that should have been warning enough.

But what no one realised at the time was that Mutsvangwa wasn't going it alone. He was building an intricate network, a base for himself, courting allies in the most unlikely of places. And so it was that one day in that winter of 2016 he opened his Hushmail account and sent a message to Johannesburg.

It was time.

He was ready to go further.

❖ ❖ ❖

The meeting was held at the Green & Gold, a rugby-themed pub on the edge of a business park in the blue-collar Johannesburg suburb of Roodepoort. Green and gold are the colours of the South African Springboks and the bar's wood-panelled walls are adorned with signed jerseys and framed photographs of famous games. Banks of TV sets show live matches.

At around 4pm one afternoon in June or July of 2016, four

middle-aged black men, none of them rugby fans, shuffled in and took seats at a table on the left. They waited anxiously.

Presently two vehicles pulled up in the sprawling parking lot outside and two men got out of them.

The Sundowner wasn't the only bar Tom Ellis held meetings in, and he liked this pub just as much, especially on game days. He opened the swing doors for his guest, Ambassador Christopher Mutsvangwa, then lingered for a while outside, surveying the parking lot.

He was about to enter when he saw a white Toyota Legend, with two men inside, pull up and park.

Ellis felt his heart flutter.

He entered, joined the table on the left, made introductions and bought a round of beers.

The four men waiting at the table were senior members of various Zimbabwean exile, refugee and diaspora groups, all aligned with the opposition MDC. They already knew who Ambassador Mutsvangwa was.

Ellis had now met the war veteran leader four times and, despite everything, come to respect him.

By rights they should have been enemies: Mutsvangwa was a famous member of the political party that had laid waste to Zimbabwe. He was the Chairman of an organisation that had taken his sister's farm and those of dozens of his friends; it was war veterans who had assaulted white farmers, beaten and killed their workers. War veterans were the shock troops Mugabe could always call on for violence.

And yet, Ellis had come to re-evaluate Mutsvangwa. They had first met a year earlier in a hotel in Fourways, a meeting Ellis, ever the connector, had helped set up. It was mediated by the former South African politician Roelf Meyer, who had helped negotiate South Africa's transition from apartheid to democratic rule. Morgan Tsvangirai, the MDC leader, was there, as were other senior MDC officials, including the white former MP and economist, Eddie Cross. Mutsvangwa was happy to meet them all and stressed that he did so in his own capacity, not on behalf of ZANU-PF, or Lacoste, or the war veterans. Ellis had liked it that Mutsvangwa was his own man.

For the four diaspora men in the Green & Gold, Ellis recounted a story of a more recent Johannesburg meeting with Mutsvangwa, in February 2016. Mutsvangwa had told him that on his return to Zimbabwe he was going to denounce Mugabe in public, just as he had in private. Sure enough, days later, he did exactly that. It was after a one-on-one meeting with Mugabe that he had made that statement – "I came out unsure of whether I could hang onto his word. I left with a distinct feeling of mistrust'," – and was soon fired for it.

The four men had even more reason to distrust Mutsvangwa than Ellis. They were all in exile; they represented disparate groups of activists and refugees who had been through hell under ZANU-PF. They wanted to go home, but could never do so under Mugabe. Even in exile, they feared Mugabe's assassins.

Politics makes for strange bedfellows, though, and Mutsvangwa acknowledged that afternoon what they had all gone through. He didn't apologise – that would come later – but he spoke of the future, his vision for a Zimbabwe without Mugabe and, to the men present, it sounded a lot like the MDC vision.

It would be a country that allowed free elections, free speech; the right to assemble; a country open to the world, not angry with it, that invited investment and economic growth.

He told them he had been saying as much to the President and others in cabinet and politburo meetings for years, but that Mugabe didn't want to hear it. It had all become about staying in power, and his wife was forever whispering in his ear...

The diaspora men listened intently. It's possible they were flattered by a powerful politician coming to court them – even one from the party that they hated. Who doesn't like to be wooed? South Africa's ANC had relied heavily on its vast diaspora to bring down apartheid, but since 2013 there had been little communication between the MDC leadership and the Zimbabwean diaspora in South Africa, the majority of whom would have supported the movement. Even during the Government of National Unity (GNU) power-sharing agreement between 2009 and 2013, little had changed for activists in exile; they remained marked men by Mugabe's assassins, just as they had been at home.

They all vouched for Mutsvangwa's courage too.

He had stood up to Mugabe in Zimbabwe, something new for a senior member of ZANU-PF. It was dangerous enough to do so in exile, they knew, but in Zimbabwe, that could mean death. Over the years Mugabe's internal rivals had disappeared, one by one. On December 26th, 1979, mere days after the end of the long and bitter liberation war, guerilla commander Josiah Tongogara, tipped to be Zimbabwe's first president (Mugabe was to become the first prime minister), was killed in a suspicious car crash in Mozambique, when his car hit a military vehicle on an empty stretch of road while travelling at night from Maputo to Chimoio, central Mozambique. More recently, in 2011, General Solomon Mujuru, the husband of the then-VP Joice, was killed in that house fire on his farm. It was declared an accident – he liked a whiskey (Johnny Walker

Blue) – and the verdict was that he'd passed out with a lit cigarette by his bed and died of smoke inhalation. But traces of an accelerant – phosphorous, possibly from a grenade – were found in the bedroom, and the emergency fire truck called to the scene had no water. Both of these men had survived the long liberation war against the racist white Rhodesian regime, only to die by what appeared to be the hands of their own brothers.

A roar went up in the bar. The Lions had just scored a try against the Crusaders and the crowd was delirious. Mutsvangwa didn't flinch; he was focused on his pitch. He told the four men that he wanted to find ways for the diaspora to cooperate with the growing internal opposition to Mugabe. According to one of the men present: "He knew that the institution he represented had lost credibility with ordinary Zimbabweans and the international community, and in order to reclaim that he wanted to partner with groups like us, who had a base and a network in exile."

The four men said that their groups could find ways to cooperate but they wanted a further statement of intent. They wanted Mutsvangwa to keep the pressure on Mugabe and, if he did so, they would assist him in South Africa. It would be his bolt-hole if he had to go on the run. They had networks he could rely on, media contacts through which he could get the message across, and people to meet. He had lost that in Zimbabwe and to succeed in a war without allies, without media, without a base, was impossible. In the meantime, they would play their part against the regime and G40.

And so the diaspora and Mutsvangwa agreed to find ways to work together.

"It was an unlikely marriage between ourselves, as people

who had fled the country, and an organisation that had entrenched the dictatorship that had produced suffering in the country," one of the men present said later. "An alliance between an organisation with very unsavoury democratic credentials – and we who were democrats. We would be assisting our nemesis. But it so happened that we said let's put our differences aside. The country is bigger than us, and as long as the war veterans spoke about transformation and the removal of Mugabe, then it was worth working with them."

❖ ❖ ❖

The meeting ended at 6pm and the group toasted with more drinks. A photograph was suggested, and one of the diaspora men, Denzel Zibhodha, jumped up to take it. In the picture Ellis, Mutsvangwa and the three other men are shown seated at the table, raising their glasses, grinning.

Half an hour later Ellis was ordering another round at the bar, keeping one eye on the rugby game, when his phone pinged. It was a WhatsApp message. He opened it. At first it confused him. It was the group photograph Zibhodha had just taken. But Zibhodha hadn't sent it to him – *Kasper had*. How was that possible? Kasper had never entered the bar – although he knew Kasper was always following him and he had seen him pull up and park outside. Then Ellis saw a dateline on the thread: the picture had been forwarded to Kasper from Harare.

Kasper had written a simple message to Ellis – *I told u*.

Jesus. Ellis realised with mounting horror what had happened.

Denzel Zibhodha had taken the shot. He had then gone to the bathroom and while there had forwarded it to the CIO in

Harare who had, in turn, sent it to their top man in Johannesburg – Kasper.

Ellis looked over at his table and his eyes blurred. A red mist descended and he was overcome with rage. Denzel was chatting away happily with Mutsvangwa. "That fucking snake," Ellis snarled. Ellis had known and worked with Denzel – DeeZee they called him – for years. He was a logistics guy for Tsvangirai when he visited South Africa. He arranged transport and hotels for the MDC leader. In truth, Ellis had never much liked him, but he never thought him a spy. They would be laughing their heads off at CIO headquarters in Harare just then: not only was their guy at meetings with the opposition and Mutsvangwa; he had photographic evidence of these clowns!

Then again Ellis knew trade craft too. He'd read *The Art of War*. The CIO would not know they knew about DeeZee, and neither would DeeZee know. That made him what Sun Tzu called a "doomed spy". A doomed spy – a spy who did not know he'd been discovered – is useful for deception.

The drinks ready, Ellis composed himself, took a deep breath and carried them over to the table. He resisted the urge to drop one of the glasses on DeeZee's lap.

Later that evening, when the others were gone, Ellis told Mutsvangwa the news.

"I'm sorry, Chris. We have a big problem."

Mutsvangwa listened, nodded and shrugged. He knew the game. It didn't even surprise him much.

Leaving the bar later, Ellis noticed the Toyota Legend was no longer in the parking lot. He was about to get into his Land Rover when he felt a tap on his shoulder. He spun around and his heart leapt. Kasper had appeared out of nowhere in the darkness. It was just the two of them, no one else around. Ellis tensed up. He preferred meeting Kasper on his own turf, in busy, well-lit bars; this – a dark parking lot, no one else in sight – made him nervous.

Kasper pointed a stubby finger at Ellis's face.

"I told you," he said.

Ellis nodded slowly. "You did."

"So are we together, Tom?"

Ellis paused. He thought for a bit. Then he nodded again. He trusted him. He trusted him 75 per cent, and in this game, that was enough.

❖ ❖ ❖

Not long after the Green & Gold meeting, Ellis found he could trust Mutsvangwa, too, for on July 22nd, 2016 the ZNLWA made an official statement on the crisis in Zimbabwe – and it was brutal.

It was a formal severing of ties with Mugabe, denouncing the "cult of personality" that had sprung up around him:

> We note with concern, shock and dismay the systematic entrenchment of dictatorial tendencies, personified by the President and his cohorts, which have slowly devoured the values of the liberation struggle in utter disregard of the Constitution…

The war veterans announced that they would not be supporting Mugabe for re-election in 2018, and in November 2017 they officially removed Mugabe as their patron.

It was a political earthquake in Zimbabwe: the most powerful wing of ZANU-PF's base, the party's muscle, the ones whose guns had delivered Mugabe into office 36 years previously, the ones who had forced him to pay them those pensions in 1997, crashing the economy, the ones who had carried out the land invasions and been at his side all these years, had officially abandoned him. An analyst in Zimbabwe at the time recalls being asked by a UK journalist whether growing street protests against Mugabe might topple him. He laughed: "They mean nothing. The war veterans splitting from Mugabe – that's a time bomb."

Back in South Africa the ZNLWA statement received instant support from the Zimbabwe Exiles Forum (ZEF), one of the diaspora groups Ellis had invited to meet with Mutsvangwa in the Green & Gold bar. The ZEF said they welcomed the war veterans' "Damascene moment", noting that the former combatants had, until now "constituted the bulwark of Mugabe's unquestioning support", and that their sudden change of heart was "a vindication of what civil society and opposition political parties have been proclaiming for years."

With Zimbabwe rocked by dissent as civil society organisations staged waves of mass demonstrations against the regime, the diaspora groups swung into action in earnest, doing their part. They blocked the movement from South Africa into Zimbabwe of trucks, cars and commercial vehicles owned by G40 businessmen at the country's borders; released information in the South African media about homes and property purchased in South Africa by Grace and her G40 allies; and exposed the close ties between G40 leaders and the firebrand populist South African politician, Julius Malema, who was proving to be a thorn in the side of the ANC establishment, and whose race-based politics calling for redistribution of white farms and white businesses echoed the language coming out of G40 in Harare.

As for Mutsvangwa, there was now no going back. And when, a week later, word got around of a photograph of him with a white man in a bar in Johannesburg, he laughed it off. For months to come, at campaign rallies and politburo meetings, Mugabe mentioned the photograph, and said that Mutsvangwa had been plotting with white Rhodesian mercenaries in South Africa to overthrow him.

"It's just a picture of me in a pub," Mutsvangwa would shoot back. "The Old Man has lost his marbles and is being manipulated by his mad wife."

Chapter 4

GABRIEL: THE ADVOCATE

The early-morning phone call unnerved Gabriel Shumba. He never gave his cell number out; but a stranger had called him on it at home, said he was a potential client and that he wanted to meet him to discuss a case. The man spoke scattershot fast, in strong Shona-accented English, and he appeared to be on speaker because Gabriel could hear a second man chuckling in the background.

Gabriel asked what the case was about, but the man said he didn't want to discuss it over the phone.

"I tell you when I see you," he said breezily. "We are waiting for you at your offices."

Jesus. He knew where he worked, too?

Gabriel asked his wife to accompany him to the office that morning but she was taking the kids to school so he gave her the caller's cell number instead and told her to contact the police if she didn't hear back from him that day. Then he kissed her goodbye and walked the two blocks from their apartment to his offices at Pitje Chambers, 81 Pritchard Street, adjacent to the Johannesburg High Court. His sensors were up. He kept an eye on the slow-moving traffic and tried to stay clear of pedestrians en route.

Gabriel was used to looking over his shoulder.

Forty-two years old, an advocate in the South African High Court and a renowned human rights lawyer, he was, in 2016, in his 13th year of exile in South Africa from Zimbabwe, on the run from Robert Mugabe's hit squads. Gabriel had lost count of the threats, assaults and attempts on his life over the years but some incidents were seared into his cortex and still gave him nightmares. He had first been abducted at his own graduation ceremony at the University of Zimbabwe in 2000. He had worn a black armband at the graduation to protest against the breakdown of law in Zimbabwe, and was about to hand a petition to Mugabe, the university Chancellor, when he was bundled off by security agents and driven away, still in cape and gown. He escaped with his life only because a team of BBC journalists followed the agents' car. As a young lawyer, he then started defending opposition activists from state persecution, and in 2003 was abducted with his client, MDC MP Job Sikhala, from a hotel room, by CIO operatives. Detained for five days, he was electrocuted, brutally assaulted, urinated on and forced to drink his own blood. Denied legal representation, he was made to sign a confession admitting that he wanted to overthrow the government. On his release, pending trial for treason, he was followed and threatened by the same men who had tortured him.

Opposition activists were routinely "disappeared" at the time, so he skipped his trial and went into exile in South Africa, smuggling himself out the country in the boot of a car on March 24th, 2003.

"Better to be a living dog than a dead lion," he would always say of his decision. The name Shumba means "lion" in Shona, but he didn't feel like one.

He had not set foot in Zimbabwe since.

Ironically, in exile he became more of a thorn in the side of the regime than if they'd left him alone in Zimbabwe. He got a Masters in Human Rights Law and began travelling the world, speaking out against the abuses of the Mugabe regime. He addressed the United States Congress, Britain's House of Lords and House of Commons. In 2004, he founded the ZEF, which provided legal advice, immigration assistance and humanitarian support for the 2.5–3 million Zimbabwean exiles in South Africa. More than half a million have since been granted right to remain in South Africa, thanks to Gabriel and the ZEF.

The thing was, he didn't look like someone who lived in fear, and he never saw himself as a victim. There was an almost angelic joy and innocence to him that suited his name. He had an easy-going, boyish manner with an infectious, high-pitched laugh. He dressed like an urban hipster – trendy shirts, tailored jean jackets, designer glasses – and was as comfortable among the abused and desperate refugees he helped as he was at cocktail parties with diplomats, ambassadors, journalists and human rights groups.

"All I want is to be able to go back to my homeland," he would say.

His offices were on the top floor of Pitje Chambers, a 12-storey, polished-brown-glass building. He half-hoped that the morning call had been some kind of prank. But as he made his way to the elevator two men appeared from opposite sides of the lobby and stood close to him, one on either side. The larger man put one heavy hand on his back and held out the other to shake. He wore jeans, dirty trainers and a white polo shirt. "Hi Gabriel, thanks for seeing us," he said. Gabriel instantly recognised his voice from the call. The second man was smaller, with thick wire-rimmed glasses. He wore a blue jacket with the letters FBI on it. He never spoke. His handshake was powerful, like a vice.

Gabriel knew instantly they were CIO agents. He knew the type too well. He wanted to run but that muscular hand was still on his back. He noticed the smaller man kept his right hand in his jacket pocket.

"Your security is not too good here, Gabriel," chuckled the talkative one. "They did not even search us."

The elevator was taking for ever, enough time for the bigger man to get a phone call.

He answered it and spoke in some sort of code.

Gabriel only recognised a few words: "We are in position, comrade, all is well."

If they were trying to intimidate him, it was working. Gabriel was terrified.

The elevator arrived and they stepped inside. Gabriel was nothing if not a survivor, though. Education – two university degrees – hadn't robbed him of his instincts. His offices were on the 12th floor: a long way to fall – or jump. A very long way. His friend Morgan Tsvangirai had once been hung out of the window of a tall building by CIO assassins. Gabriel thought fast and pushed three. The third floor was the library and he knew other advocates would be in there, reading and researching. They reached the floor and stepped out. It was a carpeted open-plan room. Gabriel started talking loudly, greeting other lawyers, drawing attention to himself and the two men with him.

Then he led the way to a corner area with a desk, near an open window.

"So guys, what is this case?" Gabriel said, trying to sound calm, but his heart was pounding.

The men took their time. Only the larger one ever spoke. Gabriel was put in mind of a hawk and a dove. They surveyed the layout of the room, analysing who was where; distances, possible escape routes.

Gabriel glanced at the open window. He thought: If I don't survive, at least I end it quickly.

"We have a project we can work on together," said the talkative one, and Gabriel noticed how he smiled when he spoke, completely confident.

"What project?"

"You are a hard worker, Gabriel. Influential. You know many people. And you know the law. You are a key component of the change we need in Zimbabwe."

He saw the smaller guy flex his right hand in the jacket pocket. Gabriel knew it was a gun. He inched closer to the open window. If he moved fast he could make it before they grabbed him or shot him.

But nothing escaped the bigger man. He shook his head, stepped closer and smiled.

"Relax, Gabe. Don't think too much. Relax yourself. I need to be your friend. Don't worry. Here..." and he broke off to write some digits on a scrap of paper. "I am giving you my number for the sake of confidence. I will call again and then we can meet to discuss."

He handed the scrap of paper to Gabriel, then he whistled to his partner to leave and the two calmly walked to the elevators without looking back. Just as quickly as it had begun, it was over.

Gabriel stood there, shaking, out of breath. He felt dizzy and slumped into a chair.

Then, after a few minutes, he did exactly what Agent Kasper of the CIO predicted he would do.

He made a phone call to Tom Ellis.

"Tom, Tom – two guys just tried to kill me in my offices!"

"Slow down, Gabe. What happened?" Ellis said, speaking softly as usual, unperturbed.

"Two guys, they were CIO hitmen, I am sure. They visited me in my offices. One had a gun."

Ellis asked Gabriel to describe them to him.

"One was big, he talked too fast. The other... the smaller guy... he had a very tight handshake."

"Gabe, the smaller one – does he wear thick glasses?"

"Yes!" said Gabriel, confused as to how Ellis knew who he was talking about.

"It's okay Gabe. I know them. That's Kasper and Magic. They tried to kill me a year ago. They were going to shoot me at an ATM. But I turned them. I think they're okay now. They're working with me."

Gabriel couldn't believe what he was hearing.

"What do you mean, working with you?" he stammered. "Those guys are CIO – they are killers!"

"Ya, they are, but I think I got them on-side. I think they're with us."

"You *think*?" spluttered Gabriel, incredulous.

"Well, of course I don't know for sure. I wouldn't put my life on it. Or yours, come to think of it. But go with your gut, Gabe. Your instinct. You decide. I would say about 75 per cent I trust them."

Gabriel wasn't buying it. He had too much past experience with the CIO and he wasn't going to go with a 75-per-cent guarantee from Tom Ellis. What experience did Ellis have with the CIO? He hadn't been arrested, imprisoned, tortured, beaten to within an inch of his life. When he called his wife and told her the story that morning, she also thought Ellis was nuts to suggest Gabriel should "trust them".

Then again… Gabriel had to concede that Ellis did have a way of making things happen. They had known each other for years. Gabriel had represented the white farmers and black farm workers Ellis had brought to him. It was Ellis who had arranged, two years earlier, meetings with Joice Mujuru, the former VP, to discuss a possible collaboration with her against her former party ZANU-PF. It was Ellis who had got Morgan Tsvangirai and other senior MDC officials in a hotel boardroom with war veterans leader Chris Mutsvangwa. It was Ellis who had arranged a meeting between Mutsvangwa and various diaspora groups in mid-2016, where they agreed that they could help each other. Gabriel thought back to that meeting, in a rugby bar. How he, like Ellis, had found himself strangely persuaded by Mutsvangwa, and come to respect him.

Then he recalled the strange phone call a few days later from Ellis asking vaguely about Denzel Zibhodha – DeeZee – and whether Gabriel trusted him.

"I know him pretty well. I've worked with him a lot. He does Morgan's logistics when he's in town."

"Do you trust him?"

It was an odd question.

"I don't trust anyone, Tom!" Gabriel said with a laugh, "that's my method for staying alive!"

❖ ❖ ❖

Later that afternoon Gabriel received a WhatsApp message and then a call from his morning visitor.

"Hello, my friend!" said the now familiar voice. "It's Kasper. I saw you this morning. Listen, I am driving to Harare for meetings but I am back in four days. When I come back we will meet."

The same thing happened at exactly the same time over the next four days: Gabriel would get a WhatsApp message saying 'Hi", and then a call straight after. It was like clockwork, routine.

Sure enough, four days later Kasper phoned and said he was back in Joburg and wanted to meet.

Gabriel agreed but he made sure it was in a public place. He decided on Capello, a lively bar in the Carlton Centre, a towering high rise in downtown Johannesburg. It would be busy and Gabe wanted people around. When he told his wife about the meeting, she insisted on being there.

With Magic having returned to his job with the South African Rugby Union in Cape Town, Kasper came alone. After small talk and a round of drinks (on Gabriel's tab), Kasper gave him his pitch.

"You are a vital element of the change we want to see in Zimbabwe, Gabe." He looked straight at him when he spoke and he talked fast, as if it was a foregone conclusion that Gabriel would sign up so he might as well do it now instead of wasting any more time.

"These G40 are dangerous people. I know them well. I know Grace, how she works, how she thinks. I know the security sector. I have all the best moves. I can see beyond. And what do you bring to the party, Gabe? You have the diaspora. You have a lawyer mind. You have media, ambassadors, human rights, NGOs. You are respected. Let us join together and make some change."

Gabriel listened. Screw that. Thirteen years on the run from men like Kasper gives you a preservation instinct. He knew the way they operated. A few years earlier, three exiled MDC activists had been abducted from South Africa and taken back to Zimbabwe. They'd been interrogated and tortured in Bulawayo. Two of them were later found dead, one with gunshot wounds.

Gabriel suspected Kasper had the same plan for him. He suspected he knew of the meeting at the Green & Gold with Mutsvangwa. Mutsvangwa had become a lightning rod in Zimbabwe and the diaspora groups had partnered with him and This Flag – the growing popular democracy movement led by a brave young pastor, Evan Mawarire – and Tajamuka, a union-based civil society protest movement, to sabotage G40.

Still, it didn't mean Gabriel wouldn't listen to what Kasper had to say.

He just made sure Kasper did all the talking.

The meetings continued for several weeks into 2017, often in the same bar at the same table.

Magic was around some of the time, but mostly it was just Kasper and Gabriel. At the first meeting, and for many after it, whenever Gabriel needed to go to the bathroom, he made sure to take his beer with him. He didn't trust them not to poison it.

Then, at one meeting, something astonishing happened.

Kasper was making his pitch – his "sweet-tongue", as he called it – when he turned and whistled to a man sitting on his own a few tables away and motioned for him to come and join them. The man stood up and walked over with his beer.

He was thick-set, in dark trousers and black leather jacket.

Gabriel stood up to shake his hand when he suddenly felt winded, dizzy. He slumped back in his chair. The man looked at Gabriel and his mouth fell open. His lips started quivering; his eyes darted around. He looked as if he wanted to run. They stared at each other, as if they had each seen the other's ghost.

Kasper said: "I think you know each other. You should meet again. Outside of that environment. . ."

It was Gabriel who spoke, and his voice trembled.

"It's okay," he said. "That was in the past. I am happy to say you are my brother."

It had been 13 years but Gabriel still remembered the face of one of the men who had tortured him in a Harare jail cell in 2003. That face had woken him from nightmares. And now, somehow, for some reason, Kasper had plucked him from Harare to come meet with him.

Gabriel saw tears welling in the man's eyes. Then, without saying a word, the man stood up and left, leaving his beer untouched. He never returned.

Kasper shrugged and sipped his Castle.

"It's important for these people to meet you, Gabe. Let's put things right, so we can join hands."

He brought other men to see Gabriel: war veterans, intelligence agents, military officers – men who had either personally pursued him, or been part of the vicious state apparatus that had done so. Gabriel had no idea how Kasper, who on the surface appeared to be a street thug, a stone-cold killer, had the power or influence to summon such people at will. *Who the hell is he?*, he started wondering.

"This is the lawyer Gabriel Shumba who we forced to leave the country," Kasper said to one. "Do we really want to hound this man to his death? Look at him, a simple lawyer. How can we say he is a traitor?"

Another man, who Gabriel did not recognise, got heavily drunk with him and then broke down in tears.

Gabriel, crying too, hugged him: "It's okay. That's in the past."

Gabriel said he had no animosity towards any of them.

He just wanted to be able to go back to his homeland.

Kasper called these meetings "Shock Tactics". Gabriel later learned that Kasper had words and phrases for every phase of an operation he ran. "Shock Tactics" were part of "The Move" – the move being to get Gabriel and his former enemies talking, working together. That would lead to "The Final Push": the push to join forces to take out G40 and remove Mugabe. "The Final Push" would at some point become "Full Scale". Kasper had been Full Scale before. The Congo war was Full Scale. Working undercover destabilising the MDC, that was Full Scale. Full Scale meant all-out war, life or death, no going back.

Perhaps, if Gabriel had known what lay in store for him and his wife in the year ahead, he would never have signed on, but, gradually, and despite himself, he found he came to trust Kasper. Indeed, at one meeting in Capello, Gabriel got up to go to the toilet and Magic called out to him as he was walking away. He and Kasper were grinning, holding up his drink: "Gabe, you forgot your beer!"

Gabriel finally trusted them not to poison it, and when he returned he took a big sip and they all laughed.

It was a meeting in early 2017, however, that finally persuaded Gabriel to trust Kasper fully. Kasper told him he had someone he wanted him to meet, someone he – Gabriel –

already knew. They drove together to an upscale hotel in Sandton and Kasper walked with him into the lobby.

"He is waiting," he told Gabriel.

"Who?"

"Morgan," said Kasper.

Morgan Tsvangirai, the MDC leader, was dying from colon cancer in 2017, and as he was spending so much time in hospitals in South Africa, it was hard for anyone to meet with him, even old friends like Gabriel who'd known him almost 20 years, since the founding of the MDC in 1999. But somehow, Kasper had located and contacted Tsvangirai, the man he had once spied on as his bodyguard, and had taken Gabriel to meet with him.

It was just Gabriel and Tsvangirai in the hotel room. The opposition leader was no longer the burly, full-faced trade union boss who had fought ZANU-PF so ferociously, surviving multiple attempts on his life. In truth he had never fully recovered from the death of his wife, Susan, killed in yet another suspicious car accident: a head-on collision in rural Zimbabwe in 2009 in which many believe Morgan, who was in the vehicle with her, was the intended target. He was thin now and those cheeks had hollowed, but he still had a glint in his eyes and a quick wit. They made small talk and then Gabriel mentioned his dilemma, the strange meetings with Kasper, and Kasper's insistence that they cooperate, work together.

"I know Kasper," Tsvangirai reassured him. "You can trust him."

And so it was that in February 2017, Gabriel agreed to sign on for "The Move".

He would team up with Kasper and Magic, agents in an organisation that had tortured him and tried to assassinate him, and they would work together against G40 and the dictator Mugabe.

It was only then that Gabriel discovered that Tom Ellis and Kasper had already been working together – for more than six months. Hell, they had even signed an agreement – a "declaration" – formalising their partnership.

Kasper said: "You are a Johnny-come-lately, Gabriel, but we can't do it without you."

Chapter 5

THE TEAM

Madcap coups, bizarre comebacks and strange political alliances have been hatched all over Joburg, Africa's richest city, usually in the plush lobbies of five-star hotels or the leather booths of oak-panelled steakhouses. Ellis and Kasper's agreement was hammered out in Ellis's Land Rover late one night in the parking lot of Northgate shopping centre. Ellis was having money trouble again and couldn't afford another night of burgers, beer and Johnny Walker for himself and Kasper at the Sundowner.

They called the agreement the Northgate Declaration for want of a better name: the Northgate sign was what they saw when they looked out of the 4 x 4's front window.

The location was not without symmetry: it was around the corner from the Total petrol station ATM where, less than a year earlier, Kasper and Magic had planned to put a bullet in Ellis's head.

As for the agreement, it wasn't exactly Magna Carta.

There was no document to sign because neither of them

had bothered to write or print one out.

It was a verbal pact: an old-school honour-between-men kind of deal. Neither of them can even recall the exact date, but it was sometime between June and August of 2016, not long after the meeting with Mutsvangwa at the Green & Gold, where Kasper had revealed to Ellis the spy in his side's ranks.

The essentials were thus: Ellis and Kasper would team up to oppose Mugabe and G40, and to push ED, the Crocodile, for the presidency. Kasper, tired of doing dirty work for Mugabe and contemptuous of G40, saw ED as the best option. "He did make some mistakes, he realised, he repented," Kasper said of him. "Of Grace and G40 he is the better." Ellis had come to see ED as the best alternative too. He couldn't stand ZANU-PF, but the MDC was divided and in disarray and Grace and G40 were rising fast. He believed G40 coming to power would be a disaster; ED's emissaries, on the other hand, had told him he would open the country to business and repair relations with the whites and the West. He also believed that removing the Mugabes would invigorate the democratic space in Zimbabwe and give the moribund MDC new life. In return, Ellis wanted a transitional national authority, much like the unity government that existed between 2009 and 2013. This was what had been discussed and agreed upon at the various meetings Ellis had set up between anti-Mugabe elements in ZANU-PF and MDC officials and the diaspora groups.

When they shook hands to seal the deal, Kasper said: "Northgate Declaration for ever – united we stand, divided we fall!" It became his catchphrase.

Later, when Gabriel and the others came aboard and the team grew, it came to be known as the Northgate Diaspora Group and sometimes the Core Group.

It was *Boy's Own* stuff and, on the face of it, quite absurd.

What power did Ellis and Kasper have to remove Mugabe and install ED?

None.

They notably didn't advocate a military coup, and they didn't have the ability to carry one out anyway.

Ellis believed in democratic change, the idealistic notion that there could be free and fair elections in Zimbabwe. And while Kasper, a spy, didn't exactly come with democratic credentials, he knew a coup would mean bloodshed and he had seen enough of that in his time. "Tom, it is easy to destroy," he would tell Ellis during their late-night Sundowner drinking sprees. "Our move – it must be clean."

What they did have was a unique set of talents, skills and contacts – networks – that, when combined, made a potent combination that could influence events over time. *Over time* being the operative words. They were in it for the long haul, activism being an often thankless long game. They knew it might take years to remove Mugabe and stop Grace, but they were prepared. They just had to keep chipping away.

There was never any expectation that any of them should switch political allegiances.

"We never asked, they never asked, and it was not expected," said Ellis of his partnership with Kasper and Mutsvangwa and the others the two of them would bring in from ZANU-PF. They were individuals, patriots, acting alone, without knowledge or approval of the parties or institutions they represented.

They were also using each other, and quite open about it.

Ellis had seen first-hand since meeting Kasper the true strength and reach of the CIO. He had always known they were ruthless, but now he understood to what extent. With DeeZee they had literally infiltrated the senior ranks of the MDC diaspora: a spy had been right under their noses all these years and they'd had no idea. Ellis had learned that the CIO knew all about him, too. Hell, Kasper had followed him, built a file on him, could have killed him any time, and Ellis would never have seen it coming.

Was it a surprise the MDC kept losing when this was what they were up against?

But now, with Kasper, they had an opening: a converted spy who knew their common enemy better than any of them. Kasper could not only provide cover for the team and protect them from his CIO pals who would no doubt be coming after them; he could feed disinformation and maybe even recruit some of the agents for their anti-G40 effort.

For his part Kasper saw in Ellis a man of calm, influence and courage who could "make things happen". Ellis had a vast network and access to donor funds. (Ellis never told him this was an exaggeration and that he was frequently personally broke). Kasper respected Ellis for the "James Bond move" he had made that afternoon in 2015, stopping his car and coming over to ask him and Magic for a drink; and also for having had the vision to approach Mutsvangwa, who Kasper considered a tactical mastermind. "Tom," he said, "let me tell you, war veterans are the most powerful institution in Zimbabwe. That Mutsvangwa – he can be kingmaker!" But Kasper also saw in Ellis something more personal: he was the first white man who had ever treated him as an equal. He'd introduced him to all his white friends at the Sundowner and the two of them would always be the last to leave, having drunk Ellis's mates under the table. Ellis marvelled at Kasper's ability to booze heavily but never seem to get drunk. Kasper didn't tell Ellis about his CIO training; how as freshmen recruits they were plied with alcohol for weeks at a time, conditioned to cope with hard liquor so that they could function in any situation. For his part, Ellis had spent so much time in bars he didn't need training. The two men shared a bond. Perhaps it was because their fathers had both been cops; in another world,they might have been brothers.

As for Gabriel – he saw that powerful elements within the political movement he had lived in fear of for years were finally coming to see what he had been telling them all this time: that Mugabe was a cruel and ruthless despot. He had realised that the way to change the regime was from the inside. For four years the MDC had been part of a unity government with ZANU-PF, and how had that changed things? He was still looking over his shoulder, living in fear. No, if it took cooperating with spies, war veterans or soldiers, his one-time nemeses, to change the system, he would do it.

Of course Gabriel gave them something they needed: legitimacy. He was respected and admired among human rights groups, diplomats and journalists all over the world. He gave them validation.

And Mutsvangwa? Well, he could use them all: he needed all the friends he could get. The diaspora groups had a safe haven for him, media contacts and the kind of respectability ZANU-PF had frittered away. He had seen the strength of their networks, and he could harness that, but he had also come to respect the urban strength of the MDC in Zimbabwe. He knew his side would need that one day too.

At the same time, he gave them something: confidence. Here he was, one of the most senior representatives of the ruthless machine that was ZANU-PF, and he was now on *their* side? That was invaluable. He knew how the system worked and the strengths and weaknesses of the enemy. He wasn't only the leader of the powerful war veterans; he was a diplomat, an intellectual gunslinger and a man with connections to the very top, including the Zimbabwe military, whose senior commanders were themselves war veterans, thus de facto blood brothers to his war veterans' association. It was like a failing soccer side signing Messi or Ronaldo; he knew how the game was played and when the time came, he would become their leader.

❖ ❖ ❖

Things started heating up pretty soon.

By August 2016 Mutsvangwa was back in Johannesburg, lying low. The explosive statement by his ZNLWVA announcing its divorce from Mugabe had produced an instant backlash in Harare, and a wave of arrests of war veterans.

He had immediately hooked up with Ellis. And it was then, at Centurion golf club outside Pretoria, that Ellis first introduced him to Kasper. There was a golf tournament on and the three men sat at an outside table watching the players hit their drives down immaculately manicured fairways.

"Chris, if you want to be safe in this country, you will need this guy," said Ellis, pointing to Kasper.

Mutsvangwa and Kasper nodded at each other and were soon getting along. He and Kasper spoke a common language, as men from military or intelligence backgrounds do. Mutsvangwa didn't appear remotely curious as to how Ellis, this *murungu* (white man) aligned with the MDC had come to know or trust Kasper, a black man from the CIO. He just shrugged and accepted it, as he had the earlier revelation at the Green & Gold bar that one of the diaspora guys he had just met with was a spy. He was used to the game.

As 2017 ramped up, Kasper became Mutsvangwa's eyes and ears in South Africa and they communicated constantly. "You are my first port of call," Mutsvangwa told him. Kasper would pick him up from the airport on his many visits, drive or follow his car to meetings and book his hotels, always selecting properties with front-gate security and open layouts where he could see who was coming and going.

Mutsvangwa used the time in South Africa to update the ZEF and other diaspora groups who were already guardedly cooperating with him. Meanwhile Ellis often took him to meet his white pals at the Sundowner and other Joburg bars. Some of his mates were dispossessed white Zimbabwean farmers. What could have been awkward or volatile gatherings turned out to be the exact opposite: "He fitted in and became the life and soul of the party in a short time," said Ellis.

Mutsvangwa told them terrible mistakes had been made.

❖ ❖ ❖

Kasper's role was riskier. In between running protection for Mutsvangwa, Ellis and Gabriel in South Africa, he took it upon himself to make frequent trips to Harare in the Toyota Legend, on his own dime, to recruit or "turn" people he knew within the state institutions: the CIO, CID, police and military. He would call Ellis en route and explain the goal. "I go talk with those people who are too influential within the systems, the institutes. I know these people, I tell them: listen, we can do this other thing, forget about G40; let's try this. . ."

Ellis called these trips suicide missions and thought he was crazy. "*Shamwari*, you are going to get yourself killed."

"Tom, if they kill me you will soldier on with the struggle. United we stand!"

That was Kasper: *Wairasa*, unpredictable: "Left signal, I turn right."

The first recruit to the team, however, was not in Zimbabwe but South Africa: his protégé Magic.

Ellis was shocked to discover that Magic had initially had no idea that Kasper had taken a decision to work with him. Magic thought all the meetings with Ellis were standard spycraft, part of a long-term move by Kasper, who could always "see beyond". But when Kasper told him about the Northgate Declaration, Magic was on board. Kasper knew he would be; he was Magic's mentor – Magic would follow him.

Soon after Magic joined, Kasper introduced another recruit, an avuncular, soft-spoken Military Intelligence agent with the mien of a school teacher, code named Horse. Kasper wooed Horse in Harare with the promise of a partnership in a lucrative agricultural project. The company didn't exist – it was another Kasper front – but by the time Horse learned this he was in too deep and couldn't turn back.

Kasper put his ability to convert people down to sheer charisma.

"Myself, I'm a crowd puller, I can persuade anyone!" he would say, and he used the metaphor of a swimmer in mid-ocean to describe the method: "Once you are crossing the ocean, to go back from halfway you can't… you have to go all the way to the banks on the other side… it's too late to stop."

So now there were three spooks on board and they would become the eyes, ears, security and muscle for the team, first in Johannesburg, and, later, when it all went down, Harare.

They needed them.

On Christmas Eve, 2016, Gabriel was almost murdered by a CIO assassin in his home on Pritchard Street. It was the period when Kasper was still wooing him. Gabriel got a knock on his door early one morning. Expecting a friend, but always wary, he opened the door slightly. Suddenly a shoulder smashed into it, flinging it open, sending Gabriel reeling backwards. A slim, wiry, wild-eyed man, aged about 30, stood in the doorway, then slunk in. He looked anxiously at Gabriel, then around the room. Gabriel found his cell and frantically dialled 10111, the number for the South African Police Service, but in his panic his fingers couldn't find the right keys. Besides, what was the point? The police would never come in time. The man walked to the living room now and sat on the edge of a couch, half on his haunches, eyes darting everywhere. He looked more nervous than Gabriel. Gabriel was dialling his wife's number now. He asked the man what he wanted. The intruder mumbled something incoherently. What happened next took place in a blur: in an instant the man drew a sharp, wooden-handled Okapi knife from his back pocket and, like an uncoiling spring, leapt off the couch, lunging at Gabriel with the glistening blade. Gabriel had done some karate and managed to repel him, knocking the knife under the couch, but the assailant was soon on top of him and hitting him over the head with a heavy stone ornament – a Zimbabwe Bird carving of all things – knocking Gabriel out. Blood spooled on the floor around his head. Sometimes you need a miracle. Gabriel's wife chose that exact moment to return home and, seeing her, the assailant panicked and fled. Gabriel was rushed to hospital for stitches and fortunately soon recovered. The story of the attack on the prominent human rights activist made the Johannesburg press. He just added it to the growing list of attempts on his life.

Kasper claims there were at least two assassination attempts on Mutsvangwa in Johannesburg that he foiled. The first, at a hotel in Fourways in 2016, he won't speak of, except to say the hitmen came face to face with him in the parking lot one night and would not want to repeat the experience.

The second, in mid-2017, when things were Full Scale, he describes in almost comic detail. Kasper, ostensibly still an agent in the CIO, heard chatter of plans to take Mutsvangwa out on his way from his hotel to OR Tambo International. Agents had been sent down from Harare to do the job. "I knew they wanted to hit Chris. I told him, I need to transport you to the airport this day." Kasper met Mutsvangwa at his hotel, put him in the front seat of an Uber, and followed close behind in the Toyota Legend. Halfway there, on the N3 highway, two cars appeared out of nowhere and attempted to pass Kasper to get to Mutsvangwa's Uber. Veering left and right, using the Legend as a dodgem, Kasper blocked them for several minutes until they gave up and peeled off. Mutsvangwa, oblivious to it all in the lead car, arrived safely at the airport, cursed Kasper for not being around and checked in for his flight. Kasper never mentioned the incident to him. He was that good, that loyal, and he needed little thanks.

By March 2017 Magic and Horse were accompanying Kasper on his "suicide missions" to Zimbabwe and they would often meet with Mutsvangwa in Harare to strategise, meet allies and woo potential recruits.

Incredibly, they usually met in public, at popular Harare hotels and restaurants, "hiding in plain sight". Chang Thai in Gunhill (later to feature in ED and Junior's escape) and

Shangri-La, a Chinese restaurant on Enterprise Road, were often used. Perhaps Mutsvangwa liked the familiar taste of Asian food, a reminder of his years as Ambassador in Beijing. Those were the good old days, back in the early 2000s, when he was head of mission, mapping out new avenues for Zimbabwe's economy and trade – what was called the "Look East" policy. China would soon become Zimbabwe's biggest investor and trading partner, replacing Western nations that had now turned against Mugabe's draconian rule and imposed sanctions on leading members of the regime (although Mutsvangwa himself was never on any sanctions list.)

Their favourite spot, though, was the far table in the tranquil courtyard of the Bronte Hotel, a quiet colonial-era establishment in the Avenues straight out of a Graham Greene novel. The Bronte is popular with politicians, foreign investors and blindingly obvious low-level CIO agents in suits and dark glasses who listen in on them.

The guys always had a cover. Their most common front was as owners of a solar power company Kasper and Magic registered in South Africa named DAKO. They would switch the SA plates on the Toyota for the trip, paste on DAKO Solar Power signs, and drive around Harare with glossy company brochures and packages of boxed solar lamps that had fallen off the back of an NGO's truck. *Dako* means "ass" or "backside" in Shona, and when Harare pedestrians and motorists saw them they would point and laugh. Kasper, Magic and Horse would laugh back. The fact the company's name was a joke made it the perfect cover: who would suspect these clowns? Once they actually got a meeting with a senior G40 politician who made a large order of lamps, handing over his South African bank account details.

Chapter 6

A DIRTY GAME

By June 2017 winter had come, but the political temperature in Harare was rising.

June 2nd marked the first of the ten planned Presidential Youth Interface Rallies to be held in the country's provinces that winter, with Grace centre stage, ED and his Lacoste faction her target.

Grace's insults against ED and the war veterans continued apace, while Jonathan Moyo was now feeling confident enough to mock ED's military ally, General Chiwenga, the head of the country's armed forces, on Twitter about his education, claiming he never authored the PhD dissertation he was awarded from a South African university in 2015. It appears there were a lot of fake doctorates circulating around Harare at the time, although Moyo never questioned Grace's. Why would he? Grace was their ace.

It was all parry and thrust. The game wasn't really even about ideology or ideas.

It was about succession – who would win the crown.

Both factions were corrupt. They had all been part of a

government and party that had pillaged the nation for decades. Those mansions in the northern suburbs weren't built on government stipends.

The top players – Grace, Moyo, Saviour Kasukuwere, ED, General Chiwenga and other senior military brass – were all on targeted sanctions lists imposed by the US. Grace lived in the US$23 million Blue Roof; had that profitable fruit farm and dairy in Mazowe which was seized from a white farmer, and her husband frequently commandeered the national airline's plane to fly to Malaysia and Singapore.

Saviour, Minister of Youth Development, Indigenisation and Empowerment from 2009-2013, had driven the controversial Indigenisation and Empowerment Act to place all foreign-owned businesses under 51% local control (a cousin of the disastrous land reform bill which frightened off investors). Yet, at the youthful age of 47, he had accumulated multiple farms and businesses of his own. Talk about empowerment. Then again, the indigenisation act was passed in 2008, before Saviour was put in charge, and ED and what was now his Lacoste faction had all been in favour of it.

During hyperinflation, members of both factions had got rich on exchange-rate looting, whereby senior party officials had access to the absurdly low official rate at which the US dollar was pegged to the local currency. They could buy US dollars at the low rate, exchange it on the astronomical black market, where greenbacks sold for tens of thousands in local currency, return to the bank to buy more US at the low rate and, lo and behold, in a few swift moves, literally become US dollar millionaires.

ED for his part had multiple mining interests, starting from the Congo war days and his deals there with his military allies and wealthy white Zimbabwean businessmen who were also on sanctions lists.

Meanwhile, members of both factions did very well out of Marange, a lucrative alluvial diamond field discovered in eastern Zimbabwe in the early 2000s, and now overseen by the military on behalf of the Chinese.

The key dividing line wasn't philosophical, left or right; no, it was a war to claim a throne. And to do this both camps had to best apply their strengths and tactics to assert control of the party, their supporters, key state institutions and, importantly, perceptions.

Mutsvangwa and his war veterans group soon made moves to remove Saviour from his position as ZANU-PF Political Commissar. Grace was the figurehead of G40, Moyo purportedly the tactical brains, but Saviour brought rock star charisma and a massive youth following. As youth minister he had started hosting live, online sessions with young Zimbabweans on Facebook and Twitter and had driven an image rebranding of the party that saw Grace and her elderly husband wearing trendy Kangol hats and brightly patterned floral jackets to political rallies. Enough young Zimbabweans loved it: a dramatic increase in the youth vote for ZANU-PF in 2013 allowed them to defeat the hapless MDC again. The war veterans clearly marked Saviour as a powerhouse and a future leader and soon got the provinces to pass a vote of no confidence to remove him; Mugabe and Grace intervened to protect Saviour, with Grace vocally defending both him and Moyo at the winter rallies.

❖ ❖ ❖

Then, on July 19th, 2017 Jonathan Moyo dropped a bombshell. During a ZANU-PF politburo meeting, he presented the President with a slick, 72-minute video (replete with a thrashing crocodile graphic in the corner), outlining how ED was planning "an illegal and unconstitutional secession-ist" coup against him. Incredibly, ED was in the room for the entire presentation, sitting a few seats away from Moyo, fuming. You had to hand it to The Professor: There were no half-measures; he punched up.

The video claimed ED's faction had even published a blue-print of their strategy in 2015 – the Blue Ocean Strategy Doc-ument – outlining exactly how their succession plan would work. The video named leading foot soldiers of the plot, Christopher Mutsvangwa being the main one. ED continued to "work hand in hand [with Mutsvangwa] under the cover of darkness…" the narrator announced ominously.

Now is perhaps a good time to introduce Moyo in detail, for he, as much as Grace, was ED's nemesis in the game, and there was certainly bad blood between the two men.

Tall and thin with an egg-shaped head that rests large and unsteady atop his lanky frame, Moyo, 60 at the time, was a mercurial figure in Zimbabwean politics, admired and loathed in equal measure, impossible to ignore. Known as the Profes-sor, (his wire-rimmed glasses fit the bill), he has multiple de-grees, including a Masters and a PhD in Public Administration from the University of Southern California.

He applied to USC to study film and music in 1978, but at the time Africa was in the throes of multiple wars for inde-pendence, and the organisation funding his scholarship said the continent didn't need more black artists – it needed black politicians. So, public policy it was.

Still, he took screenwriting courses in his spare time. A little film called *Star Wars* had just been released, and the director happened to be a USC alumnus. Moyo attended numerous lectures by George Lucas and Lucas's friend, Steven Spielberg at the university. He also took songwriting classes with one Lionel Ritchie. Forty years later, film and music remained his primary passions – and you could see his dramatic narrative style and production verve in that Blue Ocean video.

His stint at USC was followed by a period at Stanford, where his contemporaries included Susan Rice, Barack Obama's future National Security Advisor, and Jendayi Frazer, who would become US Assistant Secretary of State for African Affairs in the George W Bush administration. They often met socially, sharing meals together on campus, discussing the political issues and ideas of the time.

But if his academic credentials were stellar, his time in America also proved to be a curse: whenever he did something to annoy his rivals within ZANU-PF – which was often – they accused him of being a CIA spy. His whiplash tongue gave back as good as he got, but the accusation rankled.

He didn't help himself. In 1993 he was programme director for the Ford Foundation in Kenya, but left under a cloud, accused of embezzlement; and in 1998 he lectured at the prestigious Wits University in South Africa, where he was accused of absconding with part of a research grant. In the early 1990s he was a lecturer at the University of Zimbabwe and an outspoken critic of the Mugabe regime, calling for democratic governance and pushing for a more progressive constitution; in 2000, with the rise of the MDC, Mugabe cannily appointed him Information Minister, a role in which he transformed himself into a fierce defender of the President. Erudite, whip-smart, famous for withering put-downs of opposition politicians and journalists, he was brilliant at the job. He turned state propaganda into an art form, moving the Information Ministry into offices close to the President, making the ZBC run all local programming and leading ZANU-PF's relentless anti-colonial, anti-Western messaging. (If he was a CIA asset he was Langley's worst hire.) It was during his tenure at Information that draconian press laws that saw the banning and expulsion of foreign journalists and media organisations from Zimbabwe, including the BBC and CNN, were passed. His methods helped mastermind ZANU-PF's 2002 election victory over the MDC, who Mugabe accused of being puppets of the West and the "homosexual government" of Tony Blair.

He must have had charm, though. Consider this tale. In a blistering essay published in 2004, a talented young Zimbabwean editor and media entrepreneur, Mduduzi Mathuthu, compared Moyo to Hitler's propagandist Joseph Goebbels. It was not a compliment. And yet, not long afterwards, Mathuthu enlisted Moyo to write for his popular webzine, *New Zimbabwe*. That's some turnaround. Years later, in 2013, Moyo returned the favour and appointed Mathuthu editor of the state-controlled *Chronicle* newspaper. Moyo had other young allies installed in state media then, too. He was nothing if not strategic.

In 2005 Moyo's position at the centre of state power came to an ignominious (if temporary), end, however, and the reason for that had everything to do with ED.

Moyo had been close to ED those years, so much so that in November 2004, planning for the future, he arranged a clandestine meeting of party insiders in his home district of Tsholotsho, outside Bulawayo, to decide on the party's next VP – and thus Mugabe's likely successor. In what came to be called the Tsholotsho Declaration, the group chose ED. But news of the gathering leaked, ED failed to show up for it, and Moyo was left exposed. He was censured and soon expelled from the party. ED denied all knowledge of the secret meeting, never defended Moyo, and while he was passed over for VP in favour of Joice Mujuru, remained in the party and in Cabinet. Moyo never forgave him.

As was his nature, Moyo made his way back into Mugabe's good books, and was reappointed Information Minister after helping ZANU-PF achieve another landslide 2013 election win over the MDC.

A year later he was almost on the outs with Mugabe again, but in timely fashion he attached himself to Grace, becoming an informal advisor to her when she made her spectacular political debut that year, taking down the then VP Joice Mujuru during the course of those brutal rallies.

There was another reason for the bad blood between Moyo and ED which we will come to later; suffice to say they could not stand each other.

The Blue Ocean video accusations were naturally denied by ED, who promptly sued Moyo for US$3 million. He also wrote a long response to Mugabe outlining the disloyalty Moyo had displayed towards Mugabe and ZANU-PF over the years, including at Tsholotsho, and he wheeled out the usual claims that Moyo was a CIA spy.

Back in South Africa, meanwhile, the Northgate team responded with their own media hit. On July 31st Kasper messaged Mutsvangwa to say that he and Ellis were meeting with journalists in Joburg.

Super stars you both are! – Mutsvangwa replied all in caps. Then, ever the big-picture guy, and clearly aware that the lives

they were all leading resembled an espionage thriller, added –
Protect IP - intellectual property for film rights

Yaa cde definitely – Kasper replied.

Weeks later Reuters published a blistering investigative piece quoting "two Zimbabwe intelligence agents" and reports from leaked intelligence documents that ED Mnangagwa, "a 73-year-old lawyer and long-standing ally of Mugabe, envisages cooperating with Tsvangirai to lead a transitional government for five years with the tacit backing of some of Zimbabwe's military and Britain".

It was a year since Ellis and Kasper had signed the Northgate Declaration and the essentials of the pact were now in print. The article caused tremors in Harare, suggesting that intelligence agents were divided, plotting against each other, and that the Zimbabwe military would never accept Grace Mugabe as President.

Things were coming to a head and something had to give.

August turned out to be an even hotter month for the team than July.

On the 2nd of the month Kasper sent Mutsvangwa an oblique message – *there is a time bomb cde.*

Kasper had been hearing constant chatter that there was going to be an attempt to poison ED, and he let Mutsvangwa know. Then, on Saturday August 12th, it happened: that Gwanda rally in southern Zimbabwe where ED got stomach cramps and sweats in the VIP tent and began projectile vomiting. He knew he had been poisoned because he had received multiple warnings.

Four hundred and fifty miles away in Johannesburg that night, oblivious to the events in Gwanda, Ellis was out with Clare, enjoying a rare date night. He'd forgotten to charge his cell phone so he was free from the constant calls and WhatsApp messages the political game required. They returned to Randburg at around 10pm and had just reached their front gate when a vehicle, headlights on full glare, screamed up behind them. Ellis thought they were being hijacked. Then, in the bright light, he heard the voice of a white businessman he knew named Robert Hillman, who he was keen on getting to invest in Zimbabwe. Hillman had helped organise a conference on investing in the country in Sandton that June (ED had attended as the headline speaker), and Ellis had taken the time to introduce him to Mutsvangwa.

Hillman had his cell phone in his hand and was shouting: "Tom, where the hell have you been?"

"Out for dinner," said Ellis. "My cell's been off, what the hell's happened?"

"It's Chris Mutsvangwa," said Herbert. "He says the VP has been poisoned!"

Ellis took the phone and Mutsvangwa's voice came to him from Zimbabwe. He'd been trying to get hold of him for hours. He told him about the rally, the poisoning, the emergency evacuation by Chiwenga. It was touch and go whether ED would survive. Ellis's heart pounded. Their whole project was about to fall apart. But Mutsvangwa was also calling to check up on Ellis because he thought he might have been poisoned too. There were assassins everywhere and Ellis was as much of a target as Mutsvangwa and Gabriel. Ellis was touched that Mutsvangwa was as concerned for him and the team as he was for ED.

Kasper hit the roof at the news of the poisoning.

Things were now Full Scale, he raged, "this is war."

In a flurry of messages to Harare early the next morning,

Kasper asked Mutsvangwa if he had relayed the warnings he had given of plans to poison the VP.

Several times – Mutsvangwa replied in all caps. *I had this eventuality on my radar… I even told him to stop eating State House cooked dinners as way back as early 2015.*

Worry not – said Kasper – *there will be a lot of surprises they are the ones started. they played their game on a wrong time.*

It appeared he had a plan to hit back.

Recall the earlier mention of a time bomb?

Initially, this appeared to refer to the possibility of ED being poisoned.

But what if it was about something else?

What if he was referring to an operation so audacious it belonged in the realm of Cold War spy movies?

The odd thing about the Gwanda rally was that it was the only one at which Grace Mugabe was not present. She had flown to South Africa that weekend to tend to her wayward sons, Robert Jr, 25 and Chatunga Bellarmine, 21, whose hard partying ways had become a source of great embarrassment to the First Family. Robert Jr had been evicted from a Dubai apartment the Mugabes owned and he and his brother were now living in a suite in the swanky Capital 20 West Hotel in Johannesburg's upscale Sandton. Bellarmine would soon scandalise Zimbabweans by posting a Snapchat video of himself pouring a bottle of Armand de Brignac champagne over a £45,000 diamond-encrusted watch, captioning it: "$60 000 on the wrist when your daddy run the whole country ya know!!!"

But a bigger family scandal was just around the corner.

At 9pm on Sunday, August 13th, a young fashion model named Gabriella Engels came to see the boys in their suite.

The sons weren't in so Engels waited. At this point someone in the hotel – a doorman, a guest, or one of the boy's bodyguards – made a phone call to an intelligence agent in Joburg. It was common for girls to visit the boys in their room but it didn't happen when their mother was around.

The agent said: "It is time. Call the mother."

What happened next was brutal.

Press reports and court documents describe Grace Mugabe entering the suite and, on seeing Engels in her sons' room, picking up an electrical extension cord and beginning to beat her with it, lacerating her face. According to Engels, the bodyguards just stood there, doing nothing.

Soon after the assault Grace tried to flee, but South Africa's elite anti-crime unit, the Hawks, had received a tip-off and were quickly on the scene, preventing her from going. Was it just a coincidence that a Zimbabwean CIO agent watched it all go down from a Toyota Legend parked outside the hotel?

The story was front-page news around the world, a national disgrace, and the First Lady was charged with assault.

Kasper messaged a friend when news of the assault broke: *Now is the end of game for G40. . .*

Nail on the coffin & 6 feet deep – came the reply.

You would think so; as first ladies go, Grace was making Imelda Marcos look like Mother Theresa.

And yet, for all the mastery of the time bomb, G40 wasn't six feet deep at all, and neither was Grace.

Days later, far from facing charges in South Africa, she was granted diplomatic immunity and was soon back in Zimbabwe, parading across the stage at rallies, denouncing ED and assorted other enemies.

ED, meanwhile, his body flushed of most of the poison

after a week of treatment at the Donald Gordon Medical Centre in Johannesburg, was also back home, attending those remaining interface rallies, sitting stoically on the provincial stages, taking his latest punishment from Grace.

It was hard to look away. Two immovable forces were thrashing, and it couldn't last.

And so it proved. On November 6th, after the brutal weekend rallies in Bulawayo and Harare, Robert Mugabe fired his long-time friend and ally ED, and sided with his wife.

And then, when ED went on the run, fearing for his life, the wheels came right off the Northgate Declaration plan.

It was a batshit crazy idea to begin with.

Chapter 7

THE ESCAPE

The three cars gunned it east at high speed.

It was 1am on Tuesday, November 7th, 2017.

During the day there's no way a three-car convoy carrying a fugitive politician could make it from Harare to Mutare without getting caught. A scenic valley town in the tumbling Eastern Highlands, Mutare is 220 miles away and there would probably be as many as six police roadblocks on the way. The police, allied with G40, were everywhere in Zimbabwe at the time, hassling and fining motorists for the most minor offence. The fines filled police coffers and also funded their G40 benefactors. At night, however, the police rested from their plunder, the roadblocks shut down, and the only stops were for three toll booths.

After the drama near the gas station, the going was surprisingly good. The air got cooler outside and large domed rock formations loomed out of open savannah on either side of the road, like the humps of marooned whales.

Men on the run don't care for scenery, though; they raced on, heads down, for the border town.

They had changed the order of the convoy at the gas station. The front car, a white Mercedes C-Class, owned by a friend of Collins, was driven by Jenfan Muswere, with cousin Tarirai (Tarry) in the passenger seat. ED had switched to the middle vehicle, a Mercedes ML350 owned by Hosea "Limping Jack" Manzunzu, who sat in the back with big Richard Mavhoro, while Wise Jasi drove. The three brothers brought up the rear in Collins's brand-new white Mercedes C-Class.

By 3am they had made it through the last of the toll booths, ten miles from Mutare, and rested up for a while in a rustic lodge on the right-hand side of the road, at the foot of Christmas Pass. Then, at 5am, the sun not yet up, they made their way over the pass, towards Mutare, the city lights twinkling below.

Forbes border post, the official crossing into Mozambique, was on the far eastern edge of town, at the base of a winding valley road. They curled their way down as a fresh sun peeked up over Mozambique, burning off the mist shrouding the canopy of acacias and msasas in the valley. The land was a resplendent dewy green. A string of commercial trucks lined the side of the road waiting to be processed, but it was easy for the three cars to nudge past them to the front and wait at the gate. They were the first in line for the 6am opening. A handful of Black Boots guards lounged within the perimeter to the right of the gate under a large fig tree and in front of a military-style canvas tent; the customs building, a low-slung brick structure barely changed since colonial days, was straight ahead.

The plan was simple. The three cars would enter and park to the left of the building. ED, being easily recognisable, would stay in his vehicle, while Limping Jack and Tarry would process the four passports of those who were going across into Mozambique – Limping Jack, ED, Emmerson Jr and Tarry. The rest of the team would return to Harare once they were safely through.

"They will be looking for me," ED cautioned Limping Jack as he exited the vehicle.

How right he was.

According to the CID report of the events that followed, at 5.30am that morning instructions had come from Mutare Central District Police to "be on high alert and monitor movements of high-profile politicians at Forbes border post to alert the command for further instructions."

To begin with, things went fine. The four passports, including ED's diplomatic one, were stamped in 15 minutes. Limping Jack and Tarry returned to the ML350, and Emmerson Jr, breathing a sigh of relief, now joined his father in the back seat too. The vehicle proceeded slowly to the boom gate, where Limping Jack handed over the exit stamp to the guards on duty.

The safety of Mozambique – freedom – was only 20 yards and a stamp away.

But then there was a delay. Five minutes passed. Then ten. Then 15.

Three men in suits, probably CIO or plain-clothes police officers, ambled over to the car.

Sean, Collins, Muswere and Mavhoro observed them from the other two parked vehicles a few yards back. Collins now saw that the immigration officials in the customs building were looking over at the ML350. It was clear to him what had happened: they had seen the names on the passports, knew who was in the vehicle and had alerted the police. He glanced towards the gate they had driven through; the Black Boots were no longer lounging under their tree. They were suddenly very active, conferring with each other, speaking on cell phones, looking in the direction of the Mercedes at the boom.

Soon there were seven CIO officers in suits milling around the vehicle. They didn't appear threatening but they weren't letting the car pass either. One knocked on a back window and asked who was inside.

ED, heart in mouth, sat paralysed in the back.

"I know what this means; they are waiting for reinforcements to come and arrest me," he muttered.

He said there was no way they were getting through and they had to try to get back into Mutare.

It was time to revert to plan B.

The following events happened in a blur but are largely confirmed by the CID report.

Limping Jack, Tarry, and Emmerson Jr stepped out of the car now and started negotiating with the gate guards and CIO officers. They offered a bribe to be let through. It was refused. An argument broke out. Behind them, Sean and Collins made their move. Collins asked the truck driver blocking his vehicle to give him space so he could reverse, and slowly drove back towards the entry gate they had come through, parking just beyond the perimeter, pointing towards Mutare. He watched events unfold in his rear-view mirror.

Now Tarry and Limping Jack were arguing loudly with officers on the exit gate. It created the distraction ED needed: he lumbered his large frame out of the back of the car and started walking briskly towards Collins at the front gate, 100 yards away. Collins, looking in the mirror, did a double-take:

his father had on a wide-brimmed veld safari hat and oversized women's sunglasses. It wasn't much of a disguise. He looked ridiculous. Incredibly, the CIO officers on the boom, distracted by the argument, didn't notice at first. ED had made it 30 yards when they spotted him. Now all hell broke loose. The lead CIO officer pointed and shouted and he and six others ran at the escapee, shouting for him to stop. By the time they reached him Sean and Mavhoro were already at his side. Fists started flying, jackets were grabbed; men in suits fell to the ground: Sean, pint-sized but a soldier, and Mavhoro the burly security guy were getting the better of them. ED was running now – fast for a 73-year-old man – and Collins was willing him on from the getaway car. A command rang out from one of the officers to the police at the exit gate: "*Tora AK! Tora AK!*" – Get an AK!

ED had 20 yards still to go; then ten. A guard at the gate tried to apprehend him; the old man brushed him aside like a buffalo does a fly and made it to the front passenger side of the car, literally diving in. By now one of the policemen had collected his gun from the tent and reached the vehicle. Behind the wheel Collins was frantically trying to get the car in gear. A back door was open, though, and the wheel-mounted gear drive on the Merc wouldn't engage. Now the soldier was at his window and the barrel of the weapon – an FN, not a Kalashnikov (Collins, a gun enthusiast, recognised it) – was pointing through it right at his head. Watching from 50 yards away, open-mouthed in horror, Emmerson Jr waited for the gunshot that would blow his father or brother away. But suddenly the FN barrel was yanked in the air and the policeman holding it twisted and fell backwards to the ground. Sean had reached him, pulled the gun up and tripped the man with his right foot. The two of them rolled on the ground, trading punches, wrestling over the FN. Now Mavhoro had made it to the car; he leapt in the back seat and slammed the door. The gear finally engaged; Collins couldn't wait around for his brothers or the others. The Merc sped off up the hill at high speed in a cloud of dust, a single shot fired after it.

Junior had watched events unfold in the no-man's-land between the entry gate, the exit gate and the immigration building.. He was holding his father's heavy brief case which he had retrieved from the back seat of the car. He knew it contained vital documents and cash that they would need to get out, and he knew he couldn't get caught with it. A nearby passenger bus had its doors open and he stepped aboard. From inside he made out Jenfan Muswere in the melee below. He stepped off, reached Jenfan, handed him the briefcase and told him to lock it in the boot of the Merc that Jenfan had driven down in. Then Junior made his way to the entry gate. Chaos reigned among the CIO officers and the police. Frantic cell phone calls were being made; arguments broke out as to who had or had not fired a shot; who had allowed them to escape. Junior reached the gate, which was now half-closed, but a policeman, seeing him, turned his back and calmly opened it, letting him through. That one act saved him.

Junior started walking up the road now, back to Mutare, trying to appear inconspicuous. He looked to his right and spotted Sean running through the bush below and called him on his cell. Sean answered, frantic, out of breath. Seconds earlier he'd got the better of the policeman he had wrestled with, thrown the FN over a fence and scrambled down the slope below the road into the bush.

"See the white taxi up ahead?" said Junior.

"Yes."

"Meet me there."

Minutes later, hearts racing, they were in the cab, heading back into Mutare, unaware of where their father and brother were or what had befallen the rest of the team back at the boom gate. On the way up the road they passed six open-back Land Rovers hurtling down, carrying 40 or 50 helmeted riot police: the back-up the guards had called for to arrest ED.

It was 7am on Tuesday morning and Junior was freaking out.

This wasn't the life he was used to.

❖ ❖ ❖

"We're fucked, Kasper. It's over. ED is finished. We're fucked!"

"Tom, relax yourself. Don't think too much. Don't think."

"*Shamwari*, he's on the run and he's probably arrested or dead already."

"Tom, relax. If you think too much you will have doubts."

It was mid-morning, 700 miles away in Johannesburg, and Kasper was on the phone with Ellis.

Kasper had just got off a call with Mutsvangwa, who had also spent a restless night. He had fled Harare 24 hours earlier for Johannesburg, knowing for certain that ED was about to be fired. He was fine with ED getting fired. He wanted it. It was the war veterans and youths loyal to ED who had been bussed to Bulawayo to boo Grace. They wanted to bring things to a head. What he didn't anticipate was that ED, fearing for his life, would go on the run. There was no word of his whereabouts and panic was setting in. Without ED their plan was dead in the water. They needed him and they needed him alive.

For all his outward calm, Kasper was also worried. He had spent much of Monday evening and Tuesday morning sparring on text and WhatsApp with Agent DeeZee, who was in Harare, jubilant at the demise of the Crocodile. Kasper had tried to keep communication with DeeZee to a minimum the past year since DeeZee openly suspected he was now a double agent, working with Ellis and Mutsvangwa.

Now, DeeZee was delighted because Kasper had clearly backed the wrong reptile.

Kkkkk... – he cackled – *Garwe Raakagama Zvaro!* – the Crocodile is finished!

The game has just started cmde – Kasper replied.

Grace for President!

Who is Grace Mugabe against the whole country?

Is ED the whole country, cmde?

Kasper had heard through intel chatter about a skirmish involving ED in Mutare on the eastern border that morning, but he fed DeeZee false information anyway, knowing it would get to other agents in Harare and might confuse things.

Just got off call w Emmerson Jr, they are at the farm. Still in country.

Kkkk... – laughed DeeZee – *fake news.*

After reassuring Ellis, Kasper spent much of the rest of Tuesday sending out false flags into the intelligence ether, writing "BREAKING NEWS" followed by headlines such as "GENERAL CHIWENGA FIRED"; "HARARE NO-GO AREA", "SOLDIERS *TOI TOI* [MARCH] IN STREETS", and sending them to all his military and intel contacts. None of the stories were true but he was doing whatever he could to cause panic, chaos and confusion. He wanted G40 to think the military were rising up against them.

Then he made further calls to Mutsvangwa, Gabriel and Ellis. The mood was sombre. With ED probably arrested or even killed, G40 would be entrenched: there was no alternative leader in Lacoste to ED, no one who could rival the star power of Grace, Moyo and Saviour. Mutsvangwa, usually so confident and cavalier, had sounded troubled on the phone, and even Kasper was worried.

❖ ❖ ❖

Collins flattened the pedal and screamed up the hill, glad of the state-of-the art car he'd recently bought. In the passenger seat he heard his father mumbling incoherently to himself. He had a faraway look in his eyes. Collins had never seen him like this before. He looked like a broken man.

As ED knew Mutare would soon be teeming with police and CIO officers hunting him, he ordered Collins to turn left, away from the city. They drove in silence, climbing higher on winding roads around hairpin bends, making their way up to the Bvumba, a lush mist-shrouded mountain region overlooking Mutare to the north, and with dramatic views of Mozambique below to the east. Collins remembered the area: his sister had got married up here a year earlier, at Leopard Rock, a famous casino hotel and golf resort. He wished he was back at that wedding, the family all together; a simpler time.

After a few more miles, when they passed a sign for a police training post pointing to the left, ED, deadly serious from the passenger seat, barked at him to turn right onto a dirt road, and a few miles further on, to pull over.

"You can say goodbye to this car," he told his son.

"What?"

"We're going to have to destroy it. It's white and easily

spotted and they can trace the registration."

Collins didn't want to destroy his car – it was worth a fortune. They came to a compromise; he moved it closer to a clump of bushes and the three of them, big Mavhoro leading the way, started ripping off branches from nearby trees and covering it up.

Then they walked on until they reached the foot of a rocky hill, and came to a property with a house on it, a separate cottage and a collection of mud huts. The villagers in the huts, on seeing them, lowered their heads, bowed and kissed the ground. Collins, a rich city boy, thought it bizarre, something from another world: "It was different to anything I have seen or known of our culture."

According to Collins, his father knew the place from the guerilla war, and knew the people there would shelter them.

Indeed, stories circulated months later that ED had spent the day in a cave that he had hidden in during the 1970s guerilla war. The eastern mountains lend themselves to story-telling, though – the great novelist Doris Lessing lived in the Bvumba for years – and this to me sounds like myth-making. ED was not actually deployed to the front during his Mozambique years; he was Special Assistant to Mugabe in Maputo, running his security, and while he would visit the training camps, he was not an insurgent. It's possible he knew of the village and caves from combatants under his command, or visited them later as spy chief or Defence Minister. Either way, the villagers welcomed him and seemed to be expecting him.

ED entered one of the huts and Collins took the chance to call his brother Sean. He knew there was a risk that the call could be traced, but he needed to find out if his twin was still alive. They were identical and inseparable, and the last time Collins had seen his brother he had been wrestling with a policeman over a gun; Collins recalled the gunshot as he had driven away... Incredibly, Sean answered immediately. He was in Mutare with Emmerson Jr. They were both okay but police were all over town hunting them. They had hidden in an abandoned car wash at first, among some torn car seats and old tires. Then they'd made their way to a fish-and-chip shop, just off the town's main street. They had been joined by Jenfan Muswere now, who had also made it out. Jenfan said the others had been detained at the border.

ED emerged from the hut and grabbed the phone. There was no "Are you boys okay? Are you safe?" He had switched to military mode and demanded to know where his briefcase was.

Junior told him they had had to hide it in one of the cars at the border post.

His father was livid. "You're of no value to me unless you've got that briefcase – get it back!"

Jesus. Junior didn't fancy going back there. He knew it was teeming with police and CIO officers.

They made a quick plan as they spoke: ED and Mavhoro would remain in the mountain hideaway; Sean would take a taxi up into the Bvumba to collect Collins and bring him down to Mutare to help plan another exit; and Junior and Jenfan would work out a way to retrieve the briefcase.

Fortunately, both Junior and Sean had contacts in Mutare who could help them. Junior called a woman named Gertrude Mutandi, a prominent local tavern owner and fellow ZANU-PF Youth League member whom he trusted. Buxom and business-savvy, Gertrude owned PaGetty, a popular nightclub near the museum in the centre of town. As with any self-respecting tavern owner she had a rolodex of important contacts herself. If anyone could help them, she could.

Sean, a captain in the army, called some military personnel he knew based out of 3 Brigade, Mutare, the largest military barracks in eastern Zimbabwe. They all met in the parking lot behind the local Spar supermarket. Gertrude had brought with her three friends who said they were distraught at ED's firing. They had two vehicles and wanted to help.

Sean's contacts arrived from 3 Brigade – three middle-ranked men from Military Intelligence: Staff Sergeant Sango, Staff Sergeant Mahluale and Sergeant Mhlanga. They were dressed in plainclothes. Junior explained the briefcase situation, and the MI guys agreed to return to the border with Jenfan Muswere to retrieve it.

November 7th, 2017 turned out to be an eventful morning at the usually sleepy Forbes border post. According to Muswere, when they got there, the C-Class Mercedes with the briefcase in the trunk was surrounded by a dozen CIO officers. They came up with a plan: Distraction 101. At around 11am, two gunshots rang out on the opposite side of the parking lot to the car. The police at the tent and the officers by the vehicle raced over to where the shots had come from. Muswere, calmly moving from where he had positioned himself 15 yards from the car, opened the trunk, picked out the briefcase, and walked towards the exit, completely unseen. In turn, the MI officers casually moved from the now crowded area where the gunshots had come from and joined him, the handguns in their belts still warm from the firing.

While Sean took a cab to meet Collins in the mountains (he made sure to get a scruffy-looking driver; "well-dressed taxi drivers are all CIO", he said), Junior went to buy some new shirts at Edgar's on main street. He knew that descriptions of what they had been wearing at the border would have been distributed to police and CIO hunting them. He had no cash to pay for them, though, and had to use his credit card. The cashier read the name on the card, looked up at him nervously and whispered: "I pray for you."

Word had got out that the ex-VP had disappeared and was on the run with his sons.

When Sean returned from the mountains with Collins, they met with Junior outside Edgar's. He had their new shirts. Jenfan and the three MI officers then joined them at Gertrude's house. The briefcase, more trouble than it was worth, was safely back in Junior's hands.

It was not yet noon.

While the MI guys stayed in town to plan possible escape routes, the brothers decided to return the briefcase to their father in the Bvumba. Gertrude's friend drove them in his battered BMW, with Collins directing from the back and Junior in the front passenger seat. Just after the Bvumba police training post sign, a Toyota Corolla passed them on the way down, did a sharp U-turn and started chasing them up. Was it the police from the training base? Had CIO officers spotted them?

Junior urged the driver faster but his Beamer didn't have the gas – hell, the ceiling lining had caved in and its doors had no handles. Within seconds the tail car had caught them and was forcing them over. They were on the edge of a steep ravine; Junior thought of leaping out and throwing the briefcase into it. Then he looked over at the vehicle. His mouth fell open. It was his father and Mavhoro! Police were now searching hotels and homes in the Bvumba, and ED had been lent a car by the owner of the hideout property to get away. By sheer stroke of luck, Mavhoro had recognised Junior in the front seat of the BMW as they'd passed by.

The sons looked at their father. He was a mess. He was wearing a black SWAT cap and a tight grey tank top that he had found in the back of Collins's Merc.

Junior chuckled: "That's not much of a disguise – it's just a tight shirt and a hat."

They made their way back to Mutare now, ED lying down on the back seat of the BMW as they drove through two police roadblocks: no one was looking for the fugitive former VP in such a battered car. ED had contacted someone who had a safe house for him to hide in; it would be too dangerous for them all to be there. He gave Junior firm instructions: come and collect me when you've worked out a way to get us the hell out of here.

It was 2pm.

At Gertrude's house the brothers and MI officers now brainstormed possible escape routes. One plan – so audacious it might work – was to actually return to the same Forbes border post in the MI vehicle, ED hiding in the boot. MI officers were not usually searched and who would think he might try to escape from the exact same place again? But another recce to Forbes quashed the plan: there was a massive roadblock there and the MI vehicle's trunk was opened. Another option was to try another border post 80 miles to the south, but they found that too was on lockdown. They were having the same problems they had had when trying to escape Harare the night before. Junior shook his head: had it only been 24 hours ago?

Other men came and went from Gertrude's house, including soldiers. Soldiers were not normally free to leave their barracks without permission from their superiors. If the family had felt abandoned in Harare, it was apparent in Mutare that certain senior commanders knew of their whereabouts and were lending a hand, while being careful not to do so openly. To take sides in this political spat – that was treason.

It was finally decided that the best option would be to cross the border on foot, at night, through the bush, near Marymount Teachers' College, a frequent illegal crossing point for thousands of informal traders – "border jumpers" – who make a living buying goods in Mozambique to resell back home.

Part of the crossing was through a minefield, a remnant of the liberation war 37 years earlier, but if they crossed at night with a guide who knew the path, the MI guys reckoned they could make it. The MI guys would alert a Somalian they knew on the other side to pick them up ten miles into Mozambique and drive them to Manica, the next town. Departure time was set for 11pm that night.

By now they had all received calls and messages from their mother and sisters pleading for them to return home. ED refused. He wasn't going back. At about 10pm at Gertrude's that night, Collins fielded a very odd call. Actually, two calls. The first was from an associate from the same chrome mining company that had refused them use of their plane in Harare. This time, the associate said to wait for a very important call in a few minutes. Collins waited, and when it came, he put it on speaker so Junior could quietly listen in. The call was from the son of Defence Minister Sydney Sekeramayi, a Mugabe loyalist and potential VP replacement for ED.

The reception had an echo so the boys reckoned they were on speaker, too.

"*Mudhara ari kupi*?" Sekeramayi's son asked – where is your old man?

"I don't know," Collins replied. "We are looking for him. Maybe you can tell us where he is, we're worried."

"We are worried too," said Sekeramayi's son. "I thought you were together. I have a message from Number One [the President]. If you are with him, tell him everything is fine and he's safe and we want him to come back."

Sekeramayi's son said they wanted ED to return for the next day's politburo meeting. Collins said he would pass on the message if he heard from his father.

It's possible the call was genuine: that Mugabe had read the letter ED had written in his office and, moved by its tribute to him, was calling off the hunt; it's also possible Mugabe had no idea of the plans to arrest ED in his home and kill him – that G40 elements were to blame – and it was only now, on hearing of the incident at Forbes, that he learned ED had gone on the run. Bolstering this possibility was news they had got late that afternoon that Limping Jack, Wise Jasi and Tarry had been released by the police at the border. Junior still thought it a trap, though, and when Collins passed on the message to his father later, ED said the same thing: it was a trap; he wasn't going back.

It was time to move. Junior drove to collect his father at the safe house. As he was entering the yard he almost stepped on a black snake that had half-swallowed a frog. The omens weren't good. . .

Two cars proceeded in convoy towards the crossing point on the eastern edge of Mutare, taking the back roads to avoid the police checkpoints the MI guys had marked out earlier. Vehicles across the city were being searched. At various points on the drive the front car carrying Sean and the MI would turn off its headlights and stop, and the back car carrying the others would follow suit. It was painstaking progress. They saw searchlights at times; heard sirens and police dogs: the hunt was very much on.

Just before midnight the cars came to a gravel road, tall gum trees and high grass all around. Crickets chirped; the near full moon ducked behind heavy cloud. They exited the cars and spoke in whispers.

The three military guys, armed with rifles, would lead with the border guide; ED, Emmerson Jr and Mavhoro would follow. Sean and Jenfan would accompany them to no-man's-land then turn back. Collins would stay with the two cars in case the group had to run back and needed a quick getaway.

And that was that. It was their final gambit. If this crossing didn't work they were out of options.

Collins watched as his father and two brothers stepped onto a narrow dirt path barely visible through the high grass. They took a few steps, were enveloped by bush and disappeared into the unknown.

It was just after midnight, the early hours of Wednesday, November 8th.

Chapter 8

MOZAMBIQUE TO MENLYN

The flight of ED *from* Robert Mugabe to Mozambique is Shakespearean in its pathos. In 1977, aged 34, he had travelled on foot to *join* Mugabe in Mozambique, and continue the armed struggle against white rule. It was a journey thousands of young black Zimbabweans made at the time (Christopher and Monica Mutsvangwa included), many crossing at the exact same point that ED and his son were now. It was why the minefield was there: Rhodesians laid those mines in the 1970s to stop insurgents crossing this precise section of border. It said something about the factionalism within ZANU-PF, the betrayal of its revolution and the disaster they had made of the country, that one of its heroes was now running for his life not from white Rhodesians but from his friend and former brother-in-arms.

In the mid-1970s ED had been a lawyer in Lusaka, Zambia, married to Jayne, the sister of revered liberation army commander Josiah Tongogara, when word came that they could use a sharp mind at Mugabe's side. He "walked the walk", became security chief of ZANU, and then Mugabe's Special Assistant in Maputo.

ED's own time as a guerilla fighter, however, had come a decade earlier, in the mid-1960s. He was a young radical in Rhodesia when he co-founded the Crocodile Gang, the first guerilla group to take up arms against white rule since the First Chimurenga, a brief and bloody uprising against white settlers in 1896–97. ED's war record was patchy: he trained in Egypt and China, returned to Rhodesia and blew up a train in Fort Victoria (today's Masvingo) in 1964, but was promptly arrested by the Rhodesians and sentenced to death. His lawyers successfully argued he was under 21, and therefore too young for execution (he was actually 22), and he served ten years instead. He met and befriended Mugabe in prison, hence the touching words in the letter:

I wish to express my gratitude for the role you played in saving my life in 1965 when I was facing the death penalty...

One holdover from those years was his nickname: the Crocodile. It derived from the Crocodile Gang, although decades later most Zimbabweans had no idea of that: they assumed the name was due to his reputation: the silent, cunning, heavy-lidded assassin by Mugabe's side all these years, running the spy agency, then the Defence Ministry. Of course, it didn't hurt to be thought of in such a way. "Better to be feared than loved if you can't be both," Machiavelli wrote in *The Prince*, a book commonly found on the shelves of ZANU-PF politicians. ED (christened Dambudzo), had actually adopted the name Emmerson in high school after reading the American philosopher-poet Ralph Waldo Emerson, but Machiavelli would have been on his bookshelves too.

Now 73 years old, still suffering the after-effects of arsenic poisoning, he was fleeing his country pursued by his longtime friend, accompanied by a portly 34-year-old son used to the good life. And yet, according to that son, the old man still had it. They followed the three armed MI guys and the guide from a short distance. According to Junior, at various points, seeing searchlights or hearing voices or police dogs, ED would dive to the ground and snake-crawl, military style. Junior did the same but he found it hard; his back hurt, his butt poked in the air. His father rolled his eyes at him. "I walked for hundreds of miles through this bush when I was your age!" he scolded. That ED still had on his suit trousers and Italian dress shoes made it more embarrassing for Junior, who was made to lug the heavy briefcase.

When they came to the minefield, about 50 yards across, ED told Junior to follow his footsteps. The guide knew the path, though, and they followed him. Sean, heart in mouth, watched from the fence, and on seeing them safely through, hurried back to join Collins and Muswere at the cars.

From a vantage point just past the minefield, the MI guys noticed flashlights below them to the south, close to where they planned to meet the Somalian by the road. They assumed it was a Zimbabwean police search party pursuing them across the border; it was too dangerous to go that way so they tracked north to stay safe, making a large loop that added miles and hours to the journey.

"The ground was either up or down, never flat," recalled Junior, "and we had to grab onto branches of overhanging trees and clamber over big rocks. My father fell down at various points."

At around 2am, on a hilltop a few miles into Mozambique, with the reception on his cell showing three bars, Junior sent a message to Jenfan Muswere back in Zimbabwe:

We are through. Make the call.

Jenfan, returning to Harare on back roads, contacted a number in Pretoria, South Africa.

A man named Thabiso answered. He had been expecting the call.

"My brother, things are bad, can you arrange for pick-up for the former VP?"

"From where?"

"I will let you know soon."

Jenfan hung up. He had to keep the calls short in case his or Thabiso's phones were tapped.

Thabiso, a South African security aide to a multi-millionaire, Zimbabwe-born IT entrepreneur in Pretoria named Justice Maphosa, started making evacuation plans. ED had contacted Maphosa during the panic in Harare the night before, and the wealthy businessman had agreed to assist.

❖ ❖ ❖

The full moon was stuck behind thick cloud now and the path was muddy and slippery. The guide led them to a village and told them to wait while he entered a mud hut. He emerged with an elderly *n'anga* (witch doctor), who called the group over to sit under a plastic gazebo in the middle of the village. The gazebo, of the kind seen in cheap weddings, seemed surreal and out of place in this ancient world of mud huts and magic. The *n'anga* explained this was tribal land and the spirits required permission for them to pass through. A monetary donation usually works and

Junior funnelled some cash his way.

"A very African toll gate," he muttered to his father as they walked on.

An hour later, still in darkness, they hit trouble.

As Junior recalls it, his iPhone was in his back pocket and whenever a call came through a light would flash on it. He didn't notice this, but from the shadows someone had. They had turned a corner in the path, briefly out of view of the MI guys ahead, and a stranger stepped out of the bush and held an AK47 to the guide's head. They froze. Junior thought him a RENAMO rebel, a fearsome soldier in Mozambique's resistance army, but Junior's probably seen too many movies; the man was mostly likely a lone bandit, a rural African highwayman. The man made a gesture with his trigger finger: cash. Junior forked over more funds. By the time the MI guys had tracked back to find out what was causing the delay, the bandit had vanished, several hundred US dollars richer.

They walked on, through muddy fields, across streams and even through a dense banana plantation. The land got flatter, the air more humid. "The mosquitos were big as birds," Junior recalled.

Their feet were blistered, their clothes caked in mud. Junior wanted to collapse. It was then that they heard an engine; the putt of a motorbike. They scrambled up a slope. They had finally reached the road.

The MI guys sent a text message, and ten minutes later the Somali cab driver appeared from the west. He had waited for them all night eight miles closer to the Zimbabwe border; their detour must have added ten miles to their journey. He drove them east to a fleabitten hotel in Manica, a one-horse Mozambican town, where they checked into where a room cost US$6 a night. The sun was coming up. At 6am ED dismissed the MI guys. He gave them instructions: return to barracks; do not say where you were.

They shook hands, wished him well and, taking Mavhoro with them, hit the road.

At 7am, Junior sent another message to Muswere, who in turn contacted Thabiso in Pretoria.

"Pick-up location: Beira."

❖ ❖ ❖

Back in South Africa, at the Crowne Plaza Hotel near OR Tambo airport, Christopher Mutsvangwa was ecstatic. Kasper had delivered the news to him early that morning: ED had crossed safely into Mozambique with MI. He would soon be on his way to an undisclosed location in South Africa. Kasper, Gabriel and Ellis celebrated too – the Northgate Declaration was not dead yet!

The anxiety temporarily lifted, Mutsvangwa immediately decided to host a press conference in Sandton, to denounce "the G40 cabal" and the firing of ED. He asked Gabriel, as Chairman of the ZEF, to introduce him. Gabe was wary at first: it would be the first official acknowledgment that his MDC-aligned diaspora group and the war veterans, once sworn enemies, were working together. He ran it by Ellis and others who said he should do it – "Who better to speak for the diaspora?"

The press conference was set for 1pm at the Radisson Blu Gautrain Hotel in the upscale Johannesburg suburb of Sandton. Gabriel, Ellis and Mutsvangwa contacted news organisations and journalists they knew; Kasper, Magic and Horse staked out security at the venue.

At 9am Mutsvangwa was picked up at his hotel by Bernard Pswarayi, a jovial, broad-shouldered 40-something Zimbabwean. A schoolboy cricket prodigy, once tipped to be Zimbabwe's first black opening bowler, he now ran a branding agency in Joburg and had co-founded a promotional investment website called ZimVive. He and Ellis had met years earlier and bonded over business ideas for Zimbabwe and a love of sport. Ellis reckoned Bernard could be Zimbabwe's Sports Minister one day. In early 2017 Ellis had introduced him to the Northgate team at the Sundowner and Bernard had started running "logistics" for them: booking venues, driving Mutsvangwa and others to meetings. "It was an exciting time. I would get a message from Kasper: 'Pick up so and so at 6am, drive to this address for this time.' Then I would return to my normal desk job." Incredibly, his wife had no idea that he spent his mornings driving around the Chairman of the ZNLWVA, being tailed by spies from the CIO.

This particular day Bernard cried off his regular job altogether; the press conference was too important. He recalls looking in the rear-view mirror for CIO tail cars while Mutsvangwa, dapper as ever in designer suit and silk tie, prepared notes for his statement. He took him to get a haircut at a barbershop in the Firs Mall in Rosebank, before going on to Sandton for the press conference.

The Radisson Blu Gautrain has a swanky high-ceiling lobby, a long bar at one end and tall windows facing the street. By 12 noon a large crowd had gathered, among them reporters from Reuters, the *Guardian*, the *Wall Street Journal* and the *New York Times*, but there was a problem: payment for the venue hadn't gone through. The ZEF had no money and the Northgate group's credit card didn't work either. It was typical:

they always ran out of cash. There were times they couldn't afford to buy bottled water.

Kasper saw other problems: half a dozen cars outside, some driven by CIO agents he knew, others with tinted windows driven by agents sent down from Harare. Nor did Kasper like the look of a number of men in suits and dark glasses milling around the lobby.

Gabriel and Kasper conferred: there was another venue, a café in an office complex up the street they could rent cheaply. They could control who they let in there. Gabriel called and paid for the venue on his personal credit card. In the meantime Kasper went around and whispered to the journalists and attendees he trusted the new address and time – 2pm – and asked them to keep quiet about it.

❖ ❖ ❖

ED and son weren't out of the woods yet.

The Somalian found a friend to drive them to Beira, Mozambique's second city, a steamy, run-down port on the Indian Ocean, four hours east. They arrived at 1pm in swampy heat, and were dropped off at a bus stop downtown. Junior told his father to wait while he went to buy a new SIM for his iPhone. He looked back at his father as he walked away. The old man's status had fallen with the altitude: 48 hours ago he was the Vice-President of Zimbabwe; now he sat stooped on a bus stop bench in a mud-caked suit, shoelaces undone for his blistered feet to breathe. The only thing that differentiated him from a peasant was that he was sitting atop an US$8,000 Louis Vuitton briefcase.

The 16 member countries of the SADC – the Southern African Development Community – are more than just regional neighbours: most of their governments are all still dominated by parties that won liberation from European colonial rule. Many of their political leaders trained and fought together in those wars for liberation and thus they share more than borders: they share a blood bond forged in their respective struggles for independence. It was one of the reasons Mugabe had survived so long: despite the cruelty, corruption and economic chaos he had unleased on Zimbabwe over 37 years, neighbouring leaders revered him because he had won a war against white rule. The SADC countries cooperated on everything as a result of that blood bond, including military and intelligence matters. Over the years ED had personally helped draft defence and security cooperation agreements within the SADC and the African Union to protect and support member countries from internal and external threats. Now those same networks were working against ED: Junior knew Harare would have alerted Maputo that they had a fugitive on their soil; and if the Mozambicans didn't arrest them, the South Africans would when they arrived there.

With the new SIM, Junior sent a WhatsApp to Muswere in Zimbabwe, who contacted Thabiso in Pretoria: *Hi boss, now my team is in Beira. Can you arrange for the jet ASAP.*

For the first time Muswere gave the names and identities of the two passengers.

Hi boss – he added ominously – *also send security.*

If they managed to get out of Beira, Junior wanted a ton of armed protection on the ground when they landed in Johannesburg.

He went to collect his father at the bus stop and they found a good hotel in town where they could clean up and put fresh clothes on. By 3pm they were on their way to the airport.

The charter jet had been ordered and was winging its way from South Africa to collect them.

Departure time for Johannesburg was set for 6pm.

❖ ❖ ❖

And there they were, Gabriel Shumba, Chairman of the ZEF and Christopher Mutsvangwa, Chairman of the ZNLWVA, sitting at a table together: a torture victim side by side with the Chairman of one of the institutions implicated in that torture – and much worse.

It was 2pm in a café a short walk north of the Radisson Blu Gautrain Hotel, Sandton. Two men guarded the café entrance while a third, driving a white Toyota Legend, prevented the progress of tinted-windowed cars on the streets outside. "I know the game, how they drive – I block them," said Kasper.

Mutsvangwa began by reading a long, meandering prepared statement from the ZNLWA released to the media that morning:

> We, the veterans of Zimbabwe's liberation war… do hereby state as follows… that the party (ZANU-PF) and the nation is being traumatised by one person, Robert Gabriel Mugabe, who is bent on maintaining his hold on power, and ensuring he passes on his power to his wife in a dynastic fashion… contrary to the principles that guided our liberation struggle.

He said that Mugabe's new principles were defined as being "loyal only to Mugabe and his family…" and that this had led to economic meltdown and great suffering in Zimbabwe. As a result, the war veterans had reconstituted and were going to fight Mugabe and the "dynastic cabal".

In response, Gabriel's statement for the ZEF followed on from the "Damascene moment" words he had written a year earlier, when the war veterans had officially divorced themselves from Mugabe:

We embrace the message from the Chairman of the war veterans for the mere reason that the aspirations of the diaspora, which we have been articulating for years, are now resonating with the war veterans, the vanguards of our liberation from colonial rule. . .

Lest his friends in the opposition jump to the conclusion he had joined ZANU-PF, he added:

Our partnership should be guided by principles not fear: we want a Zimbabwe where we don't have to watch our backs; we want the values that underpinned the liberation struggle to be restored...

It's worth clarifying here that Gabriel's public role for the ZEF was different from the private one he was playing with Kasper, Mutsvangwa and co. It had been a personal decision to work with them and Ellis, and his diaspora friends had no idea that he was doing so. Gabriel hadn't wanted the ZEF to be compromised by the risk he was taking: too many exiles had gone through too much to fully trust the other side. But, in taking that leap of faith (and he and his wife had had stand-up rows over whether they could trust Kasper), Gabriel was having his own Damascene moment, and he was now nudging the ZEF towards the new approach too.

"As an individual, I found I came to convey less bitterness

and anger about the past violations I had experienced," he would say later. "I learned to moderate my speech and to talk more of reconciliation and healing than revenge and retribution. I grew up a lot as a person as a result. It made me look realistically at relationships with erstwhile adversaries. What changed was not the ideology or goals, but rather strategies for collaboration to achieve a better Zimbabwe."

Official statements over, it was Mutsvangwa's turn to speak his own mind, and that thesaurus in his brain began working overtime. It was rhetorical gymnastics, linguistic sorcery.

He started by announcing that "the assassins" had failed: that he had learned that morning that ED was safe, and would soon be arriving in South Africa.

He went on to address the elephant in the room: how his organisation, an institution implicated in so much brutality and cruelty over the years, had come to see eye to eye with the Zimbabwean diaspora – the *victims* of that cruelty. "Puppies are born on the same day to the same mother," he said in Shona, "but they do not open their eyes on the same day. On behalf of the war veterans I would like to apologise for the agony that Zimbabweans have gone through all these years."

Then he tapped Gabriel on the shoulder and said, "Who would have imagined that I would be sitting side by side here with Gabriel Shumba?"

After that it was down to business.

Having spent two years speaking to any Zimbabwean with a pen and a microphone – and they all thought his crusade against Mugabe delusional and doomed – he relished addressing the world's blue-chip media. That they were even in attendance was justification of his strategy two years earlier to court allies in the most unlikely of places: would any of the press have even turned up if it wasn't for Ellis and Gabriel; if the democratic opposition were not at the table, part of the deal?

He spoke about how he had reached out to the MDC and the diaspora "24 months ago" to form "a broad-based coalition" against Mugabe. Leaning against a wall near the back, unnoticed by anyone, the Who the Hell Is He Man quietly nodded: it was almost exactly two years ago, at the hotel in Fourways, that Ellis had got Mutsvangwa together with Morgan Tsvangirai, Eddie Cross, Gabriel Shumba and other senior opposition figures, a meeting mediated by the former South African politician Roelf Meyer. A lot had happened since then. . .

As if privately acknowledging his friendship with Ellis, Mutsvangwa then spoke of white Rhodesians and white Zimbabweans of the diaspora, and said their suffering should be acknowledged and they should be welcomed home. "We did not fight a racial war – we fought a war against injustice." He mentioned that he had been attacked by Mugabe and G40 for embracing whites – a reference to that picture of him in a Joburg pub with Ellis that had done the rounds – and that he wore such attacks with pride.

But there was something else he said that afternoon that was more intriguing than the story of bitter former enemies working together. He went out of his way to praise the Zimbabwean military, and said that it was "conscious of its obligations" to arrest "some of the excesses of this mad cabal".

"If any spilling of blood happens [in the days ahead] we will hold G40 to account…"

It was an odd thing to say because at this point his side was reeling: barely eight hours earlier he'd been in a cold-sweat panic, unable to locate ED on whom his future plans depended, and the military had not said a word. Yet now, even before ED had got out of whatever country he was currently hiding in, Mutsvangwa seemed to be suggesting inside knowledge that the military were going to step in.

Did he know something – or was he willing it?

When a reporter in the audience asked him to clarify whether he was calling for a military intervention he said no: "As revolutionaries we don't subscribe to coups, we work on the premise of organising the populace. We do not want to abuse the military to settle political scores…"

But then he added something so cryptic and left field – and yet weirdly brilliant – that you have to read carefully to decode what he meant. "You don't go and teach the American army to restore the rule of [King] George III," he said, "because it's the army of George Washington – a revolutionary. It's the same as Zimbabwe – you don't allow a feudalist woman and a cabal of thieves [to seize the state]."

In that odd verbal formulation, using the foundation of the United States as an analogy, Mutsvangwa was saying that a coup had *already taken place* in Zimbabwe – "a coup by marriage certificate" – carried out by the feudal wife of a senile king, and he was saying the military *had a duty* to intervene to reverse the coup in order to restore democracy and the constitution.

Whether the region, the world, or even the Zimbabwe military would buy his formulation was another story, but he had laid down a narrative marker, his persuasion gambit, for the dramatic events to come.

❖ ❖ ❖

At that precise moment, 900 miles away at an airport in the Mozambican port city of Beira, a uniformed immigration official took the passports of two passengers and told them to wait. He entered a separate room and locked the door. The airport was spookily quiet; there were no scheduled flights.

Junior looked at his father – why did the man lock the door?

They waited… and waited.

An hour went by and panic started setting in, a familiar dread: the immigration official was alerting the authorities that they had the Zimbabwean fugitive and his son. Junior asked his father for money. He'd been dishing out cash like a game show host all day and there was no reason to stop now. His father handed him a fistful of US dollars and Junior took it and shoved it under the locked door.

After 45 minutes the door opened and the official came over to them. He held out his hand and gave them back the money. Then he returned to the room and locked the door again.

Father and son stared at each other, bemused.

After a while a young white gentleman in a pilot's uniform appeared and apologised for the delay. His name was Marius Bekker and he was due to fly them out. Bekker, from Johannesburg, was a good-looking guy in his late 30s who bore a passing resemblance to Tom Cruise. He'd been in the corporate charter pilot business for a while, but said this delay was unusually long, even by Mozambican standards.

Bekker started banging on doors asking what the problem was. "This is unacceptable!" he railed.

He had no idea at the time who he was transporting – "a lot of clients prefer to remain anonymous" – and the client in

Pretoria had made sure their names would not be on the flight log until the last minute.

Bekker recalls the passengers being "tired and anxious, but well-spoken and perfectly polite".

After another hour a uniformed man approached from the arrivals section, flanked by seven armed men. This was it, thought Junior – the game was up; the authorities had arrived to arrest them.

The uniformed man introduced himself to ED. He said he was the immigration chief at the airport and he wanted to apologise. He'd gone home early that afternoon, not expecting any further flights, and had locked all the computers needed to process passports through immigration. His staff, desperate to find him, had been too embarrassed to tell the waiting passengers that they had no access to their computers.

He handed back their passports and said they were cleared to leave.

Bekker now saw their names, and for the first time worked out who they were.

They boarded just after 8pm, exhausted, with a single piece of luggage: the Louis Vuitton briefcase.

Junior collapsed into his seat and closed his eyes. He had barely slept in 60 hours.

His father said: "Do you want to die in your sleep?"

"What do you mean?"

"If I'm Robert [Mugabe] I'm shooting this plane out the sky – no one will ever know."

He reminded Junior what had happened to Samora Machel, Mozambique's President in 1986: a mysterious plane crash one night on the South Africa–Mozambique border, no explanation.

Was his father kidding with him, playing a cruel joke?

Junior was now very much awake.

He spent the first half-hour of the flight in sheer terror, his hands gripping the armrests.

Only when they crossed into South African airspace did he breathe easier.

They were still not in the clear.

Coming in to land at Lanseria, a private airport north of Johannesburg, Junior noticed the runway was lined with about 20 police vehicles with flashing lights. Out of the frying pan into the fire: the flight plan would have gone out and the South African authorities would know who they were.

When the plane stopped he closed the blinds and turned to his father.

"You wait here, I will deal with it," he said.

He disembarked from the plane to be greeted by two large, bald, white Afrikaner police officers.

"Where is the luggage?" they asked.

Junior knew the code – his father was the luggage.

"Guys, let's talk about this, can we negotiate?"

"If you're carrying anything let us know."

"Guys, please, is that necessary? What can I do to make things comfortable?"

Just then the pilot appeared.

"They don't have any luggage," he said, "just one briefcase."

The two big men shrugged, nodded and walked off.

Junior had seen too many movies. Luggage really did mean luggage.

As for the police vehicles, it turned out they were there for a dignitary from another fight.

Junior collected his father and they made a beeline for the

airport building. The arrivals area was crowded, mostly with burly tattooed white men in black paramilitary gear carrying automatic weapons. In the middle of them all was Justice Maphosa, the Zimbabwean-born tech millionaire whose security expert, Thabiso, had been communicating all the way with Junior and Jenfan Muswere. Maphosa had only known ED for a year – they had met at a business event – but had stayed in touch, and he'd been willing to help ED when he'd called on Monday evening, before leaving Harare. Everyone may have abandoned ED but Maphosa had been there, ready to take him in.

They were rushed outside, where a dozen black Range Rovers and BMW X5s waited – the number plates and registration discs all removed. Junior thought he was in *Mission Impossible*. "They threw us in one of the middle vehicles and the cars drove off at high speed, around the parking lot, mixing up the order to confuse any people following us. We were thrown around in the back seat. I thought we were going to crash into a wall and then the driver swerved at the last second."

They hit the N14, heading east, then the N1 north, to Pretoria. They assumed they were being followed, either by South African or Zimbabwean intelligence, if not both. Indeed, when Thabiso left the airport building two men asked him where the plane that had just landed had come from.

"Swaziland," he said.

He overheard the men arguing with each other, "It's not the one – the Beira flight is still to come."

On the highway the vehicles raced in convoy and Junior recalls the pattern: when they came to an off-ramp two vehicles would exit; at the next off-ramp another two; then another two until, nearing Pretoria, the only vehicle left from the convoy was theirs and they were clear of any possible tail cars.

Maphosa's multinational IT company, Bigtime Strategic Group, is headquartered in Menlyn, Pretoria, but the safe house Thabiso had secured was in a different suburb: a small comfortable home with easy vehicle access, yet "hidden in plain sight", close to a busy shopping mall.

Their vehicle pulled up to a large automatic gate, it opened, and they were rushed inside.

They were starving, and after they had freshened up, a meal of chicken and salad was laid out on a large dining table in the living area. Maphosa called them over to the table. A devout Christian, he founded and funds the annual International Gospel Music Festival in his home town, Gwanda, in southern Zimbabwe, ironically the same town in which ED was poisoned three months earlier.

"The food should be better here," he grinned.

Before eating, Maphosa, ED, Junior and the four white security guys (four others patrolled outside) linked hands to pray. The security guys had to unload their weapons onto the table to free their hands: handguns, pistols, rifle clips and ammo tossed among the bowls of chicken and chips.

Junior couldn't close his eyes to pray.

He stared wide-eyed at the guns and bullets in front of him.

Then they said grace and sat down to eat.

It was 1am, on Thursday, 9th November.

Chapter 9

G40 CELEBRATE

Back in Zimbabwe, ordinary people had watched events unfold since the weekend rallies with mounting alarm. It had all happened so fast and now it was dawning on them: G40 had triumphed, Grace looked almost certain to be crowned Vice-President, and after that, well, the presidency was her oyster. One day she would roll out of bed and step into the shoes of the man lying next to her.

Her vulgar and violent behaviour during the past few years had turned most of the nation against her, and although there wasn't much love for him in the general population, ED's stoicism during the winter rallies, refusing to respond to her abuse, had earned him respect and sympathy, even from those in the opposition who hated him. Grace was G40's ace – she gave them protection – but she was also their Achilles. She won them no new friends, a PR disaster.

But what did they care now?

If most people were horrified by her triumph, G40 were

laughing their heads off. And you had to hand it to them – they had played a blinder.

In the space of one year, over a series of targeted political rallies, and with a relentless character assassination campaign, they had taken out the second-most powerful man in the country – the much-vaunted Crocodile. Turns out the Crocodile didn't have much of a bite. ED had not only been fired; he'd been expelled from ZANU-PF and the politburo and, frightened and humiliated, fled the country. Now the provinces were all lining up to nominate Grace as their VP for the upcoming ZANU-PF congress.

It had all been so easy.

What was incredible was that the country had seen it all before.

It was the exact same playbook that Grace – newly transformed from typist and profligate shopper to doctor, African queen and Mother of the Nation – and Jonathan Moyo had used against the then-VP Joice Mujuru in 2014, when Mujuru was nicely positioned for the presidency.

Back then, over ten rallies, with the help of state media, which Moyo, as Information Minister, controlled, Grace had accused Mujuru – a war veteran – of being a traitor, a secessionist, of plotting a coup against her husband with a "putschist cabal".

Recognise the language?

It's almost exactly the same words she would use against ED three years later.

Towards the end of the rallies, Grace's language regarding Mujuru had turned truly sinister, and it was possible to believe that even Moyo and Mugabe, who appeared to let his wife say and do as she pleased, thought she had gone too far. She said she had urged President Mugabe to "baby dump" Mujuru, a reference to the tragic epidemic of Zimbabwean women leaving newborn babies they cannot care for in garbage bags to die.

"If he does not dump the person in the street to be devoured by the dogs, we will do it ourselves. Dumping her is the only way forward, dumping the baby so that she can be exposed to the elements. If we expose her, even flies or wild dogs will be repulsed with her corrupt activities, which stink."

But here's the incredible thing: back in 2014 it wasn't just Grace and Moyo who had gone after Mujuru: ED had done so too, as had Mutsvangwa and the rest of what became the Lacoste faction. ED went after her because he wanted the vice-presidency for himself and indeed, soon after Mujuru – broken, battered and humiliated – had been fired by Mugabe, Mugabe gave him the position. ED was now one step away from the throne, the prize he had always wanted.

Here's the other irony: in order to take out Mujuru, ED had partnered once again with his nemesis... Jonathan Moyo. Thirteen years after the bad blood of Tsholotsho they had teamed up again. It didn't mean they liked each other. It was just politics. Indeed, in a BBC Hardtalk interview in 2015 Moyo, far from condemning the character assassination of Mujuru, said it was just "political banter", and that Grace had been "courageous" for speaking the way she did.

Fast forward three years, however, and now ED was being just as brutally dealt with in the same way. He couldn't say he hadn't seen it coming. The fact that he was a man in a patriarchal society that venerates men, and an old man in a society that demands respect for elders, only made it worse. Grace and G40 had shattered all the nation's taboos – and yet they had still won. That was the shock.

Meanwhile, just in case ED thought he could stage a comeback, G40 had covered their bases too.

ED was known to have the support of the military, and talk of a coup had been rife since Jonathan Moyo's Blue Ocean Strategy video. Rumours abounded: of suspicious meetings at the garden tables at the Bronte Hotel; clandestine gatherings at the Shangri-La Chinese restaurant in Harare, and at a fancy polo estate east of the city. And Grace's words when she was booed at the Bulawayo rally – "Let me tell you this, bring soldiers with guns to shoot me – I don't care!" – indicated that G40 feared a coup.

So, it was no coincidence that Mugabe chose to fire ED the day after ED's friend, General Chiwenga, the military commander, flew to China on official state business.

The general couldn't make mischief from Beijing, several thousand miles away.

In addition, Mugabe had posted his Army Chief of Staff, Major General Trust Mugoba, to Ethiopia that weekend, to oversee an African Union Standby Force. Mugoba was in charge of military operations within the Zimbabwe Defence Forces; with him and Chiwenga neutralised, the chance of a military response was minimal.

And in case the citizenry got restless, they had advice for them too. A young American woman working in Harare, Martha O'Donovan, had been arrested days before ED's dismissal for insulting Mugabe on Twitter, and warnings now went out about posting political statements on WhatsApp, Facebook, Twitter and the like. The message was clear: watch what you say, the government is listening.

The military defanged, the Crocodile skinned, the people warned – G40 could now relax.

They did so at a celebratory event outside ZANU-PF headquarters in downtown Harare, on Wednesday. The humidity in the city was still rising, the asphalt baked, but news of ED's frantic cross-border escape had now become a meme and a punch-line allowing them to let off steam.

Leading G40 members mocked ED as a "border jumper" – nothing more than a low-rent illegal immigrant trader. "*Pasi na* [down with] *Emmerson Border Jumper Mnangagwa!*" Saviour Kasukuwere joshed, and the crowd giggled. The speakers looked up at Mugabe and Grace as they spoke, desperate for the attention and approval of the new king and queen, who were same as the old king and queen. Collins Mnangagwa, having made it safely back to Harare with his twin Sean, watched the event and noted that one of those laughing was Sydney Sekeramayi, the man whose son had called him the night before to tell him he was "worried" about his father. "He didn't look worried," Collins recalls thinking.

Grace, showing rare decorum, radiant in her triumph, quoted Bible verses, while next to her the President told the crowd that ED, despite playing the loyalty card all this time, had been plotting against him for years. "He had started to consult traditional healers [witch doctors] on when I was going to die. At some point he was told that he would die first before me!"

And the crowd roared some more.

One man in Harare wasn't celebrating yet, though.

One man took the escape of ED with the seriousness he felt it deserved; as if he wanted to make doubly certain he had been crushed before he joined the banter.

That man was Jonathan Moyo, the reputed brains behind G40, and arch nemesis of ED.

As mentioned in an earlier chapter (and despite that alliance of convenience in 2014 to take out Joice Mujuru), Moyo's battle with ED had been bitter and personal since their fallout over Tsholotsho in 2004, when ED had left him high and dry over that secret gathering.

But Moyo claimed there was another reason for his enmity towards ED: *Gukurahundi*.

Translated from Shona as "the early rain that washes away the chaff", this refers to the brutal series of massacres carried out by the Zimbabwe military against the people of Matabeleland, southern Zimbabwe, between 1983 and 1987. The military claimed to be targeting armed "dissidents" but an estimated 20,000 Ndebele civilians were killed in the slaughter, including Moyo's own father, Mlevu. The North Korean-trained Fifth Brigade carried out most of the atrocities, but ED was head of state security at the time, the spy chief, and the CIO was complicit. In March 1983, at a rally in Victoria Falls, ED had described Ndebele dissidents as "cockroaches" and "bugs" that needed to be rooted out.

And yet and yet…

None of this explains Moyo's support for ED for the vice-presidency at Tsholotsho in 2004, 20 years after Gukurahundi; his devotion to Mugabe, who was the country's leader throughout the time; or his relentless propaganda work on behalf of ZANU-PF, which ended up consuming the mostly Ndebele minority party, ZAPU, as a direct result of the genocide. Moyo, a Ndebele, has been a key figure in ZANU-PF, a party that has been complicit in appalling atrocities against the Ndebele people.

Indeed, such were the contortions required to make sense of Moyo's turbulent career in ZANU-PF that many

Zimbabweans believed he was intentionally trying to sabotage the party, to bring it down from within. This view accounts for a sizeable and often overlooked support for Moyo among younger, educated Zimbabweans, many in the MDC, who considered him one of them.

This being the 21st century, you don't kick a man when he's down – you tweet insults at him, and Moyo's tweets directed at ED during the week of November 6th read like those of a man possessed, a man channelling 34 years of hatred into 280 characters, again and again. (Twitter had conveniently increased their character count from 140 on November 6th, and Moyo made good use of the extra space.)

In terms of truth & justice, the law has a long arm which can reach anyone, everywhere, any time. You can run but you can't hide!

Then:

When a senior official is fired from a high ranking government office & they jump the border into self-exile within hours of their dismissal, you know that they are running away from being legally held to account for heinous crimes they committed & covered up while in office!

And, referencing their fallout after Tsholotsho, 13 years earlier:

I did not jump the border when I was fired in 2005. I stayed put right here in Zimbabwe as I had nothing & no one to run away from into self-exile. It's real thieves & murderous cowards who jump the border after they're fired from the high positions they abused when in office!

It was typical Moyo: driven, relentless, obsessive.
He would have been a good film-maker.

❖ ❖ ❖

By Thursday, November 9th, pundits and academics both within and outside Zimbabwe were also weighing in with their expert analysis on ED's demise, and how they had all seen it coming.

Quickly out of the gates was respected Oxford University-based Zimbabwe academic Blessing-Miles Tendi who saw ED's firing as payback for UK policy, putting it down to purported support for ED from the British Ambassador, Catriona Laing, who made no secret of wanting to reset Britain's strained relations with the former colony, and had seen ED as a man to partner with. "The UK's alleged strategy has not only... failed, but its perceived backing for Mnangagwa prompted outrage among many Zimbabweans, further weakening the UK's image in the country," Tendi wrote.

In another article, "The Crocodile who never understood himself or the waters", Moses Tofa, an academic in Johannesburg, wrote that ED was never as shrewd as he thought: "A closer look at the Crocodile reveals a man with little strategic grasp of Zimbabwe's political chessboard controlled by the grandmaster Robert and wife Grace... the majority view is that the Crocodile was merely a myth..."

Kasper, meanwhile, not afraid to give Mutsvangwa bad news, sent him a long diatribe by an analyst named Allan Wenyika, written after Mutsvangwa's Sandton press conference, which reflected the popular theory that Moyo's goal was to bring ZANU-PF down from within. It's a masterpiece of invective against Mutsvangwa, ED and the war veterans, of which Moyo himself would be proud:

>...it's you and your war vets who did everything in your power... to stop the Wits professor [Moyo] from doing something about his captured country and about your idiocy. But against impossible odds... he managed to break his way into your murderous party and stayed there long enough to enact laws and create the correct weather to disperse you all like chickens until some of you morphed from war vets and Vice-Presidents to become border jumpers and fugitives.

You can almost picture Mutsvangwa nodding in approval at the rhetoric, if not the message. Perhaps to make Mutsvangwa feel better, Kasper added a favourite Lacoste joke about Moyo: "Just because he has a rather large and irregularly shaped head doesn't mean it can't fit in the mouth of a crocodile."

The long and the short of it, the experts agreed, was that ED was vanquished, and the game was over.

Indeed, when, on Wednesday afternoon – before they had even boarded the plane in Beira – ED's lawyer in Harare, Larry Mavhima released the letter ED had written in the hours before fleeing Harare, the only people who took it seriously were ED's allies, including friends and family members, who thought it an unnecessary provocation of G40.

Take Junior, who, on waking in the safe house Thursday morning, read it on an iPad and said to his father: "Why did you write that? It's only going to make them angry."

He had got a message to his Indian friend KC Shetty in Harare to tell him they were safe but that he (KC) should get the hell out the country.

"I wished they hadn't published that statement," KC said, as he made plans to get out of Dodge.

The statement was the tonal opposite of the mournful letter ED had written to Mugabe earlier that day in his office, and the close observer might note the cunning of a crocodile in the difference: while in the country write respectfully of the Big Man; when safely out the country reveal your true feelings.

For this time ED did not hold back.

He told Mugabe that the party was now controlled by "undisciplined, egotistical and self-serving minnows…" and that the First Family had "now privatized and commercialized our beloved institution… This Party is NOT PERSONAL PROPERTY for you and your wife to do as you please".

Then he laid down a marker for the days ahead: "You and your cohorts will instead leave ZANU-PF by the will of the people and this we will do in the coming few weeks… Zimbabweans… now require new and progressive leadership that is not resident in the past and refuses to accept change…"

Then, addressing the people of Zimbabwe, he stressed again that he would be back: "We will very soon control the levers of power in our beautiful Party and country… I will be communicating with you soon and shall return to Zimbabwe to lead you."

Neutral observers in Harare tried hard not to laugh.

It sounded ludicrous. He thinks he's coming back in a "few weeks"?

The Crocodile had lost his marbles.

But if ED sounded hopelessly optimistic – a man with a

base and power does not flee a country with his tail between his legs – interestingly, Jonathan Moyo did not treat it as a joke.

He immediately fired off a tweet aimed at the lawyer who sent ED's statement to the Zimbabwean press:

So the so-called ED Press Statement issued today, which has a poor scan of his signature, was personally delivered to newsrooms as an advert by Larry Mavhima who chairs the NRZ Board & who fronts for ED at Hanawa Foods. This makes Mavhima an accessory to treason!

Then:

The difference between a Press Statement issued by a fugitive in the luxury of a 5 Star hotel in a foreign country & ZANU-PF is like that of day & night. ZANU-PF is the people whose one centre of power is Pres Mugabe who has asserted the people's authority!

Moyo was not letting up. He had tangled with ED before and lost and he wasn't making that mistake again.

And did he maybe have an unsettling feeling that his side, G40, had already made their first mistake?

They had allowed ED to escape.

Now, from outside the country, ED would easily be able to communicate with Christopher Mutsvangwa, who Moyo knew had a team in Johannesburg, and also with his military ally General Chiwenga in China.

And what on earth was up with that General Chiwenga?

By Friday, November 10th, Chiwenga had been in China

six days and no one had heard a word from him.

What had appeared, though, was a photograph of him at a military parade in Beijing, walking side by side with General Li Zuocheng of China's Central Military Commission, and now, on November 10th, news came of a meeting that very day with China's Defence Minister, Chang Wanquan.

What was that all about?

His G40 friends might have been celebrating but by the end of the week Jonathan Moyo was starting to feel just a tad uneasy.

Chapter 10

THE COMMAND CENTRE

The Holiday Inn Johannesburg Airport is located in a bustling semi-industrial area in blue-collar Boksburg, about eight miles south of OR Tambo International, Africa's busiest airport. A cut above the average airport hotel, it has an open-plan lobby hung with an ersatz chandelier, a stylish espresso bar and bistro, and glass doors that lead to a swimming pool with garden tables set under drooping palms.

It's a few miles from the gritty Johannesburg suburb of Benoni, where, on July 23rd, 1965, a baby girl named Grace Ntombizodwa Marufu was born to migrant parents from Zimbabwe. That little girl would grow up to become a typist in the secretarial pool of a Zimbabwean president; mistress and then second wife to that president; before lining herself up take over from him as leader of Zimbabwe.

So, it was not without irony that on Thursday, November 9th, 2017, in a Holiday Inn a stone's throw from where she was born, a team of men and women gathered to stage-manage Grace Mugabe's destruction.

They called it the Command Centre.

The original idea had been to base themselves in the Radisson Blu Gautrain Hotel where Mutsvangwa and Gabriel Shumba's press conference was to have been held on Wednesday 8th. But the presence of all those CIO agents unnerved Kasper, Magic and Horse. It was as if a platoon of killer ants had been let loose in Harare and sent down to South Africa on a mission: to locate and deal with ED, Mutsvangwa and those cooperating with them.

These guys were a different breed, Kasper reckoned, scurrying around in their suits, ties and shades, driving tinted-windowed cars. They looked on edge, trigger happy; he didn't trust any of them to stay cool. Gabriel had been followed home from the press conference – he knew from the Christmas Eve attack on him that the CIO knew where he lived – so after consulting Kasper, he and his wife decided to check into a guesthouse in Pretoria, 30 miles away, and sleep there until things calmed down. Coincidentally, they later learned the guesthouse was only a mile from where ED and Junior were holed up.

It's worth mentioning that at this point ED was the *least* important man in the picture.

He had done his job: he had got out of Zimbabwe alive. As long as Justice Maphosa and Thabiso kept him safe, he just had to sit tight. He would be needed again soon.

Which isn't to say that he and Junior had simply put their feet up in the safe house and were watching Netflix. From Thursday morning, communicating with sympathetic lawyers, father and son began poring over ZANU-PF resolutions and the Zimbabwe Constitution to find possible ways to contest ED's dismissal from the party, and to impeach Mugabe if the opportunity arose. Maphosa, who had made his fortune in technology, provided a steady stream of iPads and phones for them to work with. Maphosa ensured they would only use the devices a few times before handing them back to be destroyed so their location could not be traced via triangulation or voice recognition. "We must have gone through 50 phones and destroyed an iPad every three or four hours," Junior recalls. By Thursday ED was in constant contact with Mutsvangwa, although only via third parties (they never met in South Africa in person), and had also called Chiwenga in China.

Mutsvangwa, Kasper and Ellis, meanwhile, were in touch with contacts in South African intelligence to try to secure official protection for Mutsvangwa. They didn't know whether they could trust the South Africans at this point – whose side they were on – but it was worth asking them. As good as Kasper, Magic and Horse were, they couldn't protect Mutsvangwa from the killer ants for ever.

They did get one useful tip from their South African intelligence contacts: that the CIO was able to follow them easily through the geolocation settings on their phones, which record longitudes and latitudes of any pictures texted or emailed. The team was ordered to turn all their geo settings off.

Finding a safe house for Mutsvangwa to sleep in was one thing, but the team needed somewhere safe to work out of, too, somewhere they could control access to. Kasper knew Johannesburg like the back of his hand and he chose the Boksburg Holiday Inn as much for its proximity to OR Tambo airport as for its layout. It had a high, steel security fence, gate guards, and only one way in. You could sit on those plush lobby sofas or at the tables by the pool sipping a beer and keep an eye on everyone who entered.

The team had grown.

Sixteen months previously two men, Tom Ellis and Agent Kasper, had sat in a car in a Northgate parking lot and shaken hands on a hare-brained scheme to take down Mugabe and G40, and to tap ED for the presidency. By November 8th, 2017, the day of the Sandton press conference, there were more than a dozen of them, and their numbers (and levels of expertise) were expected to grow as things amped up in the days ahead.

Which was why Kasper wanted a command centre close to the airport: some new team members would be flying in from Harare; it would make it easier for him (and safer for them) if they were close by.

If the team had grown, the timeline and method had changed too.

Originally, the group had been in it for the long haul; it was just a continuation of their activism. One vague initial goal had been that ED might get the ZANU-PF leadership – and thus almost certainly the presidency – at the party's all-important December 2017 congress. But it had become apparent by the middle of 2017 that politics in Zimbabwe was blood sport. Hell, ED wasn't going to make it to congress; he might not even survive the year. Something had dawned on Ellis and Gabriel around the middle of 2017 that had probably been apparent all along to insiders like Kasper and Mutsvangwa: there could only be one winner the way ZANU-PF played the game, and your side had to make its move before their side made theirs.

Neither Ellis nor Gabriel – who were both unconnected to ZANU-PF or any state apparatus in Zimbabwe – recall exactly where or when they first heard "the rumour" but it was sometime in May or June, *before* ED was poisoned, and before the Presidential Youth Interface Rallies had even heated up.

"We're not going to congress," Kasper told them. "The Old Man will be gone by October or November."

The Old Man was Mugabe.

"What do you mean he'll be gone?" Gabriel asked.

Kasper said: "Wait and see, my friend, wait and see."

Gabriel thought at first that it was wishful thinking on Kasper's part. But then, as the months wore on, a series of strange meetings took place that made him wonder: did Kasper know something about a possible military intervention?

The first of these meetings was one Kasper arranged for Ellis and Gabriel at a resort hotel south of Johannesburg. Kasper had brought someone "important" down from Zimbabwe. It turned out to be a senior minister in Mugabe's cabinet, a well-known former war veteran and ex-military officer considered loyal to Mugabe. The four of them made small talk in the hotel lounge, mostly about business opportunities in Zimbabwe and the desperate state of its economy.

Little of note was discussed except that the minister made it clear to them that Mugabe was unpopular, even within cabinet, and that at some point soon he would have to go. Gabriel and Ellis were intrigued – less by what was said than by the fact that Kasper had plucked someone so senior from Harare to meet with them. The game they were playing had reached the highest levels and it made the heart race.

A more important meeting took place in August or September, *after* ED was poisoned, when things had become, in Kasper's words, "Full Scale". Ellis wasn't present; it was just Gabriel. Kasper asked him to meet him at a guesthouse – a stone-and-timber-built lodge in Bruma Lake – a leafy suburb just east of downtown Johannesburg. There, in a boardroom, Kasper introduced him to three large, fit, well-groomed men visiting from Zimbabwe. They wore open-necked white shirts and suit jackets and had a calm-steely demeanour. They were military officers. Kasper introduced them by rank, as Brigadier General, Colonel and Major (no given names and referred to from now on as the military trio).

He introduced Gabriel to them as Chairman, since Gabriel chaired the Core Diaspora Group.

The three men spoke in generalities at first: about their dissatisfaction with the way things were going in Zimbabwe, about the need for change, about what role Gabriel might see himself and the diaspora playing, were there to be, say, "a major socio-economic or political transition" in Zimbabwe.

Then, towards the end of the meeting, the Brigadier General said to Gabriel: "Chairman, you are a lawyer, correct?"

"Yes."

"One day, soon, we will be needing your advice."

"Advice on what?"

"On certain matters. On what is and what is not acceptable… On what is or is not legal…"

Gabriel nodded. He tried to stay calm but his heart had that familiar flutter.

Gabriel met the military trio a couple more times with Kasper before November 2017, always at the same lodge in Bruma Lake. He only ever addressed them by rank, and if he ever knew their names he was not saying. But the meetings went further and got more specific. The trio asked him what the implications might be for soldiers who took part in an operation to remove Mugabe; what the implications might be for international law if the military removed Mugabe directly; what the best methods might be to remove him as leader of ZANU-PF, or from the presidency via impeachment.

"I was just surmising, making suggestions," Gabriel recalls. "I told them the issue was that he had to be seen to be removed by legal channels, otherwise they risked intervention by the SADC and the international community. I was giving my perspective, and there may well have been people within Zimbabwe holding the same perspective. The Zimbabwe army has its own lawyers of course.

"The good thing was, we converged on the idea that whatever happened, the revolution must not be violent. It had to flow though proper legal channels."

❖ ❖ ❖

The Northgate Diaspora Group had other secret meetings between July and October: with foreign diplomats, senior war veteran friends of Mutsvangwa, Central and Military Intelligence officers whom Kasper had wooed; even a senior official from the Zimbabwe embassy in Pretoria.

The period coincided, not coincidentally, with Jonathan Moyo's Blue Ocean Strategy video claims that a coup was in the works, and increasingly loud accusations by Grace that ED was plotting against her husband. Recall her words at the Bulawayo rally when she was booed?

"Bring soldiers with guns to shoot me – I don't care!"

She *knew* something was being planned.

Even ED let it slip at one point. On October 2nd, weeks after his poisoning, at a funeral in his home province Masvingo, he made the only statement during the entire brutal factional war that indicated he knew a reckoning was coming.

For months he had sat silent and stony-faced as Grace had rained insults down on him. He had even distanced himself publicly from Mutsvangwa and the war veterans, his supposed supporters. But at this funeral he told his home crowd in Shona, referring to Grace: "Those who castigate don't know what the future holds… And when things come to a head, we will try to see where each one of us stands… Everything being said and happening now will soon be over…"

It was too pointed a comment to not be intentional. He *knew*.

The long and the short of it was that by October 2017, it was an open secret among the core of the Northgate team that the Zimbabwe military was going to step in at some point.

None of them, not even Mutsvangwa, knew when or how it would happen, nor did they have any say in it. They had just been assured by the military that there was a plan.

But plans can fall through, as they so often do, and Ellis was sceptical it was ever going to happen. What made him doubt was what he called "The Mugabe Factor". Ellis had been waging a small personal war against Mugabe since 2008, and he had always lost. In fact, if he was honest, he could trace the series of Ellis family losses to Robert Mugabe back to the 1970s, when his father fought against him in the Bush War. Ellis despised Mugabe, but he respected him too: his staying power, his incredible ability to survive against all odds. He'd been in power 37 years and seemed to have an almost supernatural hold over people – the military included, it seemed. They had done nothing when war veteran Joice Mujuru was attacked by Grace and fired by Mugabe; and they had done nothing when ED, also a veteran, was poisoned.

And so, when October came and went with Mugabe still

there, Ellis doubted "the rumour" again.

"When's he going, *shamwari*?" he would say to Kasper during a night of drinking at the Sundowner.

"Soon, Tom, don't doubt!"

"Maybe," Ellis would say with a shrug.

"Don't say 'maybe', Tom. If you are saying maybe you become a fail – a doubting Thomas!"

Ellis laughed and shook his head.

"United we stand, divided we fall, Tom!" Kasper would respond, confident as a revival preacher.

❖ ❖ ❖

It was the firing of ED on November 6th that finally brought it all to a head. The waiting was over; it was do-or-die for them all… Either the military were going to step in, or the game was over.

But the team was not helpless.

Expecting an intervention, they began to galvanise support and prepare the diplomatic ground.

There's a reason the Sandton press conference was so important to Mutsvangwa and why he was so anxious to hold it. It wasn't really about telling the international media about the dangers of Grace and G40. It was a rallying cry, and a smoke signal.

The rallying cry was to inspire ordinary Zimbabweans: here we are, the liberation war veterans hand in hand with our former nemesis, the MDC-aligned diaspora, united in a common goal: to oppose Mugabe and his wife. We have come together against a common enemy; you can too.

It was a smoke signal to all those people the Northgate team had been meeting with in secret for the past year who

169

hadn't yet come aboard: the game is on, drop what you are doing and join us.

And it was a smoke signal to the military. You said you had a plan to stop Grace – let's see it.

There was a reason that Mutsvangwa, seemingly out of the blue, paid tribute to the Zimbabwe military in his Sandton statement: they had told him many times they had a plan; now he was cajoling them to put it into action.

❖ ❖ ❖

While there was no way of knowing if the military had got the message, or were remotely influenced by it, the scene at the Boksburg Holiday Inn the morning of Thursday, November 9th, suggested a Johannesburg team invigorated. The lobby, restaurant and garden area now turned into a vast open-plan office, two dozen men and women on cell phones, huddled in conversation, poring over documents. Ellis made calls to raise money; Gabriel phoned MDC friends, diplomats and journalists; Kasper and his guys ran cover, while Mutsvangwa was the front man, leading the show.

From the beginning Ellis had seen Mutsvangwa as a leader, and Kasper had agreed.

"I told that man Chris, the only way this can work – you are in front, we push behind," said Kasper.

Still, the plotters were lacking something: the power of propaganda. You can't rally people without reaching them, and the ZBC was still under the control of Mugabe. They had to be creative. So in order to get the message out, the team got two prominent Zimbabwean analysts and digital-media personalities from different ends of the political spectrum to convey a united front in South Africa's powerful national broadcast media, as well to their own online audiences back home.

Their names were Tino Mambeu and Acie Lumumba, and initially they hated each other.

Mambeu was a spokesman for the ZEF and a long-time MDC activist. He had been in exile in South Africa since 2004, fleeing political persecution, crossing the crocodile-infested Limpopo River multiple times after various deportations. In 2005 he was sleeping rough in parks and on the streets of Joburg before finding work as a labourer. He saved to buy his own toolbox, and by 2010 had his own electrical business, employing 15 people. He re-engaged in politics, joining the ZEF, where they noted his plain-speaking manner and communication skills. He was soon a regular commentator on Zimbabwean affairs at SABC, eNews, Talk 702 and Power FM. He had been at several ZEF meetings with Mutsvangwa during 2016 and 2017 and had come to respect the war veteran, although he couldn't stand ZANU-PF, his political party.

On the other side of the tracks, representing ZANU-PF, or at least a version of it, was Lumumba: a controversial and cocksure digital-media gunslinger and political analyst – part genius, part joker. Twenty-six, devilishly good looking in Michael Caine glasses, he had a mesmerising speaking style and an estimated 300,000-strong millennial following on Facebook and YouTube for his daily video broadcast, then called Lumumba Diary, now the Lumumba Files. Educated for a time at the elite King's Norton Boys' school in Birmingham, England (his real name is the more prosaic William Gerald Mutumanje), he affected an American accent mixed with township slang and was once a rising star in ZANU-PF, a protégé of the charismatic youth organiser, Saviour Kasukuwere. In 2016, however, at around the same time that Mutsvangwa was on the outs, he had had a falling-out with Mugabe's G40-aligned nephew, Patrick Zhuwao. President Mugabe sided with his nephew. Appalled, but at the same time a showman, Lumumba called a press conference in Harare at which he literally said; "Fuck you Mugabe!" An audible gasp could be heard in the audience. He was arrested and detained for a while, and his house was firebombed, but his father was a general in the Zimbabwe military and no more harm came to him.

Lumumba was a late-comer to the team and really only arrived on board by accident. Mutsvangwa, who knew his father from the guerilla war, had heard he was in Johannesburg on the Wednesday of the Sandton press conference and invited him to attend. He then suggested he join the team at the Holiday Inn.

Lumumba drove out, entered the lobby and was hit by sudden panic.

"My first reaction was – am I lost? I saw a lot of Zimbabwe military personnel I recognised, but in civilian clothes. I saw MI guys from Zimbabwe I knew. I saw secret police from Zimbabwe, CIO agents, some of whom had once arrested me. I saw Botswana generals, South African intelligence people... My next reaction was 'hello... this is a coup and I do not want to die.'"

To be part of a coup against the President was treason, and if it failed that would mean death.

Lumumba was treading water in Kasper's metaphorical ocean: turn around or swim to the other side.

He did what everyone had done: swam on.

Mutsvangwa, ever awake to the power of media, put Lumumba and Mambeu to work as media coordinators, and from the night of Wednesday 8th, for the next week one or both of them were on pretty much every political panel about the Zimbabwean crisis.

On SABC News the day after ED arrived in exile, Mambeu said:

It would be very fair to welcome former VP Mnangagwa, wherever he is. He has joined millions of us who fled ZANU-PF and the dangerous system… ZANU-PF is a machinery that understands violence to achieve its end… Mnangagwa has now joined Zimbabweans against a system… we welcome him.

Lumumba said:

Mugabe has been trying to create a dynasty. Grace Mugabe will never be my president…We are about to change the politics in Zimbabwe… a new promise delivered by a new generation.

The team had locked down the media messaging for the region; G40 would not get a look-in.

Intriguingly, despite their major political differences, Mambeu and Lumumba became good friends.

In the meantime, Mutsvangwa and others did the diplomatic ground work, some from the Holiday Inn, some from a suite back at the Radisson Blu, where several members were still based since they'd already paid for their rooms. They made phone calls to Beijing, to British, European and regional diplomats, sounding them all out on their possible reaction to a military intervention.

Mutsvangwa was on the phone to China a lot: if there was going to be military action it needed to be cleared with Beijing, Zimbabwe's biggest investor, and he'd been Ambassador there for four years.

It's quite likely Chiwenga had cleared things with the Chinese while he was there anyway.

Another war veteran, a man known as the American, since he lived in the US now, cleared things with American officials, asking them what the US would do if there was a military intervention. One team member said he heard the American telling Chiwenga in China that the US was on board.

How much of this was gung-ho talk from people who may or may not have seen or heard what they claimed?

Some of it perhaps, but this was Mutsvangwa's goal at this point: to prepare the diplomatic ground.

That said, by Friday, November 10th, there was still no sign of the military making a move.

By Saturday 11th, South African intelligence came through with news: they had a safe house for Mutsvangwa and would give him full state protection in a "military cantonment" near Pretoria. South Africa did not want a political assassination on their soil.

By Sunday 12th, however, the team were nervous. They were all dressed up with nowhere to go. They were the maestro on stage at La Scala, an expectant audience in the balcony, but the orchestra hadn't showed up. Was General Chiwenga bottling it? Was he afraid to risk returning to Harare? Rumours flew around that he had been fired already and did not want to risk going back. Kasper had passed on intelligence that if Chiwenga re-entered Zimbabwe at the airport, Mugabe's police would arrest him.

The whole team was on edge and some of them thought the game was up.

Tino Mambeu, the ZEF media spokesman, fed up with all the big talk from ZANU-PF, started provoking that side of the team. "Is Mnangagwa a crocodile or a lizard?" he asked in one radio appearance.

You might want to be careful what you wish for.

It just so happened that at around that time, early Sunday afternoon, November, 12th, somewhere over central Africa, an Emirates flight was headed for Robert Mugabe International Airport, Harare.

In first class, a burly, broad-shouldered passenger in a dark suit and tortoiseshell glasses finished a glass of Johnny Walker Blue and shouted up for another.

The hostess brought it over.

"Your drink, General Chiwenga," she said.

The General was winging his way back, and the country would soon be hearing from him.

And when they did, Zimbabwe would never be the same again.

Chapter 11

THE AIRPORT

What apparently took place at Robert Mugabe International that afternoon might one day be taught in military academies or espionage school. It was a turning point in the great game: an operation so stealthy, flawless and precise that hundreds of people in the crowded airport at the time appeared to have no idea it had even happened. They saw nothing. No one in the country knew, and even the team in Johannesburg was unaware of what had gone down until days later. Zimbabwe's military is a dark and brutal force and when they strike it's usually with raw power and much spilling of blood. The airport operation, however, was more akin to light-fingered jewel thieves pulling off a sneaky heist.

No military official has spoken on the record about the operation so we are left with media reports, eyewitness accounts and interviews for this book with an anonymous retired senior military officer. In years to come the full truth will emerge, but let's see what we can make out through the shadow and fog.

It is learned that General Chiwenga is due to land in Harare on the afternoon of Sunday, November 12th, 2017, on a commercial flight, thought to be the 17.10 Emirates EK713 from Dubai. What day he has left China is unknown, but it's likely he stopped in Dubai en route to meet with another senior military commander who is said to have been there: Air Marshall Perence Shiri. Shiri going to Dubai the exact weekend Chiwenga flies via Dubai to Zimbabwe seems too convenient for it not to have been planned.

The Dubai–Harare flight stops briefly in Lusaka, Zambia, Zimbabwe's neighbour to the north. Chiwenga had originally toyed with the idea of disembarking there and travelling to Zimbabwe by car, across the Zambezi River, but, after consultation with fellow officers, the plan was shelved as too risky. He flies on to Harare.

What makes this move so much more daring is that he knows the danger that awaits him there.

According to many news reports, sometime earlier in the week, the President has met with his Police Chief, Augustine Chihuri, a Mugabe loyalist and G40 ally, and instructed him to arrest Chiwenga on his return from China. The rumours that Chiwenga has been, or will soon be, fired (some spread by Kasper) have reached such fever pitch that Mugabe and G40 cannot risk having him back in the country, a free man in charge of a 30,000-strong military. They already know a coup is possible; ED's dismissal and rumours of Chiwenga's – no matter how inaccurate – have made the coup scenario greater.

Chihuri knows the stakes: stop Chiwenga at all costs.

It was assumed by now that if the factional political war broke out into actual war, it would pit the military against the police, particularly the paramilitary PSU – the Black Boots. When he learns what flight the General is on, Chihuri dispatches a crack PSU team to Robert Mugabe International Airport.

Exactly how many are dispatched no one knows, but eyewitnesses recall seeing a dozen police vehicles in the parking lot that afternoon. Chihuri almost certainly knows there will be soldiers coming to meet Chiwenga, so he needs a sizeable police presence to counter that.

Where they are posted at the airport also remains unclear; it's likely some are at the end of the exit bridge, should he disembark with regular passengers, some at the VIP terminal, a single-storey building nestled between the international and domestic terminals, but most are probably on the tarmac because the General is likely to step out of the aircraft onto the air bridge, take the immediate exit door down the stairs and hop into a waiting limo which will drive him to the VIP terminal.

Chiwenga's flight crosses the Zambezi into Zimbabwe airspace at around 4pm, unseasonal grey clouds on the horizon, sun sinking low to the right. Is he anxious in first class, sweating through his suit? Or is he relaxed, tucking into another Johnny Walker Blue, confident of the outcome?

Likely the latter, because he and his fellow officers know the outcome before the operation has even begun.

Aware of the police plans, an 18-member 1 Para special forces team, a spin-off of the Rhodesian Selous Scouts disbanded at independence, has prepared itself at Inkomo barracks, west of Harare. 1 Para are part of the Parachute Regiment established in 1980 by Colonel Lionel Dyck, a Rhodesian and later Zimbabwe military officer, and apparently a friend and sometime business associate of ED. As with the Selous Scouts, whose training methods they follow, 1 Para are adept at blending into civilian populations and operating at close quarters in public spaces. The team leaves the barracks armed with handguns and rifles, but disguised in overalls – the uniform of National Handling Services (NHS), the ground operator and baggage handler at the airport, who have been persuaded to cooperate. The soldiers wear their military fatigues beneath the overalls. They probably get to the airport via the freight terminal, really an assortment of privately owned and managed businesses 250 yards west of the main terminal, one of which, Airline Ground Services (AGS), has unrestricted access to the apron and direct access to where passenger aircraft park.

❖ ❖ ❖

According to one witness, an employee of a freight company, there was a back-up plan should things go awry: at about 2pm on Sunday afternoon, he sees five armoured personnel carriers (APCs) and two armoured vehicles, about 100 troops between them, drive through the cargo village towards AGS, where they occupy the facility... If the 1 Para action went wrong, or they heard gunfire, these soldiers would be the cavalry, racing down the runway to tip the scales.

As it turns out, they are not needed.

When the plane lands and begins to taxi towards the terminal, a command is given.

What happens next might as well take place in cinematic slow motion: the special forces draw their weapons from under the overalls and aim them point blank at every member of the PSU team. Taken completely by surprise, the police are instantly disarmed and detained, their weapons tucked away in bags. Outside, in the parking lot, another team – probably MI – clamp every police vehicle. The PSU are immobilised before Chiwenga has even got up from his seat. Then, when the aircraft doors open, his security team board the plane, find him, and escort him away to a waiting armed escort on the runway.

It is all over in minutes, not a shot fired, exactly as Chiwenga expected.

There are police roadblocks between the airport and the city but the General's convoy does not slow down. It storms right through them straight to King George VI barracks, army headquarters in suburban Harare, just north of State House, the President's official residence, and not far from Pockets Hill, the studios of the ZBC.

From there, according to the retired officer, Chiwenga makes a phone call to President Mugabe.

"What have you done?" he asks, his voice deep, gravelly, seething.

"What do you mean?" says the President.

"Why did you try to arrest me?"

"I know nothing about it."

Chiwenga slams the phone down.

G40 have made their second mistake, and it's much bigger than letting ED escape: they have allowed the General back in the country and he is furious.

The rest of the country will soon be hearing from him.

Chapter 12

THE PRESS CONFERENCE

They hear from him the following afternoon, Monday, November 13th, at around 3pm, when he hosts a press conference at King George VI barracks. At least, some do.

The press conference is not broadcast on the state-run ZBC. The President's spokesman, George Charamba at the Information Ministry, turned down the General's request. There was no way he was letting Chiwenga address the nation on TV without knowing what he was going to say first. The General speaks anyway and dozens of media outlets attend.

What they record is instantly sent out on social media, and a population that had started coming to terms with the victory of Grace and G40 is stunned by the sudden reappearance of the General.

Chiwenga sits hunched and bear-like at a table in a wood-panelled boardroom. He's wearing military fatigues, a black beret and tortoiseshell glasses which he adjusts several times on the tip of his nose before clearing his throat to read. His voice is deep and sombre and he speaks in a dense Shona-accented English of the kind urban, educated

Zimbabweans tend to ridicule – the "r"s become "l"s, so when he says "beloved country" it's "beruved country" and "discipline" comes out as "disprin".

Paradoxically, his lack of sophistication only adds more menace and power to his words; he's a blunt object. He gives the impression that if something confuses him he would hit it.

The first shock is that he is speaking at all.

Zimbabwe's military commanders rarely address the public. It's even rarer for Chiwenga; few people know what he looks like. Although he's a war veteran, and Zimbabwe's longest serving full general, he is only 61 years old and he lacks the stature of predecessors such as General Solomon Mujuru. The fact that Jonathan Moyo has been brazen enough to question his academic credentials suggests people don't fear him.

The second shock is who is there: early media footage shows that he is flanked by several senior military officers, including the army commander, the army chief of staff, the air force vice-marshal and the prison boss. (Notably absent is Police Commissioner Chihuri, who was supposedly charged with arresting him 24 hours earlier, although no one watching is aware of this at the time.)

Chiwenga speaks for 15 minutes, and begins by noting the fractious state of the nation – as if things just *suddenly* turned to shit out of the blue.:

It is with humility and a heavy heart that we come before you to pronounce the indisputable reality that there is instability in ZANU-PF and anxiety in the country at large…

He doesn't beat about the bush, calling out "counter-revolutionaries" within ZANU-PF who have "infiltrated the party and whose agenda is to destroy it from within" – a direct reference to Jonathan Moyo.

He says that the "purging and cleansing process within ZANU-PF" appears to be targeting war veterans – "those with a liberation history" – in other words, men like ED and himself. Then he lays down the law:

We must remind those behind the current treacherous shenanigans that when it comes to matters of protecting our revolution the military will not hesitate to step in…

He even quotes Section 212 of the Constitution, which mandates that "the Defence Forces protect Zimbabwe, its people, its national security and interests and its territorial integrity" – to justify such a step.

His voice rising, he then lays out three key demands Mugabe needs to comply with:

To stop reckless utterances by politicians from the ruling party denigrating the military which is causing alarm and despondency within the rank and file; that the purging and targeting members of the party with a liberation background must stop forthwith; and that the known counter-revolutionary elements who have fomented the instability in the party must be exposed and fished out.

His final words contain a simple warning:

Comrades and friends, ladies and gentlemen, we remain committed to protecting our legacy and those bent on hijacking the revolution will not be allowed to do so.

By the time he has finished his voice has reached a crescendo and he appears to have physically grown at the table. It is not the statement of a weak man.

❖ ❖ ❖

A few miles away, news of the press conference has reached George Charamba, the President's spokesman, and he is horrified. He respects the General but what he has done is outrageous, verging on treasonous. He has essentially issued a public threat and ultimatum to the elected President. Such a public provocation from the military is unheard of.

Charamba has something of Jonathan Moyo about him: they're both tall, gangly, bookish intellectuals. Unlike Moyo, and despite being the President's loyal spokesman, he too has recently faced the wrath of Grace. In late July, as the winter rallies turned ugly, Grace called him up on stage in Chinhoyi and publically berated him in full view of the watching nation for not securing her and her allies more favourable coverage in the state media. You could literally see Charamba shrink and shrivel at the force of the humiliation, while President Mugabe dozed off on a throne-like leather armchair in the background. If he heard his wife's rant at George he didn't seem to mind; Mugabe never reigned Grace in, even when she went after his personal staff.

Charamba is indeed a well-read man – a fixture at Alois, Harare's vintage flea market book stall, able to quote Shakespeare at will – and he knows the Constitution like he knows his *Hamlet*. General Chiwenga has referenced Section 212 but he has conveniently omitted 213, which stipulates that *only* the President as Commander in Chief has the power to determine the operational use of the Zimbabwe Defence Forces. He's also ignored Section 208, part 2, that states:

Neither the security services nor any of their members may, in the exercise of their functions: a) act in a partisan manner b) further the interest of any political party or cause c) prejudice the interest of any political party or cause d) violate the fundamental rights or any freedoms or any person.

The General has chosen a very dangerous path and Charamba fears it won't end well for him.

So he races over to the barracks and is soon in front of him, expressing his dismay.

"What you have done?" he stammers. "Do you realise you are a dead man walking?"

Chiwenga barely bats an eyelid.

"Oh, really?" he says, and he opens a door to a side room.

In the room, staring back at him, Charamba sees the entire top brass of the Zimbabwe military – generals, brigadier generals, colonels and others – more than 80 of them. The entire upper echelon of the ZDF appear to be with Chiwenga. He's summoned them, and they've come running.

In an instant Charamba sees where the real power lies.

At this point it's not Shakespeare that comes to him but Martin Lawrence, in *Bad Boys 2:* "Shit just got real."

❖ ❖ ❖

For a man so adept at reading the winds, Jonathan Moyo appears to have completely misread this.

At 3.57pm he sends out a tweet in Shona in response to the press conference.

Kungovukura vukura, ini zete kuvata zvangu! – they keep barking (like puppies) while I am resting unperturbed.

In short, he has dismissed the General as a yapping dog.

The cavalier tweet is in stark contrast to everything Moyo has been saying for months. Does he know something no one else does? Is he confident that things will be patched up in the days ahead between Mugabe and the General, and that the tiff is not serious? After all, Chiwenga has not put a deadline on his conditions. There is no countdown. Does Moyo think that with a bit of bargaining the President can come to an amicable agreement with his General, and all will go back to normal?

Unlikely. Moyo is no fool. He's been warning of a coup for months and now the man in a position to carry one out has literally threatened to do so in front of the media. He also knows the entire command structure is with Chiwenga at military HQ, and that they will be sleeping there tonight, and for the next few nights.

Furthermore, Moyo knows much of the statement has been aimed directly at him.

There's only one plausible reason for a tweet so cavalier and out of character – and Moyo will later confirm as much for this book: it's a double bluff. He knows the military read his every utterance on twitter like teens following Instagram, and he also knows they are about to strike.

He sends the tweet in desperation, a last-gasp gambit.

He wants the generals to think he's relaxed and confident and that when they strike they will catch him by surprise in his home. Thus there's no need to watch his movements. Moyo has no intention of being at home when they come; he hopes that the bluff will save his life.

❖ ❖ ❖

By early evening every Zimbabwean with a cell phone has watched the General's threat on social media and it's like a jolt of electricity to the cortex. They're suddenly wide awake, and for the first time in years, hopeful. In 37 years they have never seen such a direct challenge to Mugabe's authority. Most of them have no love for Chiwenga or the military, but they fear the rise of Grace and G40 far more.

So they tune into the ZBC that evening, expecting a response from the President or ZANU-PF to the General's threat – or at least the ZBC's spin on the most dramatic press conference in recent history.

Instead, they get nothing. There is a total news blackout on the event, as if it didn't happen at all.

But if it's an attempt to control the message, it won't work. Facebook, Twitter and WhatsApp are on fire and the ZBC ignoring the story only adds fuel to the flames. The people sense a government in panic.

One video released on Facebook and YouTube that night is mesmerising and instantly goes viral.

It shows a good-looking young man in a tight black T-shirt and trendy glasses, speaking rapidly in American-accented English interspersed with Shona slang. He's a hipster digital-media analyst and he equates the unfolding political drama with the tactics in a deadly game.

"My fellow Zimbabweans," he says, "let me explain to you what is going to happen next..."

The President has 48 hours to make a play... Touch is a move; we are talking about Sudden Death...

The President has two options: Option 1: he can save

himself but he is going to have to abandon G40 – Jonathan Moyo, Saviour Kasukuwere, his wife Grace – Lady Gaga.

Option 2: he fails to save himself and he goes with G40. If he does this, in the next 48 hours he will no longer be President of this country.

Mark my words… in the next 48 hours he will no longer be President… He will no longer be President because the military will step in! I will tell you how they will step in. They will simply move in to all television and radio stations in the country. They will announce on the national broadcaster they have taken over the county. This time it will not be a press conference…

Zimbabweans, listen to me carefully… A perfect storm is coming… In the next 48 hours we get a chance to rewrite the story of Zimbabwe… Now is not the time to be fighting each other, now is the time to get it done. Here we are, guys, it is almost time. So, touch is a move, sudden death…

Then he catches himself, as if he's giving too much away.

"Here is the disclaimer," he says with a wink. "I am just kidding! Who am I to be talking about what the military are going to do? I'm just joking, *mafunnies!*"

The video is by the aforementioned Acie Lumumba, that cocksure digital-media analyst added last minute by Mutsvangwa to the team; and what none of his viewers knows is that he has been watching the comings and goings at a hotel in Boksburg, Johannesburg, and made his calculations. He's seen who Mutsvangwa and his colleagues have been meeting with and communicating with and he knows something big is about to go down.

Like all good analysts, he's putting all his cards on the table.

If he turns out to be right, his young followers will consider him some kind of oracle.

Chapter 13

THE STRIKE

Tuesday, November 14th starts out like all the other days that early summer: hot and humid, cloud all around, sun unable to break through the haze. But, for all the greyness, the air is filled with expectation.

If there was no ZANU-PF response to Chiwenga the night before, the citizenry get one that morning when the secretary of the party's influential Youth League, a 30-something firebrand named Kudzai Chipanga – the same man who organised the nine Presidential Youth Interface Rallies at which Grace laid waste to ED – makes a statement at the party headquarters.

That the party is sending out a youth to respond to a decorated General says one of two things: either they're intentionally insulting Chiwenga – or they've utterly failed to read the political temperature.

Before he speaks, dozens of Chipanga's fellow Youth League members sing revolutionary songs, and one of them shadow-boxes for the cameras, as if challenging Chiwenga himself to a fight.

"*Hondo, hondo, hondo!*" they chant – War, war, war!

Given that none of them fought in the liberation war, and they're about to berate a decorated general who did, one tends to lean towards the latter scenario: they're flying blind, unable to see what's happening.

When young Chipanga speaks, he's as bellicose as his chanting comrades. He's listened to Grace at those rallies and channelled her style:

We as ZANU-PF Youth League are a lion which has awakened and found its voice, therefore we will not sit idly and fold our hands whilst cheap potshots and threats are made against Mugabe… Defending the revolution and our leader and President is an ideal we live for and if need be it is a principle we are prepared to die for.

It's fighting talk, and the guy is finding his voice.

He rails that Chiwenga's press conference threat was "an assault on our freedom", and states – correctly as it happens – that the Constitution "places soldiers in barracks and civilian authority in power".

"The guns will follow the politics and not the politics following the guns."

When he's done, the youths chant some more.

But if this is the sum of the party's response to the General, it hardly seems adequate. Across town, in the Munhumutapa building, the President is hosting the weekly cabinet meeting. The meeting will go on for most of the day and apparently Chiwenga's threat is not even mentioned.

At around 2pm, rumours that the military are making their move start zinging around social media.

Someone claims they've seen tanks and armoured personnel carriers – APCs – on the Bulawayo Road, transporting soldiers into the city. Other footage shows tanks leaving Inkomo barracks, the base of the Mechanised Brigade. One tank appears to have broken down on the side of the road and is shown covered in branches. If this is the first salvo in a coup, it's off to an ignominious start.

None of the footage reveals a date, though, and many people dismiss all the reports as fake news. Memes start lighting up, one showing a photograph of a rickety old bicycle piled high with plastic water containers: "Tanks Heading for Harare," reads the caption. The President's nephew, Patrick Zhuwao, a G40 stalwart, is laughing too: *Koo baked beans is the only coup in Zimbabwe*, he tweets.

At 3.30pm, with a light rain beginning to fall, and a strangely unseasonal mist descending on the city, the rumours gain some validity. Ishe Nyamukapa, a communications director for a medical NGO, is dropping some of his staff off at their homes in Dzivarasekwa, west of the city, near the Presidential Guard barracks, when he is stopped at a Military Police roadblock. At the junction ahead he sees tanks, APCs and hundreds of heavily armed soldiers. He starts filming on his cell, adds commentary and, importantly, the date, and sends the post to a handful of friends on a WhatsApp group. It's intended just for them.

"There's a tank along Kirkman Road, Military Police and a tank!" he says. "This is happening in Harare, the date is 14th of November. This road leads to the second Presidential Guard barracks just outside Harare. Wow, it's real, guys, it's real – the danger is real!"

You want to understand the power of social media? Half

an hour later, still stuck in traffic, he's scrolling through his Twitter feed when he sees a tweet with a video showing the same tanks and soldiers at the same junction. He clicks the link, expecting another source.

Instead his own voice comes to him on his own phone via Twitter:

"This is happening in Harare, the date is 14th of November… Wow, it's real, guys, it's real!"

His video is zinging around the world.

Ishe is hit by sudden panic, terrified that he might be accused of triggering a revolution or giving away military secrets. By the time he gets home an hour later the video is on the BBC, Sky News and SABC News, and he's frantically making calls to media organisations to get them to disguise his voice. He's actually relieved when he learns that a journalist is falsely claiming credit for the footage.

❖ ❖ ❖

Eight hundred miles away in Johannesburg, the Northgate team is still on edge.

It's been an eventful 24 hours.

On the morning of Monday 13th, hours before Chiwenga's press conference, Kasper had picked up Monica Mutsvangwa, Chris's wife, at OR Tambo airport. She's flown in from Harare to attend a SADC parliamentary conference (she's Deputy President of the regional forum) and is booked into the same Holiday Inn as the team. Monica has met Kasper, Ellis and Gabriel a few times now – her husband's new friends – and frankly she isn't impressed with how their plan is panning out.

"You and your *mudhara*," she says to Kasper, referring to her husband as old man, "you have failed."

Unlike them, Monica has been on the ground in Zimbabwe, and to her eyes, Mugabe and Grace appeared more secure than ever.

Kasper says, "Mama, wait and see. We are not failures. The game is still on."

And so, when news of Chiwenga's press conference breaks Monday afternoon, it's Kasper's "I-told-you-so moment". He tells the others that this is it – the military are finally making their move. Not everyone is buying it, though. They've been waiting too long. Chiwenga never put a date on when they might step in and it could go on for months.

By Tuesday afternoon, however, they're all getting the stories of tanks and soldiers moving into the city, and Kasper's intelligence confirms it's real. It seems as if it is finally happening.

By this time Gabriel has received a message.

He'd been wondering for the past week what had happened to the military trio he'd been advising on legal matters, and it appears they've surfaced.

The message from them is simple: 2pm, the usual place.

He makes his way over to the lodge in Bruma Lake. Kasper is already there waiting for him and takes him to where the military trio are working out of the boardroom.

The officers are dressed in their usual suit jackets and open-necked shirts. They have a dozen phones between them and they're in constant WhatsApp communication with men in Harare, with whom they speak in military code, using terminology Gabriel doesn't understand.

"Hello, Chairman," says the Brigadier General, barely looking up. "It is time."

❖ ❖ ❖

The events of the night of November 14th – codenamed Operation Restore Legacy by the ZDF – have been written about extensively, but as with the airport action 48 hours earlier, the Zimbabwe military has never gone on the record about its planning, how it went down, which units carried it out, or who the casualties were. Through news reports, eye-witness accounts, interviews with an anonymous retired military officer, and information gleaned from those affected by the action, we can piece much of it together.

Suffice to say that what takes place that night is arguably the most precise, ruthless and sophisticated single-day military operation in African history – Zimbabwe's *Zero Dark 30* or *Raid on Entebbe*.

The difference being that the action is taken not against a foreign enemy, but fellow citizens; and it's not a single site that is targeted but multiple locations across the entire country.

The other difference is aesthetic. Coups tend to be bloody, indiscriminate affairs, with innocent, usually poor civilians killed in the mayhem. The November 14th operation takes place in some of the richest real estate on the African continent: Harare's lush, leafy Borrowdale suburbs, and those who are affected by it and witness to it are the nation's political, economic and social elite, the crème de la crème. It's akin to the SAS storming the townhouses of British MPs in Mayfair; or Navy Seals raiding the multi-million-dollar mansions of senators in Washington DC's Maryland suburbs.

If this seems surreal, consider the weather: it literally takes place on a dark and stormy night.

Let's rejoin the timeline.

At 6pm, the cabinet meeting over, President Mugabe's 40-car motorcade makes its way north on Borrowdale Road for the Blue Roof mansion, Mugabe in the back of his black custom-built bulletproof Mercedes S-class 600, registration ZIM 1. What no one knows is that after nearly four decades in power, this is the last time he will be making this journey in control of his country.

Back in town, the Information Minister, the same man who announced ED's dismissal eight days earlier, emerges from cabinet to deliver responses from both the state and ZANU-PF to General Chiwenga's threat the day before. "The party stands by the primacy of politics over the gun," he says. Chiwenga's statement is "treasonable conduct meant to incite insurrection and violent challenge to Constitutional order".

It's a hard-hitting rebuttal but it seems too little too late.

At 7.19pm the US embassy tweets: *Due to ongoing uncertainty in Zimbabwe, the U.S. Embassy in Harare will be minimally staffed and closed to the public on November 15th.*

They know something is about to go down.

The danger to the military (and Mnangagwa's Lacoste faction) has always been from the G40-aligned police force, particularly the PSU, those Black Boot paramilitaries. But between 7pm and 9pm that evening, tanks and soldiers lock down the PSU base and armoury at Chikurubi in Harare, and barricade the gates of the entire complex. They do the same at the three other PSU bases in different parts of the country. In one swift, coordinated move, they have confined the PSU to barracks and disarmed them without a shot being fired. Weapons secured, the tanks and APCs now move to other prominent locations in the city: the Munhumutapa building, Parliament, State House, the Supreme Court, ZANU-PF headquarters and the main police depot near State House, securing that too.

A surreal public calm remains through it all and civilians don't even know it's happening. Restaurants and bars stay open and end-of-work-day traffic returns to the northern suburbs as usual.

The rain is falling harder, though, and that strange mist is now a shroud.

❖ ❖ ❖

At 6.30pm, back in Johannesburg, night has fallen, and Gabriel and the military trio are no longer in the lodge. They're huddled in a cramped rental car in the lodge parking lot, Kasper patrolling outside.

Something strange had happened an hour or so earlier.

They were in the boardroom, manning their phones, when the door burst open.

Standing there, silhouetted in the doorway, was a 30-something man dressed in jeans and T-shirt. He said nothing, but his eyes darted around the room at the three officers and Gabriel. Gabriel recognised the symptoms… the same psychotic nervousness of the man who barged into his home last Christmas Eve, before attacking him with a knife. The military men froze and stared back at the man. They tried speaking to him in Shona. He didn't reply. Instead he motioned that he wanted a cigarette.

Kasper had sensed something was wrong and came in. He confronted the man, who still said nothing. Then he spoke to him in code and there was a flicker of recognition. Instantly they all knew he was CIO or Military Intelligence. How had he known they were here? Had he booked himself into the lodge knowing they would be coming? Was he there to kill them, but got frightened and froze?

Kasper ushered him away and out of the gate. Their position was clearly compromised now but things had kicked off in Harare and they didn't have time to find another location to work out of. So they relocated to the military trio's Nissan Altima rental car.

This will be their office for the next eight hours.

By this point it's apparent to Gabriel that the three men he is with are listening in on – and conferring with – those running the main military operation in Harare, ordering and directing the tanks and APCs.

He can hear urgent voices over the crackle of WhatsApp calls; what sounds like officers in a command centre in Harare speaking to the soldiers on the APCs and tanks. Some of the communication is in code, but the military guys occasionally translate for him as he sweats it in the back seat.

"Why have we not gone to the ZBC yet? We need the broadcaster," Gabriel hears someone say.

Someone else wonders why the military have not progressed to the Blue Roof.

Gabriel has given them his spiel many times – the advice of a lawyer versed in human rights.

"Whatever they do, don't shoot people."

He hopes and believes there are other lawyers advising the military as they make their move.

He knows the Zimbabwe military is a blunt and brutal force.

❖ ❖ ❖

If Gabriel is nervous, consider what Jonathan Moyo is going through at his house in Greystone Park, Borrowdale. Sometime earlier in the day Moyo received a message alerting him to danger: do not stay in your house tonight and make sure to take every member of your family with you when you leave.

In short: *They're coming for you.*

It's a similar message to that received by his nemesis, ED, eight days earlier.

How the tables have turned.

It's telling that Moyo is the one who has the inside scoop first. He calls his friend Saviour Kasukuwere. Saviour has received no such warning but he knows something is up, too. They sit tight, waiting.

Soon he and his family must make their move.

According to detailed accounts by Reuters and the *Guardian*, by 7pm Grace Mugabe is getting nervous too. Driving back from her Mazowe estate that evening, she sees tanks on the streets and a roadblock manned not by police, but by soldiers. Her Mercedes Maybach is allowed through but once back at the Blue Roof she confers with her husband, who has just returned from that cabinet meeting.

Then she makes a call.

Significantly, it's about message control: she calls the minister in charge of cyber security and asks him to shut down Zimbabwe's social media – WhatsApp, Twitter and Facebook. The minister tells her that's not his remit; that she must contact the State Security Minister, who oversees the intelligence agencies.

"No one will stand for a coup. It cannot happen," Grace tells him. Then Mugabe's voice comes on the line: "As you have heard from Amai (Mother), is there anything that can be done?"

The man gives the same response – it's the responsibility of state security – and then the line goes dead.

For the first time in a long time, the Mugabes are desperate. The closest they've come to this feeling before is back in 2008, after Mugabe lost the election that year to the MDC and Morgan Tsvangirai. At the time the president was unsure what to do. Concede defeat and relinquish control? Or find a way to stay longer? He chose the latter, persuaded by his generals, who helped massage the vote tallies to force a run-off. The run-off was brutal: a violent campaign of terror in which the military command, Chiwenga and Shiri leading the way, sent soldiers and militias in the dead of night to assault, brutalize and intimidate rural voters into voting the right way. The campaign got so ugly that Tsvangirai ended up conceding the run-off to stop the bloodshed.

Want another dark irony about that night? Mugabe's campaign manager in 2008 was ED, and he worked with those commanders on that violent response. He would become Defence Minister soon afterwards. Now Mugabe was without this man, his ace, who had been by his side almost 50 years. That man was ED.

❖ ❖ ❖

Rumbidzai Takawaira, 27, is beautiful – a dead ringer for the young Diana Ross. "News Bae", the fashion mags and twitterati call her. She's also tough. A black belt in karate, before she became head presenter of the ZBC's flagship 8pm Newshour programme, she pumped petrol at her uncle's garage in Mutare. She's a canny social-media operator too, and at 9.05pm, after she's finished that night's news broadcast at the ZBC's Pockets Hill campus, she hangs around the studio taking selfies to post to her Instagram account.

She's heard all the rumours during the day, but she's the first to admit she doesn't report the news: she reads what's put in front of her by her bosses. This being the ZBC, a relentless propaganda machine for ZANU-PF and the government of President Mugabe, there's been a complete blackout of Chiwenga's press conference and no mention of any tanks and soldiers moving into the city.

She's selecting which selfies she likes best when her cameraman bursts into the studio, puts a finger to his lips and in a panicked whisper tells her: "They are here! Hide! Hide!"

"Who's here?" she asks.

"Soldiers!" he says as he dives into a closet.

She hides under her desk – the same desk from which she's just read that night's news – and holds her breath. She can hear footsteps and shouting outside. She's a millennial, though, and she still finds time to update her status. She tweets that she's at the ZBC and soldiers have entered the building. Then the studio door bursts open and she feels a kick in her side.

"You!" says a voice. "Get out of there!"

She staggers to her feet and gets a slap across her face.

Three plain-clothes men are in front of her, probably MI.

The slap is nothing worse than any she's felt in karate, but still, she's terrified.

"Where are the CCTV cameras?" they ask.

She takes them to the control room, past the news room where she sees combat soldiers in uniform, their helmets covered with leaves and foliage, forcing six or seven staff on duty to lie on the floor.

The staff are petrified too.

Rumbi still has her phone on her and during a distraction

wisely finds time to delete her earlier tweet.

"Why did you not read the statement you were supposed to read by General Chiwenga?" one asks.

"I only read what I am told to read," she says.

He shrugs; he seems to understand.

Then Rumbi hears a loud rumble.

Two tanks have arrived at the front doors of the ZBC.

Rumbi thinks to herself: "Wow – this is war."

❖ ❖ ❖

Back in Johannesburg, Gabriel Shumba is frantic in the back seat of the rental car.

He knows the soldiers have reached the ZBC and entered the building.

"Guys, guys, this is important – whatever they do, tell them not to harm the journalists. They cannot be hurt. If the ZBC people want to leave they must be free to leave."

The trio relay the message but Gabriel has no way of knowing if it's received.

The adrenaline cocktail is getting to him. He's both exhilarated and terrified and the irony of his situation has hit him like a diamond in the skull. He's spent the last 15 years looking over his shoulder, on the run from the very kind of people he's now in a car with, working in partnership with. "It was because of these kinds of people that I was forced to practise international human rights law – and now they are coming to me to seek my services and resources to help them remove the man who is coming after them too."

Later, during a lull in communications, he confides to the three men something else that's on his mind.

"Guys, if this thing fails, you know they will be coming

after us in South Africa."

They turn to look at him as if he's an idiot. Two of the trio are AWOL and the third has claimed he is on holiday: if this thing fails they're never going home again; they will be court-martialled and tried for treason.

"You think we don't know that, Chairman?" they splutter.

"Guys, what I'm saying is, if it goes wrong I have to start making arrangements to go to Europe or the United States. There's an organisation in Holland I know that gives political asylum."

One of the men starts to laugh.

"Chairman, what about us? We have to be in this together!"

Then the other two start chuckling.

"Chairman, no one is going anywhere. If this thing fails we're all taking up arms. You will have to lead your diaspora to the front. You'll go through a military crash course to learn how to command them!"

The four of them are giggling now, their cigarette smoke pouring out of the windows like steam.

Before they know it they're in conversation with Harare again.

It is time to cordon off the Blue Roof. Tanks and APCs start making their way north on Borrowdale Road to the President's estate.

A strange thing has happened in the ZBC building in Pockets Hill, meanwhile.

At 9.45pm the soldiers suddenly announced that anyone who was still on their shift should continue as normal, and those who were finished were free to go home.

Staff who had spent the last hour on the floor in terror got up and dusted themselves off.

The soldiers shrugged apologetically for any inconvenience.

And, just like that, the ordeal is over for Rumbidzai. She walks out, past the tanks, shows her ID to soldiers now manning the gates and drives home to her mother through the strange mist.

She catches a flight to Namibia the following morning and does not return for a week.

The military is now in control of the national broadcast network.

❖ ❖ ❖

Jonathan Moyo is not waiting around any more. At 10pm, he drives himself, his wife and three children from his home in Greystone Park to Saviour's place on Dennys Road. It's a three-mile journey on winding, potholed roads – incredibly, some of the same suburban streets ED and his sons took at about the same time, eight nights before, also in fear of assassination.

Moyo arrives safely, soon after 10pm. His yapping dog tweet appears to have worked: he is not followed.

Saviour's wife and four children are with him in Dennys Road so there are now 11 of them in the house. Fortunately it's a big place, solidly built, with bulletproof windows. They sit tight and wait.

❖ ❖ ❖

Albert Ngulube, the CIO security director in charge of Mugabe's protection, is not so lucky. Grace has seemingly summoned him to the Blue Roof at around 9pm and asked him what the hell is going on. He doesn't know, and so at about 10pm he decides to drive to CIO headquarters downtown to find out. On his way he's stopped by soldiers heading towards the Blue Roof. There are many theories regarding exactly what happens next, all laid out in a masterfully atmospheric essay by the Zimbabwean writer Bernard Matambo. They all end in the same place: Ngulube is detained, thrown in the back of an armoured van and accused of spying for the President. Which is, as Matambo dryly notes, perfectly true: "As head of civilian intelligence it is widely acknowledged as essentially part of his job description."

At this point Ngulube appears to be fine; he's just under arrest.

But at 10.30pm his luck turns, when Grace, not having heard back from him, calls his cell. "Ngulube, a spymaster, has cleverly saved the first lady's sensitive phone number as *'First Lady'*," Matambo writes. "On noticing the identity of the caller, the troops explode and begin assaulting him."

He is apparently detained at one of the Presidential Guard barracks, stripped naked, severely beaten and only saved by the intervention of MI the following day.

❖ ❖ ❖

It's close to midnight now and the tanks and APCs are nearing the Blue Roof.

"We are ten minutes away, awaiting instructions," Gabriel overhears. He also learns that the commanders in Harare are in direct contact with the Presidential Guard unit recently rotated in to protect Mugabe. Chiwenga's tentacles are everywhere. The instructions come: the job of the soldiers is simply to cordon off the wider area. They're under strict orders not to storm the Blue Roof. No harm can come to the President or his wife, and they should be free to come and go as they please, otherwise it might constitute a coup. This is part of Gabriel's counsel (and likely to be supported by other lawyers), but Chiwenga and his commanders must know it themselves anyway.

All is going perfectly according to plan.

❖ ❖ ❖

In the early hours of Wednesday, November 15th, things start to get murky.

After weeks of intense heat and humidity, by midnight the skies above Harare start to groan, spit and spark. Lightning cracks; thunder rumbles. The strange shroud of mist enveloping the city only enhances the acoustics, trapping it like music in a theatre.

The weather gods seem to know things are coming to a head, for the literal lightning storm will soon be accompanied by a metaphorical one: ruthless coordinated strikes on three different G40 homes by Special Forces. Indeed, for months to come, the affluent denizens of northern Harare will tell of how it was impossible in those early morning hours to tell the difference between the crack of lighting and the tap-tap of automatic gunfire; between the detonation of thunder and the percussive blast of explosions.

❖ ❖ ❖

Denford Magora can't sleep. He's at his home in upscale Hogarty Hill, monitoring all the rumours and reports on Facebook and Twitter – of the ZBC being taken, of tanks and soldiers moving towards the Blue Roof. This is close to where he lives, but the roads outside seem quiet to him, deserted.

With his art director glasses, trendy sneakers and skinny jeans, Magora, at 45, looks every bit the hip advertising creative he is. In the 1990s he wrote an acclaimed play titled *Dr Government*, in which the government was depicted as an incompetent doctor, and a critically ill patient was named Zimbabwe. The play was banned by Mugabe's censors. Denford left the country, worked for leading agencies all over the world, but in 2010 returned to Zimbabwe to found his own shop, Jericho, with a slate of high-profile clients. He's done well for himself. So well that he's building a second home, a mile away, in the even swankier Borrowdale Brooke gated complex, modelled on American architect Steve Hermann's Glass Pavilion masterpiece in Santa Barbara, California. With its slabs of white cement, reinforced steel, floating glass and twin pools, it promises to be spectacular and it's costing him millions. But it's not only the design that sets it apart: it's the locale.

Perched on the southern cliffs of the Brooke, this new build is directly below General Chiwenga's Titanic mansion, and directly above Mugabe's Blue Roof. Magora can literally sit on his pool deck and gaze down on the President's vast estate, house, lawns, lake, forest, pagoda and all.

At around 2am Magora is tired of the rumours so he decides to go see for himself. How better to gauge the state of the nation than from a house that literally stands between the two warring protagonists?

"I got to my other place about 2.15," Denford recalls. There's thunder rumbling but the roads are quiet. He has to cross a rickety wooden walkway to access the top floor of the half-complete building. No sooner has he stepped onto the structure, however, than all hell breaks loose: a fusillade of gunfire from the road running past the Blue Roof below. He and his security guard dive behind the brick wall of his future living room. "I'm not sure who was shooting at whom but I didn't want to get hit by stray bullets."

The gunfire lasts for some time and he thinks it's coming from outside the Blue Roof.

But is it?

It's a dark night, and your eyes can play tricks on you. There are no bullet holes in the walls of the Blue Roof the following day; no shattered windows in neighbouring houses; no reports of casualties. There will be no claims later by those targeted by the strikes that night that there was a gun battle outside the President's house. "If it happened I would know about it and I would have told the world," said Jonathan Moyo, "and so would Mugabe." Neither does it fit Gabriel's recollection, for by 2am his and Kasper's job with the military trio is done: the roads leading to the Blue Roof have been secured; Presidential Guards loyal to Chiwenga have been rotated in, and not a shot has been fired. The President and his wife are still free to come and go as they please – all according to the plan. Indeed, wide-eyed and pumped with adrenaline, Kasper and Gabriel are heading back to the Holiday Inn to watch an expected TV announcement by a ZDF general explaining that the military have stepped in.

What if Magora is indeed hearing gunfire, but it's an echo of gunfire coming from somewhere nearby?

For it's around that time – 2.30am – that the houses of Saviour Kasukuwere, Jonathan Moyo and the G40-aligned Finance Minister Ignatius Chombo are targeted in ferocious, simultaneous, coordinated assaults.

❖ ❖ ❖

Let's start with the Chombo residence, a relatively modest

single-storey on Golden Stairs Road in Mount Pleasant. According to the senior retired military officer, a crack 18-man Commando unit pulls up and blows up the steel front gates. Chombo has private security contractors – reputed to be Israelis – who open fire. The Commandos fire back from behind an APC, killing two guards instantly. The soldiers storm the house, and go room to room before finding the elderly grey-haired minister cowering with his wife and maid in the bedroom. He is detained for a week at an undisclosed location, and later charged with corruption and fraud involving billions of dollars. No one knows what happened to the bodies of the contractors.

Three miles west of where Magora is hiding in his half-built living room, an SAS unit of between 18 and 25 soldiers storm Jonathan Moyo's house on Rosery Close, Greystone Park. They also go from room to room. Fortunately for Moyo he's already left the premises. He will later tweet pictures of the devastation.

The real action – and what Magora might be hearing – is taking place at Saviour's house on Dennys Road, a narrow lane barely a mile up the ridge as the crow flies, where Moyo has taken his family.

Their wives and seven children have gone to sleep just after midnight. Moyo stays up with Saviour in his study. They know that a coup is underway and that ZBC has been taken. "We were just wondering how it was all going to play out," said Moyo. At 2:15am they decided to pull up some chairs and take a nap. Fifteen minutes later there was an almighty explosion by the reinforced steel gate. And so it began.

Saviour Kasukuwere is a giant of a man. Big, burly, with a deep baritone voice and a loud easy laugh, he calls to mind a New Orleans jazz saint. He's given to colourful shirts and flamboyant jackets and likes to wear a leather Ivy cap jauntily to the side. His formidable size; his years as a CIO spy; his time as G40's enforcer – all this have given him a reputation. He calls *himself* Tyson. One of Kasukuwere's acquaintances in Harare says he enjoyed the big man's company, "But I always made sure I took someone with me when I met him – just in case." Even tough guys feel fear, though, and in the first seconds of the assault that night, he must have been struck by the horrific irony of the situation. He's about to be attacked by soldiers sent by General Constantino Chiwenga, a long-time friend and mentor; a man with whom he flew in military helicopters over Mozambique; a man he helped source hangover cures after heavy drinking bouts. They attended each other's weddings, they shared the same architect and they are neighbours in this glorious suburb that smells of geranium and jacaranda. Such is life in the death game of Zimbabwean politics.

As for Moyo, he has warned about this event for months and now it's upon him, the worst of all self-fulfilling prophecies. He prays that his wife and children survive. And to think this all could have been avoided in 1978 when he was at the University of Southern California: but for the conditions of a scholarship, he would have studied film-making.

Again, it's between 18 and 25 troops. They pull up quietly in two armoured vehicles opposite the steel gates. They don't open fire at first. They climb the walls of the property, lined with handsome statues of stone lions, and walk along the top of them, while others soldiers scale the balcony of the neighbour's house to the immediate left, a swooping Art Deco structure. We know this because watching it all from their bedroom windows two houses away are Shuwa Mudiwa, a former MDC MP, and his son, Tobias, a miner. "They shot from above," says Tobias. "You could see the fire from the guns." The gunfire is accompanied by grenades. Saviour has private security guards but what are they going to do? They drop their weapons and run, scrambling through the tall grass down the slope on the south side of the house and on to El Shaddai Road. Remember El Shaddai? That's where ED's house is, barely 50 yards east. Talk about coming full circle. ED is hiding out in Pretoria but his wife is home in bed listening to the fireworks, as are Sean and Collins and their wives who have moved in with her since the escape. (ED, and Junior, working through Jenfan Muswere, had boosted security around both their homes, bringing in two separate private security contractors for the duration.)

Inside, Saviour and Moyo and their families are cowering in terror, the children screaming, the house shaking, glass shattering. The alarm on the hi-tech security system is an ear-piercing shriek. The soldiers are trying to pry open the sturdy steel gates, but they're remote-controlled and hold fast. At one point, one of the group frantically calls the only people who can help them, the Mugabes. Grace answers and they beg her, "Please save us, Mama!" (Moyo later says it was Grace who called them; that she had heard the neighbourhood gunfire and got word of the other attacks). Either way, Grace tells them she will send help.

And then, just like that, after 15 minutes, a strange thing happens: the attack stops.

The soldiers lower their weapons, return to their vehicles and drive off.

Which is very strange.

They have stormed the Finance Minister's house and detained him; they have stormed Moyo's house but he wasn't in.

Here they don't even attempt to enter. Were they just sending a message to Saviour? Had the President or Grace made a frantic call to Chiwenga, begging him to call it off?

Twenty minutes later, two vehicles pull up through the mist outside the still smouldering mansion.

Grace has heeded the call and sent cars to collect her allies and their families.

She has given the drivers instructions: "You could die in the process but you need to get them."

The shaken families pile in and they arrive at the Blue Roof minutes later without mishap. They are not stopped or searched. The wives and children will be sheltered at the Blue Roof for the next week, but for Saviour and Moyo the journey has only just begun. They will soon be in another car, heading east, where – just over a week after mocking ED for being a border jumper – they will cross the same Mozambique border and go into exile.

A week is a long time in politics.

As for Denford, by 3am he's made his way back home. He notices that Chiwenga's Titanic house now has military tanks stationed at the back and front. He's well prepared. Denford gets home and posts on Facebook that the coup is real, and at 3.55am gets word to turn on the national broadcaster.

At exactly 4am, from ZBC's Pockets Hill studios, a man comes on the air to address the nation.

He's wearing a beret and camo fatigues and he's sitting at the exact same desk Rumbi "News Bae" Takawaira had dived under a mere seven hours earlier. The name embroidered on his uniform reads: Major General SB Moyo – not to be confused with the other Moyo who is now at the Blue Roof.

Unlike the other Moyo, this one is calm, steady and in complete control. He says:

Fellow Zimbabweans, following the address we made on 13th November 2017, which we believe our main broadcaster Zimbabwe Broadcasting Corporation and the *Herald* were directed not to publicise, the situation in our country has moved to another level.

Firstly we wish to assure our nation, His Excellency, the President of the Republic of Zimbabwe and commander in chief of the Zimbabwe Defence Forces, comrade RG Mugabe and his family, are safe and sound and their security is guaranteed. We are only targeting criminals around him who are committing crimes that are causing social and economic suffering in the country in order to bring them to justice.

He goes on to tell Zimbabweans to go about their business as normal. Then he addresses the international community who will, in the days ahead, have to pass judgement on what has just happened:

To both our people and the world beyond our borders, we wish to make this abundantly clear this is not a military takeover of government. What the ZDF is doing is to pacify a degenerating political, social and economic situation in our country which if not addressed may result in violent conflict…

We call upon all the war veterans to play a positive role in ensuring peace, stability and unity in the country. To members of the Zimbabwe Defence Forces, all leave is cancelled and you are all to return to your barracks with immediate effect.

It is 4.10am on Wednesday, November 15th.

Chapter 14

THE COUP THAT WAS NOT A COUP

When dawn broke and the smoke cleared, Zimbabweans woke in a strange new land.

Everything had changed – and yet nothing had.

The country had just experienced the most dramatic night in its history since independence in 1980, but the military were telling everyone that the Old Man was still President, that he and Grace were safe, and that no harm would come to them.

If he was still President, Grace still in the game, what the hell was the point?

"We yaw between terror and ecstasy," the author Rian Malan once wrote on the condition of life in South Africa, and Zimbabweans were on that precise psychological roller-coaster.

It was exhausting.

So they did what they do best: kept their heads down, went to work as normal and mined the seam of dark humour that all authoritarian societies rely on to get by.

A few bumps in the night – wrote Joanna, a neighbour

of the General in the Brooke, messaging a family group on WhatsApp – *we don't watch Game of Thrones, we live it!*

Debbie Swailes, a neighbour of Moyo, woke to find the Zimbabwe Bird stone carving in her garden had toppled over from the force of one of the blasts and its head had snapped off. Then she noticed for the first time her statue depicted a crocodile climbing the bird's side towards the now-severed neck.

She messaged a photo of it to friends: *Is this ED???!! My maid now thinks I'm a witch!*

It took a while to work out who'd been attacked or detained, who had fled or been killed, and rumours and fake news filled the void, notably reports of US$10 million being found in the ceiling of the Finance Minister's house – money supposedly intended for a team of Israeli mercenaries whom Grace and G40 had hired to assassinate Chiwenga. Another rumour was that the military operation was so precise and seamless it could never have been carried out by the ZDF and either the Mossad or mercenaries had done it.

A more plausible story, but also untrue, was that Grace had fled the country. A meme of a woman hauling Gucci bags and running down an airstrip desperately trying to hail a departing plane went viral.

What *was* true was that Youth League leader Chipanga had been arrested. He was soon on TV in a purple-patterned sweater that looked as if it had been knitted by his mother, offering an abject apology to General Chiwenga for his bellicose statement of a day earlier:

I kindly request General Chiwenga to please accept my apologies on behalf of the Youth League and myself. We are still young people, we are still growing up, we learn from our mistakes, and from this big mistake, we have learned a lot.

So much for being prepared to die for the President and the revolution.

Online wags took note of the sweater and immediately dubbed his *mea culpa* "The Apolojersey".

The President's spokesman George Charamba had also spent a restless night. Something in the tone of General Chiwenga's voice the last time they had spoken had left him terrified that the soldiers were going to come for him, too. He had hugged his pillows that night, checked on his sleeping kids and avoided all calls, but when he got a heads-up about the military's 4am statement he tuned in. Now he could breathe easier. It turned out Mugabe was still the President, which meant he still had a job.

He messaged Chiwenga. *What can I do to help?*

Charamba would now become a mediator, the go-between, between Mugabe and the generals.

And so the final stage of the great game began; the third and most important act.

❖ ❖ ❖

Once upon a time coups in Africa were as common as thunderstorms.

Military men overthrew despotic rulers, who had in turn overthrown despotic rulers. Sometimes they did it with their own armies; often they used hired guns. In the 60s, 70s and 80s, when Africa was a Cold War battleground, mercenary adventurers such as Bob Denard and "Mad" Mike Hoare became household names, inspiring best-selling books and gory classics such as *The Dogs of War* and *The Wild Geese*.

By the late 90s that had changed. With the Cold War over, the African Renaissance began, and peace, democracy and security became new watchwords. The African Union and SADC nations signed agreements stating they would not tolerate unconstitutional overthrows of member governments, and indeed would intervene militarily to stop them. In 2002 a multinational African Union Standby Force, Africa's equivalent of NATO, first mooted by a Zimbabwean (Chiwenga's predecessor in 1997), was established – security architecture for a modern Africa. Its protocols required "intervention in a Member State in respect of grave circumstances or at the request of a Member State in order to restore peace and security".

Not only was the Mugabe government instrumental in setting up these security guarantees, the ZDF, more than any other southern African military, was instrumental in enforcing them. General Chiwenga himself had helped command multi-lateral operations to quell coups in Lesotho and Burundi.

Indeed, by the new millennium it was impossible to seize power in Africa via a coup without the buy-in of the region or the international community. In 2004, for example, as documented in Adam Roberts's meticulously researched *The Wonga Coup*, the planned overthrow of Equatorial Guinea's strongman by former British SAS officer Simon Mann was foiled – at Harare's airport as it happens – after the Zimbabwean ex-military officer Mann thought was an ally turned out not to be. A year earlier a bloodless coup in São Tomé and Principe, off the west coast of Africa, was reversed in days after political pressure from neighbouring Nigeria and the US. In January 2019 a military coup in Gabon lasted three days before collapsing in on itself.

Turns out seizing power is the easy part.

Keeping it is what you have to plan for: legitimacy.

If Zimbabweans wondered why Mugabe was still in power they missed the point. The military were denying this was a coup because coups are illegal. They couldn't remove Mugabe by force because it would make them potential criminals and turn the country into a regional and international pariah.

They had to find another way. They had to make Mugabe leave voluntarily, legally.

So how do you carry out a coup that's not a coup?

Well, you call the A-Team, or, in this case, the misfit team of rivals in South Africa, whose leader, one Christopher Mutsvangwa, has been planning for this exact possibility for more than a year.

❖ ❖ ❖

Let's rejoin the group.

Tom Ellis had also had a sleepless night.

He and Clare had gone to bed early the evening of the 14th, but at 10pm his phone started pinging and 24 hours later it hadn't stopped. Kasper had sent him updates throughout the night from the lodge, but he also had friends in Harare messaging him about strange goings-on in the suburbs. Ellis had a good idea of what was going down, but he couldn't tell them. He stayed up for the 4am statement, and as he watched it he thought back to 2015 and his decision to reach out to elements within ZANU-PF, which had led him to Mutsvangwa; and his impulse, that afternoon in Northgate, when he had stopped his car at a red light and approached the two men following him – his assassins – and invited them for a drink. Those two actions had led him to this point. Mugabe was not yet gone, but they were getting close: the final push.

By Wednesday evening Kasper and Gabriel hadn't slept in 48 hours. Slugging beers and mainlining espressos at the hotel, they'd watched the Brigadier General's announcement and were still up when the rest of the team, like company men at a corporate retreat, reported for the day's strategy session.

When Gabriel addressed the Core Group's meeting that morning and the following day, Thursday 15th, he felt tears well in his eyes as he saw for the first time the seeds of what Zimbabwe could become. Here they were, former enemies, working towards the common goal of a hopeful new country.

"Our very being together symbolised for me the dream for a new Zimbabwe. In our small group you had people from the army, from the CIO, former policemen, some MDC, some business people, some NGO people fighting for human rights. Add into the cauldron the Chairman of the war veterans from ZANU-PF.

"You actually had what we envisaged a future Zimbabwe to look like – a country where you are not ashamed to be in any political party and not fearful of defending and stating an ideological position or political philosophy. It should be the model for the country."

For the first time since he had signed up for this madcap adventure Gabriel dared believe it might just work.

For Kasper, the endgame was in sight.

He expected Mugabe to resign any day. "Our mission was successful. I, as main actor on all logistics, I was very happy that it's all done at last after a hard struggle."

But he was also worried. He wanted it to end soon, for by Wednesday evening the number of people joining the team had swelled to more than 50 – there were still more based out of the Radisson Blu in Sandton – and frankly he didn't trust them all. It was impossible for himself, Magic and Horse to vet the newcomers; they just arrived, walked through the lobby doors as if they belonged and joined the revolution. Was it the innate paranoia of the spy in him that made him suspect some of them were saboteurs, G40 plants? He found he missed the camaraderie of the small group, the original Northgate team. They'd become his family over the past year – hell, past two years with Ellis – something bigger than himself, something good and decent in his work for a change, and he would literally have given his life for any of them. He almost did. But now all these Johnny-come-lateleys were jumping on board as if it was their plan. What did they know of where it all began, of the risks they had all taken? He messaged his security concerns to Mutsvangwa. Mutsvangwa replied: *Everyone has a role to play.*

So what of Mutsvangwa, the putative leader?

Well, at that point, the evening of the 15th, he'd been out of Johannesburg for three days.

He wasn't there because he'd been flown to Cape Town in the middle of Monday night by his South African Military Intelligence protectors to meet with President Jacob Zuma.

Consider the scenario: Jacob Zuma is not only the President of South Africa in November 2017; he's also the Chairman of the SADC, the regional organisation duty bound to intervene in case of an unconstitutional military takeover of a member state. Moreover, the African Union would take their cue from the SADC, and the UN from the AU.

Jacob Zuma was the most powerful and influential figure in the game at that point: the decider.

Mutsvangwa had known for a while that the day might come when he would have to persuade South Africa, the region and the continent that the Zimbabwe military stepping in to remove Mugabe and Grace was not a coup. Now that time was upon him. "We were actually anticipating the future," he recalls. "Remember we are guerillas. We have a visionary aspect about the way things go."

And so, over two days in Cape Town, he pitched the argument that he'd first taken for a public spin at the Sandton press conference a week earlier: that a coup *had* taken place in Zimbabwe, but it was in the form of state capture by Grace Mugabe and the G40 cabal. The military stepping in would only be reversing the coup and restoring constitutional order, he told them.

"There were two courts," Mutsvangwa explained later. "The court of regional opinion and the court of international public opinion. My job was to get Zuma on side. To avoid him using the C-word – the coup word. My history as a war veteran, my years as a diplomat, I knew how to handle that kind of situation."

As it happens, Mutsvangwa didn't get a personal audience with Zuma, but he did spend many hours on Tuesday and Wednesday with Zuma's aides, senior ANC officials and intelligence officers, many of whom he knew from his liberation war days, others he knew as an ambassador.

What's astonishing is that Mutsvangwa was in place on Tuesday, prepping Zuma's aides, *before* the military operation had taken place; and he was still there Wednesday morning, *after* the action. He was a hidden hand, in place to pre-empt and counter any claims coming from Mugabe and G40 in Harare.

How important is this?

Well, consider that Wednesday morning, suspecting a coup has taken place in Zimbabwe, Zuma, in his capacity as SADC chair, dispatches an envoy to Harare to meet with the beleaguered Mugabe. Zuma has phoned Mugabe, who has told him he is fine, but confined to his home. The envoy – South Africa's Minister of Defence and Military Veterans, Nosiviwe Mapisa-Nqakula – is going to see for herself. Meanwhile, Alpha Condé, the AU Chairman, has also said that what has happened "looks like a coup".

So Mutsvangwa takes his pitch to Zuma's aides into overdrive. He appeals to the liberation war blood bond between the ANC, Zimbabwe's military and war veterans such as himself and Zuma. (Zuma was head of the ANC's military wing.) Grace and the G40 cabal are not part of that bond, he warns. They did not fight. They have a different *ethos*. They represent a corrupt "oligarchy capitalism", which is dangerous to the region. You saw how she beat that poor South African girl Gabriella in that hotel, he tells them. You know of the ties between G40 and Julius Malema, the usurper who is a threat to you here? For good measure he adds that old staple: that Jonathan Moyo, the brains behind G40, is a CIA asset. You don't want these people in charge of the country and its military to the north of you, do you?

Warming to his theme, he spells out what he says would be the dire consequences for South Africa's security if Mugabe's wife were to gain power.

"You maybe have a situation where Grace is in command, Kasukuwere is in command, Jonathan Moyo is in command and then the Zimbabwean army comes to the Limpopo River," Mutsvangwa warns. "Then your [South African] army will be on the other side of the Limpopo River. This would happen because these people, they do not have the same ethos [as us] and you can't allow that."

It sounds absurd – he's saying there may be a regional war – but he has a way with words, Mutsvangwa. They flow like mercury off his tongue. And he has credentials too. He's educated, an intellectual, a blue blood, a liberation fighter, an ambassador. He's *persuasive*.

Does it work?

To a point. Mostly it buys them time. When Zuma makes the public announcement on Wednesday that he is sending his envoys to Harare to meet with Mugabe, he adds that he has "managed to get the briefing about the situation", and "given the seriousness, I have taken the decision to send an envoy to contact the leader of the Defence Forces, and to meet with President Mugabe to get a more clear picture."

It's the opening Mutsvangwa needs. Indeed, when the envoy lands in Harare she will be met not by government officials loyal to Mugabe, but by military officers. And instead of meeting with Mugabe and Grace privately at the Blue Roof, to hear their sad tale, the meetings will now take place at State House, the President's official residence, with Chiwenga and the representatives of the military present.

An extraordinary photograph is soon published in which the envoy and mediators are pictured sitting with a relaxed Mugabe on sumptuous sofas in a gold-lit drawing room at State House. General Chiwenga is there, standing rod-straight in front of Mugabe, in full military fatigues, saluting him.

If this is a coup, it's unlike any the world has ever seen.

Mugabe looks as if he's in complete control.

Mugabe might take this moment to tell the envoy it's all

a ruse. He's not in control. But he doesn't do that. After all, he's a giant of Africa, revered for his strength, for his leadership. For him to suggest he's not in charge of his own country would be an admission of weakness. So he doesn't.

By Thursday, even the AU has changed its tune.

Recall that days before firing ED, as part of his attempt to "coup-proof" the military, Mugabe had posted Major General Trust Mugoba to Ethiopia to oversee an African Union Standby Force? Well, that move has backfired too because it's almost certain Mugoba is in constant contact with his military friends in Harare and is reporting their version of events directly to his new colleagues at the AU.

Indeed, senior representative Moussa Faki Mahamat reads a statement on the crisis: "The military has assured us this is not a coup d'état. The AU is against any unconstitutional change of government."

In this backroom world of smoke and mirrors, sometimes it is the shiniest object that goes unnoticed: the AU official is presenting the Zimbabwe military's version of events as statement of fact.

The risk of outside intervention appears to have been averted for now.

Such is the art of persuasion.

❖ ❖ ❖

Winning over regional and international opinion is not enough, however.

For a coup to not be a coup, it must have a third element, beyond regional and international buy-in. It needs the buy-in of the citizenry. The people must rise up against the despised leader to give the change the required democratic legitimacy.

By Thursday this is the message from Zuma and other elements within the SADC.

So it is that on the evening of Thursday, November 16th, with Mutsvangwa now back at the Holiday Inn in Johannesburg, the team make the decision to organise a mass march against Mugabe.

Actually, the decision to march has already been made by Mutsvangwa's war veteran colleagues in Harare, apparently endorsed and encouraged by General Chiwenga, but the Holiday Inn team is in a better position than anyone to spread word of it and get people on the streets for it.

The day chosen is Saturday, November 18th, which is only 36 hours away.

How to organise a mass march in an African city as decayed as Harare at such short notice, with a population frightened that the desired outcome – the resignation of Mugabe – is already in doubt?

They all know Mugabe's staying power, and even the military appear to be hedging on getting rid of him.

Zimbabweans are not generally given to marches, demonstrations or mass uprisings either. Yes, they do hit the streets, but never in the numbers of, say, the Arab Spring.

Resilience, stoicism, dark humour, an ability to make a plan, to survive against all odds, these, for good or ill, are traits of Zimbabweans, not mass protest.

What if only a few thousand brave people show up and it doesn't work?

Their heads would be on the chopping block.

Mutsvangwa's war veteran colleagues' plan is to hold a rally in Harare's Gwanzura Stadium and then march to State House. Gwanzura has a capacity of 10,000 and the war veterans say they can fill it.

But what is 10,000 people in a nation of 16 million? It would be embarrassing.

It's at that point that the disparate members of the Johannesburg team start brainstorming.

The value of the bigger team is that they now represent every element of Zimbabwean society, and it's soon apparent that they all believe they can do a lot better than fill a minor stadium.

They already have the war veterans and the ED-supporting Lacoste faction of ZANU-PF to draw on. Through Monica Mutsvangwa, who has remained in Johannesburg since Monday, and Auxillia Mnangagwa, ED's wife in Harare, they have ties to the ZANU-PF Women's League not loyal to Grace. Through Gabriel and the ZEF, they have instant connections to three million people in the diaspora, and they can get word to *their* friends and family in Zimbabwe. They have direct links to the MDC leadership in Zimbabwe – Morgan Tsvangirai and his deputy Nelson Chamisa. This is vital because Harare, like most urban areas, is MDC territory. They also have a direct line to Pastor Evan Mawarire, the charismatic democracy activist whose This Flag movement has legions of supporters, and who is already talking of a march to catch the mood. Then they have ties to business, churches, civil society and NGOs.

And what of the nation's disillusioned youth, those all-important millennials who comprise the bulk of the population? Well, it turns out Acie Lumumba is still in Johannesburg, working out of the Radisson Blu, and his dramatic video prediction of Monday 13th – that the military were going to seize power – has not only turned out to be 100 per cent accurate, it's gone hyper-viral. He's picking up thousands of new followers by the day and they are indeed calling him "The Oracle". Lumumba pipes up to Mutsvangwa that he can get word out to an entire generation of young Zimbabweans that the others on the team have no connection to.

In other words they are all of the belief that, far from just filling a minor stadium, they will fill the city.

And so by Thursday evening the team gets to work, organising a march. They light up their networks, mine their databases, contact business people in South Africa and Zimbabwe to provide money, fuel, food, buses, sound systems, flags, printing presses, posters and transport.

"It was our D-Day," recalls Ellis. "In a few hours we had to get word out to millions of people to hit the streets of Harare Saturday morning. That takes a lot of organising. The energy was incredible."

Mutsvangwa also decides that the following day, Friday 17th, he will relocate the Command Centre to the Rainbow Towers in Harare, the former Sheraton hotel, where his war veteran colleagues have been based for months. He will hold a press conference there the following day for local and international media. The entire world must see this march and the international press, for so long pariahs in Zimbabwe, must be invited in, no visas necessary, to record the historic unifying occasion.

It was time to flood the zone.

"We were making our move, the final push," said Kasper.

It was then, barely an hour after greenlighting the march, that the team made a catastrophic mistake.

In truth it was Mutsvangwa and Kasper who blundered. After months, nay, years, of living on the edge, the end finally in sight, they let their excitement get the better of them. They dropped their guard.

Pressure had been building on Mugabe in Harare the past 48 hours and rumours were rife that he could resign any minute. It was at around 7pm on Thursday night that they got the incredible news: it was all over, Mugabe had agreed to step down. He had resigned! It was news that every Zimbabwean with a Twitter handle recalled in real time that evening, information confirmed by even reliable sources such as journalist and media entrepreneur Trevor Ncube.

The atmosphere in the Holiday Inn lobby – already electric – now exploded.

"He's gone!" someone shouted, holding up a phone. "He's resigned!" screamed another.

The roof of the hotel lifted off its hinges. Not since South Africa won the Rugby World Cup at Ellis Park Stadium down road from here in 1995 had Boksburg seen such a party.

The problem was, the report was false.

It was either disinformation designed to sabotage them, or just more fake news.

The next problem was, within minutes of getting the false report, a cell phone video of the hotel celebrations was taken and posted to Facebook. The video showed four people: Christopher and Monica Mutsvangwa, a woman named Josey Mahachi between them, and a tough-looking man, right of screen.

Josey had joined the team with two girlfriends earlier in the week, arriving on the same flight as Monica. A digital-media entrepreneur, film-maker and friend of Africa's richest man, Nigerian Aliko Dangote, Josey had been invited by Christopher because of her connections to potential investors, including Dangote. Mutsvangwa was thinking ahead, of getting Zimbabwe open for business, and Mahachi, a proud patriot, was happy to be part of it.

"This man!" she's shouting in the video, recognising what Mutsvangwa has pulled off, "This man!"

Then she turns to Monica to her right and purrs: "Monica Mutsvangwa is back in power!"

Monica smiles bashfully and lowers her head, suddenly uncertain if she wants to be on camera.

The fourth person in the video has his right arm around Christopher. He's wearing a long-sleeved T-shirt and jeans and has a missing front tooth and a meaty face. He's jumping up and down, delirious with joy, shouting over and over again: "We are the team! We are the team! We are the team!"

By the time they all learned, an hour later, that Mugabe had not in fact resigned and that the report was false, the celebration video was zinging around Zimbabwe. Intelligence agents in Harare loyal to Mugabe would take note of the man on the edge of the clip, the one shouting "We are the team".

That man was supposed to be one of them, but it turned out he'd been with the enemy all this time.

That man was Kasper, and he would soon be paying a heavy price for his precipitousness. They would make sure of it.

Chapter 15

THE MARCH

By Friday, November 17th, Zimbabwe was gripped with coup fever. Or was it *Koo* fever? The military speaking in tongues, denying a coup had taken place, had set the internet ablaze with ironic memes.

Having largely ignored the story over the past ten days, the world's media started converging on Harare for the march, anticipating the toppling of Africa's most infamous tyrant. Not since a lion named Cecil was shot by an American dentist in the south of the country in 2015 had the international press paid so much attention to Zimbabwe. "Last time it was for a lion, this time for a crocodile," another joke went.

The emotional rollercoaster didn't let up; terror and ecstasy.

At 8pm on Thursday evening, like the team in the Holiday Inn, much of the country thought Mugabe had resigned. By Friday morning they were gutted to learn he was still around. A familiar dread set in: the G40 and the intelligence agencies were regrouping, and Chiwenga, looking out for his own future, was ready to cut a deal with Mugabe. The longer the impasse lasted, the likelier it was Mugabe stayed. That had always been Ellis's fear – "the Mugabe factor" – that the wily old fox would find a way out of this like he always did. When had Mugabe ever lost a negotiation?

There was another theory doing the rounds now, too: that the military were not as united behind Chiwenga as his Tuesday press conference seemed to suggest. The top commanders certainly were, and had known all along of the plans to intervene militarily, but what of the other 80 officers at the Monday press conference? Would they all have known beforehand what Chiwenga was going to say and what he was going to do? Unlikely. Coup 101: tell as few people as possible. This theory had it that the other officers – those George Charamba laid eyes on in the side room – only came hurrying to meet Chiwenga at KG VI because he had told them he wanted to discuss salaries and pension payments. Instead, Chiwenga made his press statement – the threat to Mugabe – and they were all caught on camera with him. They were now trapped, complicit, and there's no going back once you're in the middle of the ocean.

If this theory is true, it was a cut-throat move worthy of The Godfather.

❖ ❖ ❖

At the risk of disturbing the narrative, allow me to introduce myself at this point.

As mentioned in the introduction to this book, I returned to Zimbabwe on the night of Thursday 16th, cutting short a road trip into far northern Mozambique with three friends, Michael Bowles, John Kerr and Craig Ellis (no relation to Tom). Four middle-aged men in midlife crisis, we'd gone in search of our lost youth, on a life-affirming adventure, travelling in a white vintage 1971 Mercedes 280 SE. We were ten days into the trip when we realised the adventure was happening back in our home country. It took us three days on mud-splattered jungle roads, but we raced home in time for the revolution.

We crossed back into Zimbabwe at Forbes border post – the same frontier at which ED and his sons made their narrow escape from on the morning of November 7th – and drove through Mutare, the town in which I was born, to my parents' farmhouse on the other side of the mountain in the Mutare River valley. At the foot of Christmas Pass, three miles from their home, we were stopped at that roadblock referred to in the introduction. The roadblock was now manned by soldiers.

"Got any bombs?" the Kalashnikov-wielding soldier had asked.

Then the grin and the fist bump.

In 2010 I published a book, a dark comedy titled *The Last Resort*, about my parents' unconventional methods to keep hold of their home and backpacker lodge during the violent land invasions launched by Mugabe and the war veterans. Seven years on they remained in their home, but the state had taken the title deed to it, their tourist business had collapsed, and years of stress and anxiety had taken their toll. My parents had no love for ZANU-PF, the party that has overseen this disaster, and had long since given up hope of Zimbabwe changing, yet even they had Koo Fever. We opened prized bottles of red wine and guzzled them like water that night, marvelling at the events of the last ten days. "I have to say it's strange to be supporting Mnangagwa," said my 82-year-old father. "It's like watching a snake eat another snake."

A common enemy is a galvanising thing, though.

My mother was more circumspect, as was always her way.

"It is exciting, but even if Bob goes it'll be the same bus – just a different driver. Mark my words."

Those were her final words on Zimbabwean politics.

She would be dead from a heart attack four months later.

We spent Friday November 17th in Mutare, a city on the skids in a country on the ropes.

Nationwide cash shortages meant mile-long queues outside banks and ATMs, and while there was food in the shops, it was all imported and too expensive for the average Zimbabwean. Zimbabwe, which had once fed much of the continent, now couldn't feed itself. Nevertheless there was also an unspoken frisson of excitement that day; people weren't expressing it openly yet for fear it could all go wrong, but they sensed the country was on the cusp of a momentous change. We ran into a friend of my father, a businessman named Laurence Maziwa. "Mr Rogers, this morning I saw something I never thought I would ever see," he told my father. "My ZANU-PF friends sitting down with my MDC friends to arrange joint bus transport to Harare for the march tomorrow. These people hate each other – yet here they were joining hands!"

We retired for lunch to the Mutare Club, a threadbare century-old British colonial building, and were joined by family friends from the Bvumba and other remote outposts in those eastern mountains beloved of storytellers. They reported having seen convoys of trucks crossing into Mozambique in the middle of the night. Those G40 who had not been detained were on the run, and some were making their escape.

Then, during dessert, the familiar twinge of anxiety returned: the TV in the club's bar was tuned to the ZBC and live footage showed Mugabe attending that day's Zimbabwe

Open University graduation ceremony. So much for being under house arrest, on his way to resigning! He looked as in charge as ever.

It turned out that one of the students graduating that day, and whose cap Mugabe had to doff, was Marry Chiwenga, the wife of the General who was supposedly trying to remove him.

Such was the surreal nature of the game.

By now even my parents' elderly friends had heard about the march and I marvelled at how word of it had spread so quickly. It spoke of an organisation and efficiency not common in Zimbabwe any more.

My friends and I decided we were going; we would wake early and drive west to Harare to take part.

❖ ❖ ❖

At around the same time that I was lunching in Mutare that Friday afternoon, a battered white Toyota Legend beeped outside an apartment block in downtown Johannesburg.

The driver and his two passengers were in a hurry. The driver beeped again.

Eventually a couple emerged carrying blankets and two suitcases.

"We're coming, take it easy, Kasper," Gabriel shouted.

Kasper cackled his aggressive laugh behind the wheel. "Chairman, what's taking you, you're going to make us miss the march!" He pronounced "march" as "much", taking a meat cleaver to the word.

Gabriel tossed his and his wife's suitcases in the back of the truck. He clocked the licence plates on the Toyota: Zimbabwean. Yesterday, at the hotel, the plates had been GP (Gauteng Province) for Johannesburg. Kasper and Magic had switched them overnight as was their practice whenever making a trip to Zimbabwe.

Gabriel jumped in the back with Magic and Horse and tried to get comfortable among the clutter of fuel cans, blankets, megaphones and food supplies, while his wife rode shotgun upfront.

Then Kasper hit the gas and they raced north, to the Zimbabwe border, six hours' drive away. Kasper planned to drive through the night – he never had much need for sleep – and be in Harare by dawn.

Gabriel had not set foot in Zimbabwe since fleeing in the boot of a car on March 24th, 2003, 14 years previously. He was a fugitive from his home country and hunted by Mugabe's assassins in his adopted one, but there was no way he was going to miss the event he believed would finally topple the tyrant. He wanted to be free again, to not have to look over his shoulder any more, and that time was close at hand.

Something had rankled Gabriel during his 14 years in exile: the accusation from putative allies in the opposition back home that those in the diaspora had it easy.

"There were always allegations that we had left others to fight and die. So when I made the decision to go for the march it was partly an attempt to convince myself that I wasn't a coward. I had always said I would rather be a living dog than a dead lion, but now I said, 'Let me show them I can risk it'."

Nevertheless, they had taken security precautions.

It was Gabriel's wife who had suggested they drive to Harare with Kasper and co. instead of flying. The Mutsvangwas and several other members of the team had flown to Harare that morning, but Mrs Shumba thought the airport would be more dangerous. Being wanted for treason meant

Gabriel was on a security database, likely to be arrested, and chances of escape at an airport were impossible. At the border, on foot, with Kasper, Magic and Horse as muscle – that gave them a fighting chance.

Gabriel had phoned Morgan Tsvangirai in Harare that morning to say he was thinking of coming and Tsvangirai had been thrilled. After some back and forth, the MDC leadership was on board with the march. They had been reluctant at first to be seen enabling any faction of ZANU-PF, let alone the military, but they also sensed the national mood. "Morgan said we should all come in support of the big moment," Gabriel recalls. Gabriel had also phoned contacts at the US embassy and two European embassies in Harare saying he was entering the country again, and if he disappeared to get word out.

But it was something Kasper had told him four months earlier that persuaded Gabriel he might be safe.

Back in July, returning from one of his suicide missions, Kasper told him that he had located and destroyed Gabriel's docket – the file on his case ordering his arrest for treason – and had then pulled strings within intelligence to get the officer in charge of his case demoted and transferred out of Harare.

"No one can hurt you now, Gabe," Kasper told him. "That man, he is out of the picture."

And so, despite the pit of fear in their stomachs, he and his wife decided to risk it.

❖ ❖ ❖

The going to the border was good.

They passed dozens of buses carrying patriotic Zimbabweans home for the march, flags fluttering. Gabriel,

Tino and their ZEF colleagues had been up most of the previous night sending word to their networks, helping to arrange transport, and here, in a matter of hours, was the result.

At 3pm, as was his habit, Kasper messaged Ellis back in Johannesburg to update him on their progress.

Ellis couldn't make the trip. His passport had expired, but he was also banned from Zimbabwe. During the 2013 election, while campaigning undercover for MDC candidates, a military vehicle had pulled over his Land Rover Discovery in Harare. Clare was in the car with him. The soldier in charge knocked on his window and calmly delivered a message: "You need to leave this country now. And don't come back. Understand?" Ellis got the message. He had left and never returned. Now, stuck in Johannesburg, he called contacts to donate fuel, air tickets and the like; he phoned MDC and NGO people he knew to mobilise their followers to march, and at the last minute added two rusty megaphones he'd dug out of his basement at home to the luggage on the back of the Legend.

"Take these," he told Kasper. "You'll be on the streets and you might need to have your voices heard."

Then he had hugged his assassin and wished him luck.

❖ ❖ ❖

On the road, at around 4pm, Kasper heard from Mutsvangwa, who was back in Harare already, that the war veterans press conference at the Rainbow Towers Hotel that afternoon had gone well.

Mutsvangwa had flown back to a different country from the one he'd skipped 12 days previously, the day of ED's dismissal. Back then he had feared the assassins were coming for him too, and he'd been terrified his flight might even be turned back. But now, with Mugabe on the ropes, he swaggered from the airport to the Rainbow Towers and announced preparations for the coup de grâce.

"The game is up for Mugabe, it's done, it's finished," he told the massed ranks of local and international media gathered at the hotel. "The generals have done a fantastic job. We want to restore our pride and [Saturday] is the day… we can finish the job the army started."

He had a warning for Mugabe and his "mad wife": that while the protests would be peaceful there was no telling what an angry mob might do if Mugabe failed to fall on his sword. "We could have a Gaddafi scenario on our hands," he said, "youths marching beyond State House to the Blue house itself."

❖ ❖ ❖

The Legend arrived at the Beit Bridge border on the Limpopo River close to 9pm. The queue to get in was long. Not since Bruce Springsteen played Harare in 1988, at the height of apartheid had so many people made their way overnight from South Africa to Zimbabwe.

Getting out of South Africa was easy; getting into Zimbabwe, not so much. Gabriel showed his passport and it went as he feared: his name was flagged and the official would not allow him in. They didn't sound any alarm, which was a relief, and everyone else could proceed, but not him.

Kasper wasn't having it. He wanted to assault the official, then thought better of it.

"United we stand, divided we fall," he muttered.

Then he conferred with Horse and Magic. An hour later

the Legend continued on its way across the border, while Gabriel and Horse turned back into South Africa, immigration on that side bemused as to how a Zimbabwean on a Zimbabwean passport had been denied entry into his own country.

It was there that Horse put the new means of crossing the border into action. Gabriel won't say exactly how they smuggled him in; suffice to say that having fled Zimbabwe in the trunk of a car 14 years previously, he re-entered his country in equally unconventional fashion in the early hours of Saturday morning, November 18th. They reconnoitred with the Toyota Legend at 3am, six hours later.

Sufficiently clear of the border, Kasper pulled the Legend over on a stretch of straight road and they all hopped out. There was no moon, but it was a clear starlit night and the air had the musky wet smell of weed grass, mopani leaves and wood smoke. Gabriel inhaled the smell of his rural childhood.

Then he got down on his knees by the side of the road, gathered some soil in his hands and licked it, a custom, if one has been away for a long time from home, to let the ancestors know you have returned.

As he knelt there, the taste of Zimbabwe on his tongue, tears started rolling down his face.

He turned to look up at his wife and three friends who were staring at him in the starlight.

They were crying too.

❖ ❖ ❖

That same morning, at my parents' farmhouse, Michael, John, Craig and I woke at dawn. We hopped into the battered Toyota Prado my brother-in-law always lends me when

I visit Zimbabwe, and raced west for the capital. The road is usually that gauntlet of police roadblocks but now, except for one military stop, it was completely clear. The police had remained confined to their posts since the Tuesday operation, and their absence lifted a burden.

It was apparent ten miles out of Harare that the march was going to be big.

We hit heavy traffic and weaved into the city on back roads, making our way to the Avenues, a neighbourhood on the edge of downtown which appeared to be a major gathering point for the march..

I expected a loud, angry crowd demanding the head of the dictator. What we found was a delirious city-wide block party. I had never seen Harare like this. Numbers are hard to calculate but there must have been a million people on the streets that day, dancing, singing, cheering, drinking like it was Mardi Gras or the Rio Carnival. Supermarkets ran out of Amstel, strangers passed Chibuku beer cartons and vodka bottles around, women posed for photos with smiling soldiers. It wasn't so much a march as a street party – with tanks. The song "Kutongo Kwaro", by Zimbabwe's musical superstar Jah Prayzah, about a returning hero, became the march soundtrack, blaring from every vehicle, street corner and apartment.

The organisers of the march – from the war veterans to the Joburg team to Pastor Evan Mawarire – had all implored the marchers not to make it a party political occasion, and aston-ishingly, people obliged. There were no ZANU-PF or MDC signs or regalia; no one chanted party slogans or gave political speeches. Posters had been made, but most lightheartedly ei-ther mocked Grace – "Leadership is not sexually transmitted" and "Lady Gaga Stop It!" – or implored the SADC and the AU to stay out.

What's real, and what is choreographed, though?

My friend Craig has read every book on the Rhodesian and Zimbabwe military, and he kept an eye on those soldiers, worried about their trigger fingers. "They're not wearing regimental insignia," he noted. He worried that the reason for this was to make them unaccountable should bullets start flying. Michael is a photographer, and looking now at the remarkable images he took that day, I'm struck by how photogenic the soldiers all were, as if handpicked for the occasion for their good looks. It wouldn't surprise me. Mutsvangwa had got the military to ensure immigration ignored the country's byzantine media restrictions and let all foreign journalists in. "I know the value of propaganda," he would tell me later. "As former guerillas we wanted to ensure public opinion was on our side. We carefully calibrated local and international opinion so we never fell on wrong side of it."

Having handsome, professional soldiers keeping the peace helped shape the narrative. (I later learned from Ellis that Mugabe's Friday attendance at the Open University graduation ceremony was also stage-managed: everything looked normal but close observers would have noticed his personal security detail was no longer the same.)

Helicopters buzzed overhead; it was said that Chiwenga had taken Mugabe up in one to make him see the game was up. This was later denied. Still, Mugabe shrugged off the crowd size anyway: Harare was MDC territory, he said later, so it wasn't surprising; his support was in rural areas.

❖ ❖ ❖

Gabriel, Kasper and co. arrived in the city at 10am, five hours behind schedule. They had dropped Gabriel's wife off with family members on a farm in Masvingo en route; it was decided it was too dangerous for them to stay together. They drove straight to Zimbabwe Grounds, next to Gwanzura Stadium, in Highfields, south of the city, where much of the relocated Johannesburg team began the day. The war veterans hadn't just filled the stadium with 10,000 people; they had filled the vast open grounds adjacent to it with half a million people and, as in central Harare, the atmosphere was jubilant.

Gabriel hit the ground running and never stopped. He met up with old MDC activist friends who were stunned to see him in the country; and was introduced by Mutsvangwa, Kasper and Horse to war veterans and soldiers he had once considered his enemies. Fourteen years on the run keeps you alert, though; Kasper promised they would keep him safe but, thrilled as he was to be there, Gabriel kept looking over his shoulder.

In 2008 Gabriel and his wife had bought a house in a Harare suburb where a relative now lived, but he had never seen it. He would later drive past it in the Legend, but he would not stay there now. It was too dangerous; instead, he stayed at Magic's place, not far from Kasper's two-bedroom shack in Mufakose. A successful lawyer with contacts in high places, he chose the protection of three rough township men he now considered friends.

Our paths might have crossed at one point that day.

Word came that Morgan Tsvangirai was addressing marchers near State House, the President's official residence, and Michael, Craig, John and I moved in that direction, until the volume of people proved too great and we were pushed back.

Gabriel was there, however. He had known Tsvangirai since the founding of the MDC in 1999 and been close to him ever since. He had last seen him in that Sandton hotel when he had vouched for Kasper. Now Gabriel saw him address tens of thousands of Zimbabweans right outside Mugabe's official residence: up until a few days ago, this would have been unthinkable.

Tsvangirai told the marchers that the day was not a party political event, but one of national unity. He paid tribute to the military – the same military that had brutally beaten his supporters into submission to prevent him from assuming the presidency after he'd won the elections in 2008. This time he was urging Mugabe to step down. "There is no way Mugabe can continue to pretend that everything is normal. He must go." For Gabriel that speech and the euphoria with which it was greeted was fulfilment of a long struggle.

❖ ❖ ❖

Unable to get close to State House, I recall us getting stuck outside a handsome British colonial building with high steel gates on Josiah Chinamano Avenue, not far from the Bronte Hotel.

What I know now, and did not know then, was that at that exact time, in the second-floor boardroom of that building, the next stage of the operation was falling into place.

You want the closing of a circle? These are the offices of Connecor, the investment company belonging to Emmerson Jr and his Indian friend, KC Shetty, mentioned in the prologue of this book. Junior had turned it over to Dr Jenfan Muswere, one of the people who'd helped ED escape, and Jenfan had turned it into a political command centre for

Lacoste operations. They called it The Pentagon. One of the reasons so many people had gathered in the Avenues for the march, it turned out, was because Jenfan had distributed free fuel, water and printed posters to Lacoste supporters from this very building. Moreover, these past couple of days, assisted by Monica Mutsvangwa, war veterans and allies in the Youth League, Jenfan had worked with ZANU-PF's ten provincial committees to coordinate and drive the resolutions to recall Mugabe as party leader, reinstate ED and expel Grace and leading members of G40.

Muswere communicated progress back to the safe house in Pretoria where ED and Junior were still poring over the Constitution and consulting with lawyers as to how to impeach Mugabe. Between calls to the provinces, Muswere joined the march or watched it from the windows and sent WhatsApp messages and photos to Junior about the sea of people on the streets outside.

the momentum is gathering – he says in one early Saturday morning message – *its massive*

Good work Cde well done – Junior replies.

whites in trucks walking with locals – Muswere says. (I wonder later, reading those messages, if that's me and my friends he has spotted. We were right there.)

Push comrade push, it's the last hour – Junior responds – *the old man must go*

he's gone – says Muswere confidently.

They sound like puppet masters.

❖ ❖ ❖

At around 3pm we got back into the truck and drove deeper into the throng. The crowd from Zimbabwe Grounds was now heading into the city, towards State House, planning on descending on the Blue Roof itself. Four white men driving through a politically charged crowd of black demonstrators, thousands of them ZANU-PF war veterans, might once have been a dangerous proposition.

Not this day. "You will get your land back now!" some of the protesters cheered, assuming we were white farmers. I did think my parents might like their title deed returned. There were requests for selfies, hugs from strangers, and the entire time we had 20 or 30 joyriders on the back of the truck, banging on the roof, jumping and cheering, prepared to go anywhere for the ride. "Sometimes we have to rearrange our minds and learn to live as one," an elderly out-of-work fitter and turner told me.

At the Scales of Justice monument outside the High Court, we stopped to take photos and a hand appeared from nowhere and snatched my iPhone. I turned around in panic but couldn't locate the person. The crowd pushed me forward to sit with marchers posing for pictures by the Scales of Justice. Suddenly the person with my phone appeared, took photographs of me and then handed it back.

"Happy Second Independence Day!" he grinned.

So what is real, and what is choreographed?

Politics is the art of persuasion. We like to believe we are rational, sober-minded people, but we are driven by emotion, and great political moments appeal to the irrational in us – the heart.

More than a million people of every race and political persuasion marched that day, Saturday, November 18th, and I am here to report: it felt good. In a broken, poverty-stricken country riven by hatred, anger, distrust and dysfunction, not a stone was thrown, not a window broken, not a shot fired. No one was killed, no one rioted. Organised and executed in a mere 36 hours, it went like clockwork in full view of the world. If you could bottle the planning, foresight, mood and atmosphere of that day you would have the elixir for a special country, something that usually only exists in fantasy – Black Panther's Wakanda perhaps. When I went to bed that night, I wondered how Mugabe could possibly survive.

Chapter 16

THE ENDGAME

The following afternoon, Sunday November 19th, ZANU-PF's Central Committee met to follow through on those provincial resolutions that Jenfan Muswere and Monica Mutsvangwa had helped coerce from that building in the Avenues in the previous two days. And so it happened: after almost 40 years as leader of the party that brought him to power, Mugabe was recalled, and Grace, Moyo, Kasukuwere and several other G40 stalwarts expelled.

A week earlier, every ZANU-PF provincial committee had enthusiastically lined up to expel ED; now, the power matrix having shifted, the exact same people fell into line to enthusiastically reinstate him.

Ah well, if it weren't for double standards, ZANU-PF might have none at all.

Christopher Mutsvangwa, like an African Zelig, was there too, and footage of him celebrating, dancing to Kutongo Kwaro, as the resolutions were announced, did the rounds. It was in March 2016 that he had been expelled from ZANU-PF and begun that quixotic one-man campaign against his former boss. It had taken him 20 months of planning, of forming strange alliances, but he had now helped return the favour.

The final nail in Mugabe's coffin – his resignation – was surely close.

Indeed the party had given Mugabe 24 hours to resign as the country's President, or they would begin impeachment proceedings against him.

Across town that same Sunday, meanwhile, Pastor Evan Mawarire, a thorn in the side of the dictatorship, and a victim of multiple arrests and assaults over the years, was holding a prayer vigil in Unity Square, imploring Mugabe, for the good of the nation, to go. He and his followers in the This Flag movement remained unmolested, which was also new. "My fear that day and Saturday was that people would get beaten, shot, murdered – as had happened before. But the soldiers treated us with respect and said, 'Just control people so they don't get out of hand and your guys will be fine.' That was amazing to me."

It all appeared to be coming together and on Sunday evening Mugabe seemed to have got the message too, for at around 6pm word spread that he was finally going to resign.

He would do so that night in a live television broadcast on ZBC at 8pm.

An expectant nation – and a global audience estimated at one billion people – gathered around TV sets.

I watched the speech with my friend Joanna and her husband who live in Harare.

I have mentioned her earlier. I was in Mozambique, racing back to Zimbabwe, when I received the group WhatsApp message from her in the early hours of Wednesday 15th, after the military strike: *A few bumps in the night. We don't watch Game of Thrones, we live it.*

She and her husband live in Borrowdale Brooke, the centre of the action.

Her neighbour, one street north, is General Chiwenga, and tanks were still posted out front and back of his Titanic mansion on that Sunday night, with soldiers on guard. The Blue Roof is 500 yards away, over the ridge, and for much of Saturday and Sunday helicopters buzzed over the roof, intimidating the occupants.

Denford Magora's Glass Pavilion is close by too, of course. Denford had spent much of the past few days updating his Facebook feed, correcting fake news reports that Grace had fled the country. He knew she hadn't because he could see her walking through the grounds of the estate in the mornings, deep in thought, clearly anxious about her world falling apart around her.

Few people believed what Denford had to say, however, because no one believed that someone could have such a clear and unobstructed view of the home of one of the most feared men in Africa.

Denford also noticed those days that every time Mugabe's cavalcade departed the Blue Roof to meet with the generals and the mediators at State House, his car, that black Mercedes 600, would be thoroughly searched by soldiers at the gate, who now answered to the generals.

It must have been the ultimate humiliation for the Old Man.

What on earth did they think he was hiding in there – weapons to stage a comeback?

I believe I know the answer, for as late as Sunday, November 19th, they were still searching for Saviour Kasukuwere and Jonathan Moyo.

Both Saviour and Moyo are writing books about the coup, but they spoke to me for this book without giving too much of their personal story away. I had long assumed that the pair fled the Blue Roof on the morning of November 15th, soon after arriving there, after the attacks on their homes. Not so. They left on Saturday, November 18th, the day of the march. "It turned out to be the most difficult time of all," said Moyo. "The helicopters were buzzing and the soldiers outside were on high alert." He will not say how they got out; just that it was terrifying and it was thanks to "angels" that they made it.

It would take them two more days to get to Tete in northern Mozambique, before flying on to Maputo where, according to Saviour, they were met by Mozambique's President Filipe Nyusi, an acquaintance of his, who put them in the care of his chief of police. Their lives had changed forever but the pair retained a shared sense of humour. Saviour said that when he told the police chief what their families had been through on the night of the attack, tears started rolling down the Mozambican's face. Saviour, always the tough guy, turned to Moyo and quietly muttered: "Good Lord – no chief of police should ever cry."

❖ ❖ ❖

The expected resignation speech is an hour late.

At 9pm, ZBC goes live to a red carpeted room in State House. The military commanders are shown first, seated left of screen, Chiwenga in the same fatigues he wore for his press conference. The mediators, including George Charamba and Mugabe's friend and spiritual advisor, Catholic priest Father Fidelis Mukonori, are seated right. The odd man out, next to Chiwenga, is Augustine Chihuri, the G40-aligned police chief, the man who supposedly tried to arrest Chiwenga at the airport. He and Chiwenga looked on good terms.

Mugabe finally appears, in a dark suit, looking small, frail and unsteady. He shakes hands with the commanders, who salute him, then sits at a table in front of two mics. He's immediately swallowed by the chair he's slumped in. With the military men hovering over him, it looks like a hostage video.

What follows is one of the most bizarre live broadcasts by a politician in modern television history.

As he's about to speak he shuffles some papers – one assumes the written speech – and they drop to the floor. Chiwenga picks them up and hands them to Chihuri next to him, who keeps them for the duration. This act will set off a host of conspiracy theories that are still raging today. Was the intended speech changed at the last minute?

Then he begins and he's a sad shadow of his usually articulate self. He looks his 93 years and his usually perfect diction and BBC English are gone. He rambles, slurs and mumbles for 20 minutes.

Incredibly, given the drama of the occasion and the roller-coaster of the past 13 days, it turns out to be a dull state-of-the-nation address. Six minutes in, he says the economy "is going through a difficult patch", at which point the speech itself hits a difficult patch, from which it never recovers.

It's about 15 minutes in that we all realise: he's not going! Thousands of social mediators are frantically asking, #WTF? Indeed, despite being dismissed as ZANU-PF leader earlier that day, he even says he's going to preside over the party's December congress.

By the end, when he's calling on the nation to "refocus", and put "shoulders to the wheel" for the promising agricultural season, millions of mouths across the world have fallen open in horror.

"*Asante Sana*," he says, signing off – Swahili for "thank you very much" – and with that he staggers to his feet, shakes more hands and is gone.

If it was a hostage video, he had flipped the script.

I confess I found a sneaking admiration for the Old Man at that minute.

They would have to hold a gun to his head to get him to go.

❖ ❖ ❖

The *Asante Sana* speech memes were instant and apt:

"How do you put a champagne cork back in a bottle? Ask eight million Zimbabweans."

"When you have a coup that's not a coup expect a resignation speech that's not a resignation speech."

Some people reacted with more horror than others. Recall Tino Mambeu of the ZEF? He had flown from Johannesburg to Harare for the march and watched the speech at the Bronte Hotel.

He expected Mugabe to be contrite, to say that he understood the anger and would take steps to leave office. Instead he seemed determined to stay, and Tino was suddenly gripped by fear.

"When we in ZEF started this thing back in 2016 it was just activism, a way for us in exile to keep the fire burning. I did not realise that I was in the middle of something so big, and when there was talk that this was a coup I started panicking – what are we going to do now? We are involved!"

He had reason to be afraid.

As he left the Bronte that night, a man in a suit approached him in the parking lot.

"We know who you are," the man said. "Watch out, we can kill you any time."

He took the next plane out of Harare.

I confess I exit the story at this point, too. My return flight to the US was the following day, Monday 20th, and I made sure I was on it, relieved to be flying back to my family in Virginia for Thanksgiving.

I would write a magazine piece about the coup and my experience of it that would lead to this book, but I was not around for the denouement.

I admit I got the fear.

I was frightened that Mugabe was not going anywhere and the fightback had begun.

The swapped speech conspiracies started raging instantly, and continue today.

Months later George Charamba told me his version of events. Charamba said he wrote the speech for Mugabe and the President made alterations, but the intention was never to resign. Chiwenga, on the other hand, expected Mugabe to go, and while he (Chiwenga) looks calm on screen, he's furious when Mugabe doesn't bow out.

"There was external calm against internal discord," Charamba says of Chiwenga's poker face.

Minutes after the speech, however, summoned to KG VI by the fuming General, Charamba gets a first-hand taste of some external discord when Chiwenga pins him against a wall, crushes his foot with his big military boot, and snarls at him: "What the fuck have you done, *watengesa* – you sold out!"

"Get your hands off me – don't you know I have saved your future?" Charamba splutters back.

He tells Chiwenga that Mugabe couldn't have resigned on live television with the military hovering over him like that.

This calmed the General down.

Intriguingly, given they were on opposing sides, Ellis, Gabriel and Kasper, the core of the Northgate team, were of the same view as Charamba that night, and not too worried.

"It would have looked terrible for Mugabe to resign seated in front of military officers accused of removing him," said Ellis. "When he said he was still in charge, that took away any chance of the operation being called a coup, and it took away any chance of foreign intervention to save him."

Instead, all it meant was that the game had to play itself out; Mugabe had to be removed by legal means, which was the idea in the first place, and there was still one big play left to make.

For, despite all his defiance, the Old Man was cornered. He had been fired by his own party on Sunday 19th, and by noon, Monday 20th, missed the deadline given by ZANU-PF to resign as President.

On Tuesday, November 22nd, impeachment proceedings against him would begin.

Cornered as he was, he was desperately trying to rally support, though, as was Grace.

Grace called Jacob Zuma for help, and Mugabe sent an emissary to the Zambian government to appeal to them for military assistance. To no avail. Months later Mugabe would complain of a mysterious "third hand" at play that had got to all the regional leaders before him. That third hand was Christopher Mutsvangwa.

Another cunning last-minute gambit was an offer from Mugabe to resign in favour of Chiwenga – as long as Chiwenga was in charge, not ED. Perhaps Mugabe recognised a certain ambition in his general; only an ambitious man builds the biggest house on the tallest hill. Chiwenga, no fool, refused. He'd put down enough coups to know how to carry out the perfect one. Besides, he still had time. He was only 61.

Another ploy was a call between Mugabe and ED arranged by the mediators, in which Mugabe implored ED to come back and they could talk it out. He actually asked ED why he had run away. "The people around you have caused me to leave the country. My life was in danger and they wanted to eliminate me," ED said he told Mugabe, as quoted in Ray Ndlovu's *In the Jaws of the Crocodile*.

After initially suggesting he would come back to talk it over, that plan was quickly scuttled. Instead, ED released a long statement on Tuesday 21st saying that he would not return until Mugabe had resigned. Referring to the mass march of Saturday 18th he wrote: "To me the voice of the people is the voice of God, and their lack of trust in the leadership of President Mugabe has been expressed."

And so, with desperation setting in at the Blue Roof, and hearing word of those plaintive calls to Zuma and other regional leaders, the military and the Johannesburg team upped the pressure some more.

According to Mutsvangwa, he contacted Brigadier General SB Moyo and asked him to send a tank to the Blue Roof. A crowd of demonstrators descended on the property at the same time.

They were loud and angry and they appeared to have commandeered the tank. The occupants of the Blue Roof could hear them. The generals now told Mugabe and Grace that they didn't know how long they could hold the braying mob. It was the Gaddafi scenario that Mutsvangwa had warned about days earlier. The military had now turned into Mugabe's protectors, imploring him to help himself by letting go.

What the occupants of the Blue Roof didn't know was that the crowd outside was choreographed, too. It was staged. There were only about 50 demonstrators, bussed in for the purpose, and they were in fact rather orderly, gathered at the northeastern wall of the property, near the back entrance to Borrowdale Brooke. Denford Magora could hear them from his unbuilt house, although he couldn' see them, and they were in no way about to scale the walls.

If you had been able to make your way to that corner of the property, you might have recognised three of the demonstrators on the tank. They were shouting into megaphones, getting their voices heard; megaphones lent to them by a friend of theirs named Ellis in Johannesburg. I did not know Kasper, Magic and Horse then, but they were playing the game a few hundred yards from my friend Joanna's house, and they were playing it perfectly.

And so it was that on the afternoon of Tuesday, November 21st, impeachment proceedings against President Robert Mugabe, Zimbabwe's only ruler for 37 years, began.

Let's close more circles.

So many people were present for the occasion that parliament relocated to the Harare International Conference Centre at the Rainbow Towers Hotel. The Rainbow Towers happened to be where the Johannesburg team had also relocated on the

Friday. The game had literally come to them.

It wasn't just every parliamentarian and much of the world's media who wanted to be there. The public did too, and the galleries were full. Taking their seats upstairs were four men who had spent the last two weeks running on adrenaline: Gabriel, Kasper, Magic and Horse. The latter three were just back from tank duty at the Blue Roof, while Gabriel, along with Mutsvangwa, had been to meetings at various western embassies to update diplomats and ask them what they could expect in the months ahead. Mutsvangwa had arrived at the HICC too, but was downstairs with his wife, who was a sitting senator. Only Ellis was missing from the Core Group but it was 3pm and Kasper messaged him as he always did at around that time, part of his routine.

Shamwari how are u – he wrote.

They got comfortable on the balcony, anticipating history. Only Gabriel scanned the room. He looked to his right at three men a few seats away. They were looking right at him. They did not look happy.

❖ ❖ ❖

There was doubt that ZANU-PF would succeed with impeachment on its own. The party had many G40 members and there was no guarantee they would vote against Mugabe. To avoid disaster the Lacoste faction needed the support of the opposition MDC who were tabling their own impeachment motion. There was more backroom dealing before the MDC came aboard the ZANU PF version.

Then there was the question of who was going to table the motion. If the motion failed, that person could be charged for treason, and everyone was understandably wary.

A woman stepped up. A woman who had gone to war for her country at the age of 15, in 1976, and who three months later survived an attack by Rhodesia's Selous Scouts on her training camp.

Her name was Monica Mutsvangwa. She tabled it. Mugabe was unfit for office and in dereliction of duty, the motion read; he's too old and frail; falls asleep in meetings, and in general embarrasses the nation.

The motion was seconded by James Maridadi from the MDC.

However, no sooner had Monica forwarded it than she was approached on the floor by a stern-faced, plump figure in a suit – Happyton Bonyongwe, a Mugabe loyalist who was the CIO boss for many years and was now the Justice Minister.

"You are going to lose your head," he threatened her.

She didn't flinch. "I went to war, I know what's right. You don't scare me."

And then, just before the hearing was about to proceed, something bizarre happened on the house floor. There was a sudden flurry of activity around the speaker, Jacob Mudenda. Bonyongwe, the Mugabe loyalist, had handed a letter to him, and a couple of MDC MPs had raced over to him. The speaker asked on mic if its contents were accurate, and Bonyongwe nodded.

Word spread around the great hall before it was even confirmed – Mugabe had resigned!

Indeed, by the time Mudenda read – "Following my verbal communication with the Speaker at 13.53 hours… I, Robert Gabriel Mugabe… formally tender my resignation as the President of the Republic of Zimbabwe with immediate effect," – the vast auditorium had erupted in jubilation.

Within seconds the country erupted too. You could hear the hooting and screaming from the streets outside in the hotel lobby. For the second time in four days Harare embarked on a wild and raucous party that would go on late into the night. Bars and taverns would run out of beer, soldiers would be hoisted aloft in celebration, and joyous music would blare from a million speakers.

After 37 years of rule by one man, the country would soon have a new leader and a fresh chance.

Tears rolled down Gabriel's face that afternoon as he hugged his unlikely friends. At last the nightmare was over.

He was so emotional he didn't even care when one of the surly men near him in the gallery walked past and said to his colleagues: "It's them, they must be dealt with."

Chapter 17

THE GAME WITH NO END

If this were Hollywood our story might end here.

The guys would wake up, clear their bleary eyes and marvel at how they had managed to pull off the impossible. A misfit team of rivals, a disparate group of men and women who might never have met each other but who risked it all for something bigger than themselves and won.

But Zimbabwe is not Hollywood, of course, and history does not run in a straight line.

The guys celebrated late into the night. They didn't have to go far. The lobby of the Rainbow Towers has a popular bar and it pumped like a nightclub on Tuesday evening. There's video footage of various members of the team, beers in hand, dancing, celebrating the end of Mugabe's reign and saluting the wild ride they had all been on.

"We are the liberators!" Kasper cheered. "We are the people who started this thing, way back, with this man Tom Ellis!" He messaged Ellis in Johannesburg and told him about the celebrations.

This time, unlike last Thursday at the Holiday Inn, they

hadn't jumped the gun. Mugabe really had resigned and while it would take a long time to even begin to fix the country, they had made a start.

Kasper, Magic, Horse and Gabriel drank heavily that night, then weaved their way back to Mufakose in the Legend in the early hours. But they were still too pumped with adrenaline, too conditioned to the pace of the game these past months, to sleep long. They woke early on Wednesday, November 22nd, a day of resplendent sunshine, and Gabriel suggested that they take a drive together.

He wanted to celebrate with his wife who had shouldered a lot of his pain and agony over the years, and suggested they meet her at a rural plot in KweKwe, in Zimbabwe's midlands, which he'd bought in 2002 and, like his Harare house, had also never seen. They could slaughter a cow that night, Gabriel said, grill it on an open fire, drink under the stars and finally relax after months of stress.

And so the four of them set off at 9am on a road trip, Kasper behind the wheel.

KweKwe is a three-hour drive away but Kasper had someone to meet beforehand in Waterfalls, a Harare suburb, so they headed there first. At around 10am, on a busy commercial street in Waterfalls, Gabriel and Horse banged on the roof of the Legend for Kasper to pull over so they could buy some cigarettes and Cokes at a roadside kiosk. They all got out, Kasper and Magic stretching their legs by the car, while Gabriel and Horse wandered over to the kiosk and waited in line.

There is a world of difference between the hunted and the hunter. Gabriel had been looking over his shoulder for so long now that it had become instinct, second nature. Until Kasper and co. turned against their institutions, they had always been on the other side: the hunters. They were conditioned differently.

So it's perhaps not surprising that it was Gabriel who first sensed the danger.

He was by the kiosk, watching the street, when he looked left and saw a sedan pull up about 20 yards away, with three men in it. He looked right and saw another vehicle pull up, this one with tinted windows, ahead of the Legend. Kasper and Magic were yawning by the car and didn't notice; Horse was in line for the Cokes.

Then Gabriel saw a man in a suit and tie across the road from him. He was pretending to be messaging on his cell, but he was clearly filming them through a gap in his fingers. Gabriel wondered where he had seen the man's face before. Then it hit him: he was one of the men who had been sitting near them at the conference centre the day before, the one who had been staring at them, and said, "It's them, they must be dealt with."

Gabriel nudged Horse, panic rising: "Horse, look, these guys – I don't trust them."

Horse turned around, clocked the scene and whistled, "Oh shit."

Now the men from the two parked vehicles stepped out. They wore jeans, collared shirts and shades. Kasper had noticed them too and alerted Magic: six men, three on each side, hands by their hips, walking slowly towards them, as if for a showdown in a Western. Magic had a gun on him and Kasper saw him reach for it but he knew the men approaching were armed too.

He held up a finger to his partner and shook his head. "Not this time, my friend."

Magic listened to him, as he always did.

Kasper knew they had no chance of shooting it out, and if they ran for it they could all be caught. But if the two of them – he and Magic – gave themselves up, there was a chance Gabriel and Horse could get away. Besides, it was Gabriel they had promised to protect. They would sacrifice themselves for him.

Kasper decided all this in a split second.

He gave a loud sharp whistle directed at Horse, who instantly recognised the signal: run!

Horse jabbed Gabriel in the ribs and the two of them bolted like startled antelope down a dirt path beside the kiosk that ran between two low-slung residential buildings. There was a busy road 500 yards away, beyond an area of open grassland and a stand of tall gum trees. They ran for their lives, hearts pounding, not looking back. They had no idea if they were being chased, or what was happening to Kasper and Magic back at the truck; they just knew they needed to get away.

Magic raised his hand from his hip now; and Kasper nodded at the men as they reached them.

"What is it you want?" he snarled. "Why us?"

They didn't answer.

They bundled them away in the two cars, leaving the Legend on the roadside.

❖ ❖ ❖

Gabriel and Horse ran for three miles, past the tree line and up the road until, exhausted, and finally feeling sufficiently clear of danger, they jumped on a public bus that took them into town.

Before long Gabriel's phone rang.

It was a woman's voice. "Chairman, we are at Waterfalls Police Station, come back!"

He didn't recognise the voice and he wondered how she knew he was the Chairman. Only those at the Command Centre in Johannesburg knew him as that.

"Why should I come there?"

"We are all here; come join us!"

He asked her to put Kasper or Magic on the line, but at that point the call went dead.

Lying low with Horse in central Harare, Gabriel called a human rights lawyer he knew and asked him to go to Waterfalls Police Station. The lawyer didn't want to go. The country was on a knife edge and it was clear that the side that had lost – G40 and Mugabe loyalists – were going to lash out. There were a lot of people in intelligence, the police and even the military not on board with regime change.

The lawyer eventually went but reported back to Gabriel that no one named Kasper or Magic and no one fitting their description was detained at Waterfalls.

❖ ❖ ❖

That Wednesday afternoon, two private jets landed at Robert Mugabe International, bringing ED, Junior and their entourage home from their exile. Justice Maphosa and Thabiso came too. Auxillia and Junior's wife were there to greet them, along with a massive security escort. A cavalcade of about a hundred cars and outriders rushed them home to Helensvale through throngs of cheering people.

It was two weeks to the day that ED's lawyer had released that letter to the press, the one he had written in the frantic hours before fleeing Harare, the one that said he would be home "in a few weeks" to lead the country.

Those words had been roundly ridiculed at the time.

Yet, here he was, the Two Weeks Man, ready to take the reins.

Soon after getting home to Helensvale, he was out again, for a briefing with Chiwenga at army headquarters, and then at a ZANU-PF gathering in downtown Harare, where he addressed thousands of delirious supporters.

"*Pamberi ne* ZANU-PF!" he chanted – forward with ZANU-PF – "*Pamberi!*" they responded.

❖ ❖ ❖

At that exact time, seven miles away, Kasper and Magic were bleeding heavily, getting the shit beaten out of them.

They hadn't been taken to Waterfalls but to One Commando barracks near the airport. Their captors were not CIO but Military Intelligence. Not all the military were with Chiwenga and ED, and those of them allied to G40 and Mugabe were using the brief window they had left to dish out vicious retribution.

Kasper and Magic were given a blanket each and walked to separate cells.

The cells were wet, and smelled of urine and feces.

Then, sometime late on Wednesday afternoon, the beatings began.

It turned out their captors knew everything.

They had seen Kasper in the Facebook video that went viral – the premature celebration with Mutsvangwa in the hotel in Johannesburg – and they had matched him up with video and photographs they had taken of three men with megaphones on a tank at the Blue Roof.

But they knew about him and Magic and Horse from way before that.

They knew about all the meetings at the far garden table of the Bronte Hotel with Mutsvangwa, and with military and intelligence people Kasper had recruited on his suicide missions.

They told them what they knew about their project in between beating them.

"We installed cameras at the Bronte to film you" – whack, fist to the mouth.

"You were late, my brother, it was all done," spluttered Kasper, spitting blood on the floor.

Another punch to the face – "We knew you were planning something."

"So why could you not stop us?"

"We had no proof – we could not hear what you were saying" – punch to the gut.

"We used a cover," gasped Kasper, doubling over.

"That stupid company you had!"

Kasper laughed through the kicks and punches.

"DAKO Solar Power," he said, "that was our front. It fooled you!"

"You kept moving your meeting places" – punch to the nose.

"We're not stupid," spluttered Kasper. "I was converting, left and right, full scale."

He swallowed the metallic taste of blood.

"You can keep hitting me but I am dying," spat Kasper.

"What do you mean you are dying?"

"Already I am HIV positive, I am infected."

The men stopped the beatings, looked at each other, then at the blood on the floor and on their hands.

They didn't know if he was lying or not.

Then they started again, but with their boots.

❖ ❖ ❖

Gabriel knew he had to leave Harare that night.

Horse was probably being hunted too, so it wasn't safe sticking with him.

He tried to get a message to Mutsvangwa about what had happened but Mutsvangwa was caught up with the return of ED. He tried to call a military guy Kasper had introduced him to during the march, but he was worried his phone was being tapped. He saved a call for his wife, told her he was on his way to her in Masvingo that night. Then he turned off his phone. His lawyer friend arranged a ride for him at 2am and they drove through the night. He got to his wife in Masvingo, Thursday morning, at daybreak.

They spent the morning together then decided to split up.

Mrs Shumba would go to the KweKwe plot and try to leave for South Africa from there. She had a passport and was in the country legally. Gabriel was at risk – having entered illegally – and a danger to her. "Better one dead parent than two," they decided.

He laid low on Thursday, sleeping on the roof of the farm-house in case they came for him there. He had no idea what, if anything, Kasper or Magic might reveal under torture about his whereabouts.

Gabriel did get hold of Mutsvangwa on Thursday and told him what had happened. Then he called a contact at the US Embassy and asked him to get word out to find Kasper and Magic.

Then he messaged Ellis the bad news.

❖ ❖ ❖

It turned out it was Horse the MI guys really wanted.

Horse had been one of them – MI – and they knew he was part of Kasper's crew.

But Kasper wasn't telling them where Horse lived.

More beatings, truncheons this time.

"You know Itai Dzamara came through here," they warned as they hit him.

Dzamara, a much-loved opposition activist, was abducted in Harare in March 2015 and never seen again.

Magic was having a worse time of it in his cell. He had poor eyesight – hence the thick glasses – and the punches to the head were blurring his sight even more and giving him a killer headache. He couldn't even see the blows coming.

They tortured them both for 11 hours until, eventually, worn down and exhausted, some time on Thursday 23rd, Kasper said he had had enough and would take them to Horse.

They piled into a van and headed to Mufakose.

He directed them to a small two-bedroom shack up the street from a gymnasium.

Bloodied and bruised, he stumbled out of the van in hand-cuffs.

There was a kid outside the shack, practising karate moves in the dust.

Kasper nodded at him. The kid ran off up the street.

He entered. It was a tiny room with a single bed and an old TV set with a Hello Kitty toy on it. The only wall decorations were a poster of a soccer team and a kid's silver medal from a karate tournament. There was a bag of ice in the sink keeping the milk cool.

The woman inside was shocked to see four men enter, one

of them battered and bruised in handcuffs.

"I am arrested, at One Commando!" Kasper spluttered to his wife.

The captors cursed – this wasn't Horse's place, it was Kasper's house!

They dragged him out and threw him back in the van.

He was laughing at them now.

"You think I am stupid? Fuck you!"

If his son was smart, and Kasper knew he was, the boy would now have the license plates of the vehicle he had been in, and would have run up the street to tell Horse.

❖ ❖ ❖

The MI guys took Kasper back to One Commando but they didn't keep him and Magic there.

They booked them into the police station at Waterfalls, the jurisdiction in which they had been picked up. From there they were taken to Central Police Station, to be dealt with by CID Law and Order.

Magic and Kasper spent three days in the cells there. Then they were finally taken to Mbare Magistrates Court and from there to Harare Remand Prison, where they were detailed as D Class – dangerous criminals.

❖ ❖ ❖

On Friday the 24th Gabriel escaped the country at Beit Bridge, the same frontier he had smuggled himself across a few days earlier, this time disguised as a truck driver. He had now come in and out of Zimbabwe three times illegally. He hoped that this time was the last. He found his way back to Johannesburg, his wife and kids. In the meantime, he,

Ellis and Horse had contacted NGOs and human rights groups and MDC networks in Zimbabwe, who had managed to locate Kasper and Magic.

They were released from D Block and allowed home after a week inside.

There had been nothing to charge them with.

Magic could barely see any more, even with his glasses on. His shins would soon be scarred from walking into chairs and tables, but he was home – bruised, battered, yet alive.

Kasper returned home too. His kids were waiting for him; his wife was peeling mealies under a tree out the back.

He limped into the shack, saw the medal on the wall, the Hello Kitty on the TV set. There was a cold Amstel his wife had bought for him, next to the braai meat and the milk on the ice in the sink.

He thought: one day it might be good to get a new fridge.

He walked outside into the sunlight. It was 3pm on one of the last days of November 2017.

He got his phone and sent a WhatsApp message to a friend in Johannesburg.

Shamwari – he said.

u ok – came the instant reply.

i am ok – he replied – *but its not over. the game goes on.*

Epilogue

THE HANGOVER

On Friday, November 24th, 2017, Kasper and Magic still in detention, Emmerson Mnangagwa was sworn in as Zimbabwe's new President in a ceremony at Harare's National Sports Stadium. The entire escape team was there – Junior and his twin brothers, looking snappy in designer suits, as well as cousin Tarry, Limping Jack, Jenfan Muswere and Gertrude, the tavern owner who'd drafted some friends in to help out in the border town that day. The Mutsvangwas were in attendance too; Christopher would soon be named Special Advisor to the President – acknowledgment of his role masterminding diplomatic and media efforts to sell the coup as not a coup. Monica would be appointed Governor of Manicaland and, later, Minister of Information.

ED, no great orator, nevertheless gave a rousing speech. "I intend, nay, am required to serve our country as the President of all citizens, regardless of colour, creed, religion, tribe, totem or political affiliation," he said, before adding a tribute to his friend, mentor and "father of the nation", Mugabe.

It was hard to believe that 18 days earlier Mugabe – or a

faction of his followers – had wanted ED dead.

The future looked promising.

Three weeks later Tom Ellis made his first visit to Zimbabwe since being ordered to leave and not come back in 2013. He didn't come alone. He brought an eager group of South African businessmen, eyeing investment opportunities. What started slowly soon snowballed: from January 2018 Ellis visited Zimbabwe almost every week for eight months, flying in on a Monday, returning to Clare in Johannesburg on a Friday, and every time he came with – or met with – dozens of potential investors: engineers, road builders, pipeline contractors, energy execs, airline operators, tech and software CEOs, conservation, hotel and tourism entrepreneurs, and farm and agribusiness companies.

I met with Ellis on one of his visits and watched him in action. He would host meetings in Harare's bars – Corky's and the Tin Roof being his favourite – choosing a quiet corner table, cold Zambezi beer at the ready. There would be a group of people nearby waiting to meet him, and they would come over one by one for a chat. In that soft voice of his, Ellis would offer advice, tell them about openings, suggest locals to meet or partner with, and give out the names of government contacts to ease the way. He sounded like an evangelist. "The potential is incredible," he told me. "We'll open this place up and it will fly. You'll see."

He used his talents in other ways, too; in December 2017, working with Monica Mutsvangwa, he helped a third-generation white farming family named Smart get their farm in Manicaland back after a long and agonising ordeal. The story made international news.

Gabriel also started visiting the country, and he no longer

looked over his shoulder. The November trip for the march had been a stressful blur; now he came in legally and took his time. What he saw depressed him. "There were people in my rural village who had returned from the city to live there because in Harare they couldn't afford to buy food. At least in the village they could grow something." The collapsed infrastructure – ruined roads, power cuts, abandoned farms, closed factories – shocked him. He said it looked like a different country to the one he had fled in 2003, like a bomb had hit it.

Kasper was back in Zimbabwe full time. Was he in or out of the Institute? Who could say? Can you ever leave? He and Magic (who was nearly blind now), were looking to sue the government for the torture they'd endured at the hands of MI and had found legal representation. Kasper kept in daily contact with the Team, as was his routine. Indeed it was Ellis who introduced me to him at the Bronte one morning in March 2018. We sat at the same far garden table where he, Magic and Horse had sat during the Push, posing as solar energy salesmen, persuading powerful men to turn against Mugabe and G40. The first thing he did was scowl at me, pretty much in the way he must have greeted Ellis that afternoon at the traffic light. Then he said: "I have an amazing story to tell but it's not over. We are soldiering on."

He meant G40 were still out there, but he was wary of the military, too; he knew certain elements wanted power for themselves.

❖ ❖ ❖

What coup – even one deemed not to be a coup – ever produces a stable democratic government or anything other than a strong man? Come to power by the gun you leave by the gun is the old adage. But at what point can you judge something to be a success or failure? After six months? One year? Five years? There was a famous exchange in 1972 in which the Chinese premier Zhou Enlai was asked during a visit by Henry Kissinger what he thought of the French Revolution. "Too soon to tell," he replied.

Zimbabweans didn't have that long to wait.

Immediately there were signs that ED was in trouble.

His first cabinet was a horror show: nothing but recycled deadwood from the old ZANU-PF. The Transitional National Authority that had supposedly been agreed on in all those clandestine meetings that Ellis organised between ED people and MDC brass never materialised. According to one of the Northgate team, representatives from the MDC presented a list of their names for a TNA to ED's team on the 17th floor of the Rainbow Towers in December 2017. ED's people accepted some, nixed others and sent the list back. When Morgan Tsvangirai saw it he rejected it.

"We can do better," he apparently said. "This is less than we had in the GNU [Government of National Unity]."

Is this account true? Who can say?

ED was old guard in ZANU-PF, after all. He was one of them, and he needed to keep the old guard happy. Furthermore, despite being the much-vaunted Crocodile, the strong man, he was actually politically vulnerable within his own party. If you remember, the impeachment process against Mugabe had needed support from the MDC to pass, because not enough ZANU-PF parliamentarians were on board with it. Added to which, ED owed his position entirely to General Chiwenga – a man with his own ambitions – and what did Chiwenga owe the MDC? The opposition had spent 18 years trying to get rid of Mugabe, and Chiwenga had pulled it off in about eight hours. Now they wanted a slice of the pie?

Whatever the truth, Tsvangirai tragically passed away on February 4th, 2018, after a long struggle with cancer, and the new MDC leader, Nelson Chamisa, a charismatic if callow young man with the speaking style of a travelling preacher, was made from different cloth from his sedate, conciliatory predecessor.

Chamisa and others in the MDC might have recalled how the last power-sharing agreement had come back to bite them. Back in 2009, they had helped the country – and ZANU-PF – back on its feet with the GNU and then – wham – they had been annihilated in the 2013 elections. What was the point of partnering with these guys? They were still ZANU-PF. "Same bus, different driver," they said. I recall my mother taking that line for a spin during the coup – the last words she ever spoke about Zimbabwe politics.

ZANU-PF owned it all.

ED did appear to be trying to do the right things, or at least saying the right things: he tweeted furiously about peace, unity, love, and the "new Zimbabwe" being "open for business". "Open for business" became his mantra and ZANU-PF's new slogan – quite a change from Marxist-Leninism, socialism and the violent redistribution of previous decades. But how does a party forged in bloody revolution and in power for 37 years, with all the corruption and graft that comes with that, ever change its spots?

The economy continued its slide. Nothing would improve until Western governments and institutions recognised a new regime, and that could only happen with an election.

ED finally announced one for July 30th, 2018, and said all

international observers would be welcome – a big departure from Mugabe's days. International media would be allowed in too, yet another change.

And so the parties geared up for the campaigns.

Despite the economic morass, everyone assumed that residual sympathy for ED for removing Mugabe, and the enduring weakness of the MDC – dissolute and divided, they were at their lowest ebb since their founding in the late 1990s – would mean a walkover for ED and ZANU-PF.

And here's where things began to turn.

Once upon a time political lines in Zimbabwe were simple and easily drawn: there was Mugabe and ZANU-PF in one corner, and there was the opposition. But now the old lines had fractured and blurred. Some in the MDC supported the coup; others didn't; some in ZANU-PF were with ED; others despised him. These realignments tore friendships and even families apart. Meanwhile the citizenry were impatient, opportunists looked to fill the power vacuum, and the military were waiting in the wings.

Few realised it at first but the removal of Mugabe had rendered the country a tinderbox.

That should have been evident on June 25th, 2018, when ED survived an assassination attempt at a rally in Bulawayo, all captured on film. A grenade was thrown into a crowded VIP tent just as he stepped off stage. Two people were killed and 49 wounded, but he survived. "I am used to these attempts," he said with a shrug, adding that he knew who did it – presumably the same G40 elements who tried to poison him. Incredibly, instead of responding with a brutal crackdown as Mugabe would have done had he been the target, ED played the statesman: he called for peace and unity, and continued the campaign.

By July, meanwhile – election month – Nelson Chamisa, a terrific speaker, was finding his voice; and the democratic space that the coup had opened up – as Gabriel and Ellis both believed it would – had indeed invigorated the opposition. They could campaign freely now, without threat of violence as before, and their urban supporters, social-media savvy, were energised. Suddenly their rallies were packed, seas of people wearing MDC red, and footage of those rallies zoomed around Facebook and Twitter, bringing more support. Political campaigns are about momentum and the opposition – exhausted by 37 years of ZANU-PF rule, and tired that little had changed in eight months – seized their moment.

They were also playing hardball, which Morgan Tsvangirai, often a conciliator, rarely had. Senior MDC leaders were now saying ED's government was a "military junta" and that the coup was illegal. This dismayed some people, including Gabriel, who was himself an MDC supporter. "I was mystified to hear them say there was a coup and this was a junta because I personally spoke to Morgan on the streets on November 18th. He was leading the march, as were others in MDC. I heard them call for Mugabe to go."

Moreover, the language they were using was the same as a certain spin doctor who was also finding his voice...

Enter our old friend Jonathan Moyo.

The routed members of the G40 faction had been silent since November, humiliated and afraid.

Except, that is, for the Professor. It wasn't his style to keep quiet.

After escaping to Mozambique with Saviour in November 2017, he had made his way to exile in Nairobi, Kenya, his wife's home country. He was wary the new regime would "do a Kagame" on him – a reference to Rwanda's president who is prone to sending assassins to foreign lands to take out his political opponents. Yet, so far, he was unmolested. He said that on his wife's advice he had taken to wearing a disguise in public: a tweed cap "to cover my egg-shaped head". Afraid or not, it was from Kenya, soon after his arrival, that he began tweeting furiously about the coup being illegal, the country being in the grip of a military junta, and its leaders, chiefly ED and Chiwenga, being murderous "Gukurahundists" – responsible for the Matabeleland massacres in the 1980s.

At first few people paid attention. He was on the losing side after all. But, as little improved in Zimbabwe, he started gaining traction. Indeed, by mid-2018, the Prof was very much in the picture and all he needed was a cell phone and a Twitter handle. Welcome to the 21st century. A strange and unlikely marriage of convenience now appeared to have developed between the MDC and the ousted G40. Apparently, they shared a common enemy.

A certain power couple in Harare confirmed this, in another bizarre twist in the game, on the eve of the election. The very day before voting, Robert and Grace Mugabe, who had been allowed to stay unmolested in the Blue Roof since the coup, with a US$10 million government payout, opened the gates of their palace to the world's press. Having harassed and tormented journalists and media organisations for decades, Mugabe needed them now, and they hung on his every word.

What happened that afternoon was astonishing and surreal: sliding off a leather armchair set up in the garden pagoda (that Denford Magora could see from his roof deck), the 94-year-old former President, Grace hovering over him, proceeded to denounce ED's government as illegitimate and endorse… Nelson Chamisa of the MDC for the presidency.

It was as big a bombshell as the war vets splitting from Mugabe in 2016.

And, this being electoral hardball, far from rejecting the endorsement of the man they spent 20 years trying to remove, the MDC welcomed it. Who could blame them? By voting day they were telling their supporters they were going to win and the massive sea of red at Chamisa's final Harare rally – compared to the desultory crowds turning up for ED – seemed to confirm it.

It's easy to picture panic in ZANU-PF ranks at this point, not to mention a rising anger among certain military commanders who were not used to the open, free democratic game: they didn't expect this! Besides, they might have thought: where were the MDC in November, 2017 before we did this thing – our thing? They were nowhere, and now they think they can come and take it from under our noses?

And yet and yet…

We have been here so many times before. When the results came in, ZANU-PF, whose support is not in cities but rural areas, where people don't live on Twitter or Facebook, appeared to have won parliament in a landslide. The presidential ballot turned out to be much closer but ED squeaked it out with 50.8% – conveniently, just enough to avoid a run-off.

But then, by August 1st, 2018, it had all fallen apart anyway.

Amid accusations of massive vote-rigging, a protest by MDC supporters in Harare turned into a riot. Cars were burned, buildings torched. And then the military responded. Eight months after putting on a professional and disciplined show for the world's media, they reverted to type in front of the exact same watching media: soldiers from what looked like a ragtag militia opened fire on the streets of Harare, killing six civilians and wounding dozens more, most of them shot in the back. One of the dead was a 41-year-old fruit vendor and father of four, who was just manning his fruit stand, not part of any protest.

If Jonathan Moyo, the MDC and all those saying "same bus, different driver" needed to present evidence that nothing had changed – here they had it.

And no Western government watching that disaster considered Zimbabwe open for business.

❖ ❖ ❖

I write this in the first week of February 2019, exactly six months since that shooting.

ED is still the President, but the MDC have not recognised him as legitimate. General Chiwenga is now Vice-President, removed from military command, but with what still seems like great power. After his election win, ED named an inclusive and stronger cabinet, cutting much of the deadwood and bringing in a World Bank technocrat to run the all-important Finance Ministry. He even named a white woman, Zimbabwe's Olympic swimming legend Kirsty Coventry, as Youth, Sports, Arts and Recreation Minister. (He appointed Jenfan Muswere, who had done so much of the leg work during the escape and securing the recall resolutions, Deputy Minister of Information, Communications, Technology and Cyber Security.).

But the country is as divided as ever and still on the ropes. There are desperate fuel shortages, queues several miles long and no cash in the banks. Demonstrations against an exorbitant fuel price hike in mid-January produced another brutal response from the military, with 12 dead and hundreds beaten and arrested. Pastor Evan Mawarire, who had helped lead the November 18th March, and spoke glowingly about the courtesy of the soldiers that day, was arrested too, and spent two weeks in prison.

ED was abroad during the crackdown, flying around the world in a massive private jet, courting investors, having left VP Chiwenga in charge. While away he tweeted a statement denouncing the "wanton violence and vandalism" – not of the soldiers, but of the demonstrators. He added cheerily that Alrosa, a Russian diamond company, was going to start operations in Zimbabwe.

No Zimbabwean believes Russian investment in a diamond mine will fix any of their problems.

Besides, Zimbabweans couldn't read the tweet anyway: the government had shut the internet down.

Had the entire game come down to this tawdry denouement?

It would seem so.

Then again, it depends on the length of your view.

Robert Mugabe was in power for 37 years, having come to power after a bitter 15-year-long civil war. Before that there was a century of colonialism and oppressive white rule, and before that indigenous peoples waged brutal wars against each other and all that time, empires rose and fell. This has been going on in this corner of Africa for centuries. Sometimes I look at Zimbabwe and think chaos, violence and conflict are the normal way of things; it's the few times we depart from that way of life that are abnormal.

That's the cycle that needs to be broken.

And here's the thing: there's already a template for how to break it. You don't even have to go back centuries. You only have to go back to November 18th, 2017 and a march on the streets of Harare.

The way I see it, the art of politics is to get the wrong people to do the right thing. On November 18th, 2017, the wrong people – the much-feared Zimbabwe military, the country's war veterans and elements of ZANU-PF, a party that has driven Zimbabwe into a ditch – actually did the right thing. The military sheathed their weapons and treated citizens with dignity and respect for a day; war veterans called for peace and unity; and members of two political parties who despise each other, invited to put away their hatred and enmity for a day, did the same. Yes, it was choreographed and it was manipulated and on some level it was all for show, but all politics is manipulation. Not to get all starry-eyed but the way I see it, the wrong people helped stage a day of peace and unity because, deep in their souls, they know that this is what the overwhelming majority of ordinary people want all the time. To paraphrase the conclusion to a magazine piece I published soon after the events of that momentous day: if Zimbabweans could run their country with the planning, professionalism and courtesy with which they stage a march, they would be the envy of the world.

Until then, as Kasper would say, the game goes on.

ACKNOWLEDGEMENTS

This book exists because of a road trip I undertook to Mozambique in a vintage Mercedes with my friends John Kerr, Michael Bowles and Craig Ellis. I'd like to thank them for joining me on the journey, and our wives Grace, Jane and Robin for giving us the freedom to do it. We were looking for an adventure and we found it.

My sister Stephanie and her husband Rob in Zimbabwe have always been warm and generous hosts, as have Sandy and David in Johannesburg, Helen and Barnaby in London, and my uncle Stuart Ingram.

My parents were there for me always, not just with a bed, red wine and hot meals but with comic insight on the surreal politics of Zimbabwe. It's not surprising that it was a business friend of theirs who first put me in touch with Ellis. Sadly my mother passed away during the writing of this book. She always encouraged me to write about "home" and I hope this story does her proud. I miss her more every day.

The story told in these pages was only possible because of the trust and cooperation of Tom and Clare Ellis, Kasper, Magic and Horse, Gabriel Shumba, Bernard Pswarayi and several others in their orbit who wanted their story told and who were confident telling it to me. I spent several hundred hours pestering them for information, and I only hope that I've represented them accurately and fairly here.

Thanks to Brian James, Acie Lumumba and Tino Mambeu for starting me on my way.

I owe huge thanks to all the team behind the forthcoming documentary *Two Weeks in November* of which I am a co-producer and which covers some of the same ground as this book: Claudia Walker, Julian Phelan, Rumbi Katedza, Lauren Norton, Greg Amira, Wanuri Kahiu, Marius van Graan, Nigel Munyati, Joe Njagu, Troy Reid, Theresa Muchemwa, Mike Slee, Ben Young, Spencer Young and Caleb Heyman, as well as Matt, Tatenda, Nikita, Liberty, Thomas, Kuda, Derrick, Alexi, Christian and Debbie.

During my research I relied heavily on the advice and reporting of a number of Zimbabwean writers, journalists and publications. Ray Ndlovu, author of *In the Jaws of the Crocodile*, was incredibly generous with his time, contacts and analysis, even as he was writing his own book on the subject and having to meet tight deadlines for his newspaper, South Africa's *Sunday Times*.

My friend Jono "Mvura" Waters gave me invaluable background on the geography and architecture of Harare and its suburbs, as well as unvarnished views of the characters in "the game". He is, for my money, the best analyst on Zimbabwean affairs and "only ever been wrong once".

Another friend, the author Petina Gappah, an original voice and fiercely independent mind, secured me a pivotal interview when I was getting nowhere, and I'm grateful to Dumisani Muleya of the Zimbabwe Independent and Trevor Ncube for taking time to meet with me. A superb essay on the coup titled "Army Arrangement" by Bernard Matambo, published in *Chimurenga Chronic*, got my heart racing and inspired the narrative voice I took. Bernard's work deserves a wide audience.

For background on Grace Mugabe's political debut and

her takedown of Joice Mujuru I relied heavily on the comprehensive paper 'Coupe de Grace? Plots and Purges: Mugabe and ZANU-PF's 6th National People's Congress,' by David Matyszak of the Research and Advocacy Unit.

My friend, fellow Mutare boy, and now fellow Virginian, Kuda Bhejana assisted me with Shona translations, dialogue and character development, and gave me terrific feedback on the first draft. Also in Virginia, thanks to US Army Colonel Patrick Anderson and Colonel GM of the ZDF for those late nights.

Thanks to my great friend Andy Pattenden who knows more about Harare airport than anyone else, and who also gave me an atmospheric personal account of the night of November 14th.

The authors Memory Chirere and Ignatius Mabasa explained to me the curse of November in Shona culture, and the brilliant photographer Stephen Chikosi clarified some important political dynamics.

My touchstone throughout meanwhile was Leon Hartwell, first in Washington DC, then in Sydney, Australia, who encouraged me to pursue the narrative approach, read and meticulously edited an early draft of the manuscript, provided me with vital background on the main players in "the game", and even introduced me to one of them at a memorable dinner in Sandton, Johannesburg.

Talking of those players, I met and interviewed several of them, from each faction, and always came away surprised that in person they were polite, charming, and whip smart. It confirmed my suspicion that if Zimbabwe's politicians spent their time, energy and intellect producing functional institutions, instead of pursuing personal power, Zimbabwe could be the envy of Africa.

Thanks to Jessamy Calkin at the *Telegraph Magazine* for assigning me the story on the coup that led to this book, and Andrew Purvis, my *Telegraph* travel editor, who assigned me the Mozambique piece.

Rebecca Nicolson and Jeremy Boraine, my publishers at Short Books and Jonathan Ball respectively, were cheerleaders for the book from the start, and showed incredible faith in me when I told them the story had changed. I'm hugely grateful for their trust and guidance. Thanks to the brilliant Aurea Carpenter at Short Books for her edits, advice and support throughout.

Thanks also to Anna Carmichael and Susan Raihofer at David Black and Associates, my agents.

Finally, love and gratitude goes to my wife Grace Cutler to whom this book is dedicated; and our children Madeline and Whitaker. I spent a lot of 2018 in Zimbabwe and South Africa, and when back home retreated to my study, only occasionally coming up for food, air, and advice on structure, which my wife, an expert, unfailingly gave. This would not have been possible without the three of you.